Universitext

Günter Gabisch · Hans-Walter Lorenz

Business Cycle Theory

A Survey of Methods and Concepts

Second, Revised, and Enlarged Edition

With 75 Figures

Springer-Verlag
Berlin Heidelberg New York
London Paris Tokyo

Professor Dr. Günter Gabisch

Dr. Hans-Walter Lorenz

Volkswirtschaftliches Seminar
Georg-August-Universität Göttingen
Platz der Göttinger Sieben 3
D-3400 Göttingen, FRG

The first edition was published in 1987 as volume 283 of the series "Lecture Notes in Economics and Mathematical Systems".

ISBN 3-540-51059-1 Springer-Verlag Berlin Heidelberg New York
ISBN 0-387-51059-1 Springer-Verlag New York Berlin Heidelberg

© Springer-Verlag Berlin · Heidelberg 1989
Printed in Germany

Printing: Weihert-Druck GmbH, Darmstadt
Bookbinding: T. Gansert GmbH, Weinheim-Sulzbach
2142/7130-543210

To

I.G. and K.L.

Contents

Preface

"Is the business cycle obsolete?" This often cited title of a book edited by Bronfenbren-ner with the implicit affirmation of the question reflected the attitude of mainstream macroeconomics in the 1960s regarding the empirical relevance of cyclic motions of an economy. The successful income policies, theoretically grounded in Keynesian macroec-onomics, seemed to have eased or even abolished the fluctuations in Western economies which motivated studies of many classical and neoclassical economists for more than 100 years. The reasoning behind the conviction that business cycles would increasingly be-come irrelevant was rather simple: if an economy fluctuates for whatever reason, then it is almost always possible to neutralize these cyclic motions by means of anticyclic demand policies.

From the 1950s until the mid-1960s business cycle theory had often been consid-ered either as an appendix to growth theory or as an academic exercise in dynamical economics. The common business cycle models were essentially multiplier-accelerator models whose dependence on particular parameter values (in order to exhibit oscillatory motion) suggested a rather improbable occurrence of persistent fluctuations. The obvi-ous success in compensating business cycles in those days prevented intensive concern with the occurrence of cycles. Rather, business cycle theory turned into stabilization theory which investigated theoretical possibilities of stabilizing a fluctuating economy. Many macroeconomic textbooks appeared in the 1960s which consequently identified business cycle theory with inquiries on the possibilities to stabilize economies by means of active fiscal or monetary policies.

The obvious failure of Keynesian demand policies during the 1970s - at least with respect to the postulation of a *general* validity of demand stimulating policies claimed by orthodox Keynesians - has not only initiated a critical reconsideration of Keynesian macroeconomics and revivals of what has been called "classical" economics, but has also led to a resurrection of business cycle theory. While the term "business cycle" had nearly disappeared from titles of macroeconomic papers for 20 years, the revival of "classical macroeconomics" during the 1970s became inseparably linked with the emphasis on the fluctuating behavior of an economy. However, compared with Keynesian macroeconomics, the causality is usually reversed: the emphasis is not on stabilizing fluctuating economies by means of governmental activities, but rather on the generation of cyclic motions resulting from these activities themselves. The second mainstream of macroeconomic reasoning during the 1970s, namely the rationing or non-Walrasian approach to macroeconomics, has not attempted to contribute much to business cycle theory which is mainly due to the conceptual concentration on short-term, temporary equilibria of an economy.

Although the New Classical Macroeconomics has initiated a renewed interest in business cycles, it has not provided essentially new theoretical insights into the fluctuation of an economy. The assumed mechanisms which allow for the occurrence of cyclic motions are typically the same as those in the multiplier-accelerator models. Yet, there has been some effort in dynamical economics to investigate the relevance of new mathematical techniques in explaining economic fluctuations. The theory of non-linear dynamics (bifurcation theory, catastrophe theory, chaos theory, etc.) has revealed that a large variety of dynamic phenomena emerge if the model at hand is appropriately specified. It has especially become evident that slight modifications of the models are often sufficient to generate cyclic motions. This property particular to some dynamic models suggests to reflect about a classification of business cycle models in the following way.

A text that reviews the current state of the art of static macroeconomics must certainly distinguish between the two mainstreams of macroeconomic thinking, namely the New Classical Macroeconomics (or Rational Expectations literature) and the New Keynesian (or non-Walrasian) economics. Both trends have amounted to paradigms which do not seem to be compatible, even with considerable concessions on both sides. However, a text on business cycle theory following this classification would be characterized by two basic properties: first, abstracting from the underlying qualitative economic reasoning, the text would be full of repetitions as far as the dynamic oscillatory forces are concerned. Second, the text would be very short if it concentrated only on the dynamical aspects of both mainstream macroeconomics and would definitely be incomplete, as it would neglect many interesting approaches to business cycle theory which cannot be subsumed under the two mainstream categories.

Whether or not a dynamic model of an economy is a business cycle model, *i.e.*, a model which allows for fluctuations in major economic variables for a considerable amount of time, does not depend on the general economically motivated and paradigmatic features of a model, but rather on its mathematical structure. While, for example, the introduction of a certain lag-structure in the production function can certainly not be a distinctive mark from an economic point of view, this structure may be the essential dynamic feature which allows for oscillatory motions of an economy. Therefore, this text will concentrate on those features of dynamic economic models which constitute the essential fluctuation-generating forces.

A purely formal classification according to linearities or non-linearities, time-concepts, and lag-structures, etc., would also be unsatisfactory as it would veil the interesting aspects of economic dynamics with formalism. The theoretical business cycle models presented in this book will rather be distinguished according to the dependence of their cyclic behavior on exogenous shocks. While this importance of exogenous forces for the onset of cyclic motions has been stressed especially by the New Classical Macroeconomics, a classification according to this dependence allows existing business cycle models to be distinguished very easily and categorized in two classes.

This book is thus organized as follows: Chapter 1 deals with the empirical observation of cyclic performances of major economic variables. The chapter provides an overview of distinct cyclical phenomena of an economy on different time scales and lists typical phenomena, *i.e.*, the so-called *stylized facts*, observable in business cycles. Another section is devoted to the measurement of business cycles. Business cycle theory can only have relevance beyond the pure academic concern if there is indeed some empirical evidence of this cyclic performance. Chapter 2 presents an overview of shock-dependent models. It encompasses the traditional multiplier-accelerator models as well as several special non-linear business cycle models. As these models rely heavily on exogenous shocks in order to start as well as to maintain cycles, a special chapter is devoted to these exogenous forces. Chapter 3 includes the theory of political business cycles and concentrates mainly on the Rational Expectations models. Thus, Chapters 2 and 3 should be viewed as a unit. Chapter 4 presents shock-independent models, *i.e.*, models which can generate cycles endogenously, due only to their formal structure. While the models of Chapter 4 already require the introduction of several mathematical techniques which do not belong to common knowledge in economics, those involved in the models of Chapter 5 are certainly uncommon. As the relevance of these mathematical tools and models for future research is not clear yet, they are presented in a separate chapter dealing with chaotic motion and catastrophe theory.

A short book like the present one can of course not claim to be encyclopedically complete, and it would be pointless to list all concepts and single models which are missing in the presentation. Two omissions should at least be mentioned, however: a text on business cycle theory may be considered incomplete as long as it entirely neglects the history of ideas in this field. We have omitted an appropriate chapter primarily because there are several good texts (some of which are today regarded as classics) which deal with this subject. Furthermore, recent developments in business cycle theory have initiated a revival of some historic ideas (especially Schumpeterian economics) which are discussed in many good separate survey articles and books. Secondly, we have omitted a treatment of the large field dealing with business cycles in the framework of econometrics, as a satisfactory presentation would exceed the scope of this book.

Although no attempt is therefore made to provide a *complete* survey of modern business cycle theory, it cannot be avoided that the book sometimes appears to be rather itemized. The classification according to the more formal aspects of the models necessarily implies that models which are economically quite different are presented under the same entry. The reader is requested to excuse the consequent isolation of some economic approaches for the sake of a consistent presentation of modern business cycle theory.

This textbook is suited for students on the graduate or the upper undergraduate level. In addition to a sound knowledge of advanced macroeconomics, the reader should be familiar with formal reasoning. Although the book attempts to bring together the various mathematical tools of modern business cycle theory and to comment on unfamiliar instruments as much as necessary, the reader is often requested to complete the calculations or to consult the original literature.

This book contains a revised version of the text that appeared as a *Springer Lecture Note in Economics and Mathematical Systems*. The unexpected success of the first edition showed that there is an obvious demand for business cycle texts like ours. The field is dominated by models in the New Classical tradition with an emphasis on linear stochastic approaches, but it seems as if the importance of non-linear business cycle models is steadily increasing. A major step toward the establishment of non-linear dynamical systems in business cycle theory was undertaken in the attempts to derive the necessary nonlinearities from microeconomic foundations. For example, while many non-linear elements in early models of chaotic dynamical economics were introduced by *ad hoc* assumptions, recent general equilibrium models or optimal control models are much less vulnerable to criticism on their basic assumptions.

During recent years, the literature on business cycles has grown enormously. We have tried to credit these recent developments by incorporating the relevant literature. On the other hand, when uncommon topics are mentioned in a textbook in addition to traditional themes, several items have to be dropped in the course of scientific progress as well. While the first edition included a loose collection of some theorems concerning chaotic dynamics, we decided to delete several theorems which turned out to be rather irrelevant to business cycle theory.

The main modifications of the text in this second edition involved a reshuffling of some sections and an expansion of several others:

- The numbering of the chapters has been changed.
- The first chapter has been extended and now includes a short presentation of different cycle types and the stylized facts of business cycles.

- The Hopf bifurcation is by now a standard tool in business cycle theory. Therefore, we have included material on the continuous-time and discrete-time versions in Chapter 4 dealing with standard shock-independent theories.

- Parts of the section on chaotic dynamics have been completely revised because of some imprecise statements in the first edition. This section now also contains a short survey of methods and recent findings in the field of empirical research in chaotic dynamics.

In addition, we had to revise several definitions, descriptions of established mathematical results, and misleading formulations in the rest of the text.

We are grateful to Dieter Bock, Lutz Siegmund, and the GMD-Göttingen for their assistance in preparing the first edition. Marleen Sacks made tremendous efforts to make the English of the first edition more readable (and understandable). Ralph Phillips copy-edited the new parts of the text. Richard Herrmann kindly provided the numerical bifurcation diagram used in Chapter 5. The final manuscript was typeset in PCTEX.

It is a pleasure for us to acknowledge the many critical comments made by our colleagues and students who provided many suggestions for improving the text. We hope that the reader will benefit from these modifications.

Günter Gabisch

University of Göttingen

Hans-Walter Lorenz

University of Göttingen

Chapter 1

Fluctuations in Major Economic Variables

Business cycle theory deals with approaches to describe and explain observable fluctuations in major economic variables like the national product, the employment rate, or the inflation rate. Its aim is to establish necessary and/or sufficient conditions for the existence of more or less regular oscillations in a model economy. As a theoretical model is always an abstract picture of real life, business cycle theory concentrates only on the modelling of common patterns of empirical fluctuations and attempts to isolate those essential ingredients in a model which are responsible for an oscillating behavior of a model's variables.

Theoretical explanations of business cycles require that several preliminaries have been discussed in advance:

- It had to be clarified whether fluctuations in economic variables are periodic and whether different patterns can be distinguished. If different periodic patterns have been detected, i.e., if fluctuations with different wavelengths can be distinguished in an economy, economic theory must concentrate on different aspects. For example, in the explanation of long waves with a 40-60 year cycle technical innovations will probably play a dominant role while models concerned with 2-4 year cycles may ignore technical progress entirely and may even treat the capital stock as being fixed.

- It had to be clarified which variables are to be observed over time, and the mea-

surement procedure had to be described. Different macroeconomic variables may
develop completely differently over a cycle. Several variables like total employment
in a particular industry may lead or lag the motion of aggregate employment or
may be completely disconnected from the aggregate fluctuation.

- If an agreement on the periodic pattern and the measurement procedure has been
  found, the common features of empirical business cycles must be isolated. These
  common features will be called the *stylized facts* in the following.

The rest of this chapter is devoted to a discussion of these preliminaries.

1.1. Periodic Patterns and Stylized Facts

In the history of business cycle theory several different periodic patterns were claimed
to exist when the emphasis was put on particular phenomena and associated variables.
The following list sketches only the most influential contributions which have survived
until today.[1]

Kondratieff Cycles The major inquiry into long-wave cycles is usually attributed to
Kondratieff (1892-1930(?)[2]) who, among others, studied British
and German iron consumption and arrived at the conclusion that
a cycle with a period of about 40-60 years exists. Though several approaches to explain the existence of these long waves have
been proposed, technological innovations and subsequent structural change are usually considered to be the main driving forces
of this cycle. The major technological events over the last 200
years, namely the innovation of *(i)* steampower ($\approx$ 1790), *(ii)* of
railroads ($\approx$ 1830), and *(iii)* of industrial electrification and of
the automobile ($\approx$ 1885) correspond with the three distinguished
up- and downswings isolated by Kondratieff: a first complete cycle from 1790 to 1844/51, a second cycle from 1850 to 1890/96,
and a third one from 1890/96 to $\approx$ 1930. [3]

Juglar Cycles Cycles with a period between 7 and 11 years were observed by
Juglar (1819-1905) in an investigation of French, British, and US
banking figures, interest rates, and prices. These medium waves
seemed to correspond with a life cycle of investment goods which

---

[1] *The following classification is due to Schumpeter (1939).*

[2] *The precise year of Kondratieff's death is unknown since he was banished to Siberia.*

[3] *Kondratieff himself reported only a part of the last cycle.*

initiated fluctuations in the GNP, inflation rate, and employment. For example, Schumpeter (1939) distinguished 11 Juglar cycles in the period from 1787 to 1932. Juglar cycles can be considered true business cycles, *i.e.*, cycles which are usually meant when one speaks of fluctuations in trade activities. After World War II the average length of these medium wave cycles decreased to approximately 5 to 7 years for most Western countries.

Kitchin Cycles   Kitchin (1926) concentrated on short waves with a length between 2 and 4 years in a study of British and US bank clearings and wholesale prices. It seemed as if stochastic exogenous influences dominated the evolution of the economy. Variables like inventory stocks temporarily respond to these shocks but eventually return to their equilibrium values.

In addition to this list, several other cycles are proposed in the literature. The Kuznets cycle with a length of 15-20 years is occasionally included in the list of standard cycles.[4] Table 1.1 summarizes the properties of the three major different cycles.

Though this classification has become popular, it is not definitely clear whether all of these cycles really exist. For example, Kondratieff was able to isolate only three long-wave cycles because reliable data on industrial production only exist for the last 100-150 years in most industrialized countries, and the periodicity of the major historical innovations can be viewed as being purely accidental.[5]

Schumpeter (1939) has already noted that superposition of different cycles may generate a rather complex overall motion. Even if single cycles would resemble harmonic wave motions, their interaction would probably not generate harmonic motions on top of longer-term harmonic waves. It follows that it may be empirically difficult to assign an observed cycle to one of the three different patterns mentioned above.

The models presented in this book attempt to provide theoretical explanations for cycles with a wavelength between approximately 4 and 8 years, *i.e.*, cycles that can roughly be identified with Juglar cycles. The most interesting economic variables are therefore the national product, the aggregate price level, and the unemployment rate. Some models generate harmonic time series and can be viewed as explanations for abstract and isolated Juglar or Kitchin cycles, while other models are able to generate

---

[4] *Cf. Zarnowitz/Moore (1986), p. 522.*

[5] *Recently, long waves have found a renewed interest especially in conjunction with the work on the so-called economics of evolution. Cf. Freeman/Clark/Soete (1982), Clark (1984) and the papers in Vasko (1987) for surveys on the long-wave debate. However, Goodwin (1987) notes that "...long waves appear to be facts in search of a model".*

Type	Wavelength	Major Topics
Kondratieff	40 - 60 years	technical progress, structural change
Juglar	7 - 11 years	investment cycle; $\Longrightarrow$ fluctuations in GNP, inflation rate, and employment
Kitchin	2 - 4 years	random shocks; $\Longrightarrow$ fluctuations in GNP, inflation rate, and employment; inventory cycle

Table 1.1

irregular time series with varying frequencies. The common feature of most models in this book is that they concentrate on economic variables which exhibit an upward motion for a considerable time interval followed by a downswing and an eventual recovery, *i.e.*, the models concentrate on *"...recurrent sequences of persistent and pervasive expansions and contractions in economic activities"*.[6] Phenomena like the structural change in a single industry, economy-wide technical progress, or adaptions to very short-term stochastic influences will be ignored in most models presented in this book.

Empirical investigation of business cycles suggests that common features of observed business cycles can be isolated. Broadly accepted *stylized facts* of business cycles with wavelengths between approximately 4 and 8 years are the following:[7]

i)   Observed values of economic variables can be divided into leaders, laggers, and coinciders. Aggregate output movements and profits are coinciders; different but related sectors move in conformity. Stock exchange rates, the value of sold shares, and employment in hours per week in the manufacturing industries are leaders, while factory payrolls and medium-term money market rates are laggers.

ii) Business profits show much greater amplitudes than other series.

---

[6] *Zarnowitz/Moore (1986), p. 520.*

[7] *The following list is a modified version of the one proposed by Lucas (1977), p. 217f. Compare also Zarnowitz (1985).*

iii) The production of durable goods exhibits greater amplitudes than the production of non-durables does.

iv) Agricultural production and the exploitation of natural resources together with the associated prices exhibit greater than average deviations from the scheme of leading, lagging and coinciding series.

v) Different economic variables can move in different directions: the aggregate price level and short-term interest rates are procyclical; long-term interest rates only slightly move in the same direction as the coinciding series. Monetary aggregates are procyclical.

vi) Trade cycle statistics correspond with leading, lagging, or coinciding series in many countries. The conformity is higher in small countries.

In addition to this list of stylized facts, other phenomena may be considered typical for medium-wave business cycles. It depends to some degree on a theorist's paradigmatic attitude toward reality whether these phenomena are regarded as being relevant to a description of a cycle. Some "facts" may support a specific world view and others may raise doubt in the validity of a certain class of models. The more important facts seem to be the following:[8]

vii) Labor productivity is procyclical.

viii) Real wages do not unambiguously move anticyclically.

ix) Observed cycles are asymmetric: the velocity of an upswing is typically slower than that of a downswing.[9]

x) The amplitude of observed cycles decreased in the postwar period.

The different models presented in this book are not able to generate time series which simultaneously describe and explain *all* stylized facts mentioned above. Most theoretical business cycle models deal with highly aggregated economies and are therefore unable to distinguish different sectoral motions and different kinds of goods. Sectoral aspects are the domain of econometric approaches to the cycle. Furthermore, monetary factors and international trade are neglected in many models so that statements on the interest rate, exchange rates, trade balances, the stock of money, and (in most of these models) on the inflation rate are impossible.

---

[8] Cf. *Sargent (1979)*, p. *218*; *Ramser (1986)*, p. *3f.*, *Boyd/Blatt (1988)*, p. *19*, *Zarnowitz/Moore (1986)*, p. *531ff.*

[9] *Though this statement is widely accepted, recent research has cast doubt on its validity. Cf. DeLong/Summers (1986) and Boyd/Blatt (1988) for contrary empirical results.*

It will become obvious in the course of the book that out of the remaining "facts" items *vii)*, *viii)*, and *ix)* are able to classify existing business cycle theories: classical and Keynesian models differ especially in statements about the development of real wages over the cycle; the symmetry or asymmetry of the cycle is an indicator for the dominance of linear or non-linear elements in a model, which in most cases is equivalent to a shock-dependence or shock-independence of a model, respectively.

1.2. The Measurement of the Business Cycle

While the more or less regular movements of numerous economic entities is accepted as a fact by most economists, the problem of how to measure the aggregate state of the economy with regard to these business fluctuations is difficult due to the many single economic magnitudes involved. Usually, the time pattern of these fluctuating economic activities is rather diverse. While some economic activities are expanding at a given point in time, others have already reached their upper turning point and still others are on the downswing; a few economic activities might even be at a lower turning point. Thus, the question of how to measure the aggregate level of business activities deserves some attention.

The answer to this question is, beyond the pure theoretical concern, of important economic interest. Depending on the result of this measurement procedure, (*i.e.*, the measured state of economic affairs), the political economic authorities might come to different conclusions as to how to intervene in the economic process. To be precise, the actions of monetary authorities will be different in timing and volume if they state the beginning of a recession as compared with an accelerating depression. The same is true for the fiscal authorities. Whether a budget is neutral with respect to the monetary economic business situation or not depends to a large degree on the concept of the measurement of business fluctuations. For this reason, the Council of Economic Advisers (CEA) developed the concept of a full employment budget surplus in 1962.[10] According to the change in this surplus over time, different fiscal actions seem to be appropriate. Yet, this surplus hinges crucially upon how a "normal state of business activities" has been measured. The same is true for the concept of a business-neutral budget as developed by the German "Sachverständigenrat" [11] in the Federal Republic of Germany (FRG). In this concept, the measurement of potential output plays the decisive role and - together with current output - can be interpreted as a measure of current economic activities.

---

[10] *Economic Report of the President (1962), p.77.*

[11] *Sachverständigenrat (1970), pp. 91ff. The "Sachverständigenrat" is the German equivalent to the American Council of Economic Advisers (to the President) (CEA).*

At the center of the discussion on measuring the current business activities are two concepts: the use of economic *indicators* and the concept of *potential economic output*. Both will be discussed below.

1.2.1. Economic Indicators

The theoretical concept of measuring current business activities using economic indicators is rather simple though its practical application is difficult. The basic idea of this concept consists of constructing different time series of data so that the overall movement of economic activities can be made transparent by these series.

1.2.1.1. Harvard Barometer

In the 1920s the so-called Harvard barometer or Harvard-ABC curves became very popular. This indicator had been developed by W.M.Persons (1919a,b) and originally consisted of five groups of time series. Time series belonging to the same group were characterized by roughly similar and simultaneous cycles. Twenty different series ranging from "value of building permits issued for twenty leading cities" to "Bradstreet's index of commodity prices" were used in setting up the five groups. All these groups revealed similar cyclical patterns, yet the cycles did not occur simultaneously but rather consecutively.

In order to give a clearer picture of the cyclical movements of general business activities, the five groups were later reduced to three - labelled ABC-groups - and the number of time series was reduced to thirteen by excluding those series which were fluctuating more erratically than the others (Persons (1919b)). Specifically, group A consisted of four series, affording an index of speculation, group B consisted of five series, yielding a combined index of physical productivity and commodity prices, and group C consisted of four series, affording an index of the financial situation in New York City. These three groups gave a rather simple, yet impressive picture of the cyclical movements of the US-economy from 1903 to 1914. (cf. Figure 1.1)

The Harvard barometer, like most of its followers, was constructed not only to *measure* past and present business cycles, but was also hoped to serve as an instrument in *predicting* business cycles.

Persons (1919a) specified the properties of a suitable measure of cyclical fluctuations:

> "..[the] *sort of measure desired is one that is not applicable merely to past data but that can be applied with some confidence to the present and the future"*
> (1919a, p.33).

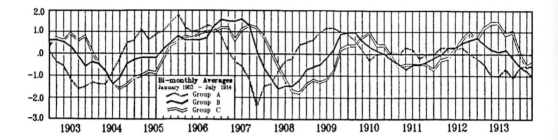

Source: Persons (1919b), p.112 f.

Figure 1.1

And after this statement he asks the rhetoric question:

> *"Is there a 'law' of business cycles which holds so consistent over a considerable period of the past that we may reasonably expect it to hold in the future?"* (ibid.)

Although his own answer to this question is rather cautious and pondering, he is in the last instance convinced that his barometer can be applied for predicting future business activities. In his opinion the ABC curves constituted

> *"...an intelligible index of business conditions which, when properly interpreted, threw new light on future tendencies as well as upon current movements."* (1919c, p.2).

According to this opinion the Harvard University Committee on Economic Research regularly published predictions of the business conditions from September 1919 until January 1924, but after initial accomplishments the predictions became unreliable and after the indicator even failed to predict the Great Depression (*"...one of the great fore-casting failures of all time."* - as Moore (1980, p.302) put it) it was totally abandoned.

1.2.1.2. NBER Indicators

Leaders, Laggers, and Coinciders

Much in the spirit of the Harvard ABC curves, economic indicators were conceived at the National Bureau of Economic Research. Originally, W.C.Mitchell and F.Burns, responding to a request by a US agency, developed the basic idea of reference cycles in 1938, which were led and followed by other ones. On examining 487 statistical series they ended up choosing 71 time series as statistical indexes of cyclical revivals. These series were ordered according to the average lead or lag with regard to the reference revivals, thus giving an impression of the scattered timing of a revival. For example, six time series had no average lead or lag; typically 'factory employment, total' and 'factory payrolls' belonged to these series. On the average, the leading series were from one to ten months ahead of the reference revivals; they comprised such series as 'pig iron production' (3 month lead) and 'bank clearings, NYC' (6 month lead). The lagging series were on the average from one to twelve months behind; they included such series as 'magazine advertising' (2 month lag) and 'bond sales, NY Stock Exchange' (7 month lag).

The idea of leading, lagging, and coinciding (reference) series was developed even further by G.H.Moore (1950). In his study he also systematically included times of recessions and based his analysis on the 801 monthly and quarterly time series for the United States which had been prepared by the NBER. From these series were chosen as economic indicators those which passed a test for conformity and timing; conformity meaning the consistency with which the series have conformed to business cycles and timing referring to the consistency with which a time series' turning point has led, lagged or roughly coincided with the reference data. Thus, 225 series out of the 801 ones were chosen and were condensed into five groups characterized by 'long leads', 'short leads', 'short leads or lags', 'short lags', and 'long lags'.

Using this classification, the number of series finally accepted as economic indicators boiled down even further to 21 series. Those series were selected which were similar in timing at peaks and troughs and were classified into three groups: leading, roughly coincident, and lagging. To name but a few from each group:

leaders: number and value of shares sold, NY Stock Exchange; average hours worked per week in manufacturing by all wage earners

coinciders: physical volume of business activities; "Babson" business profits of all corporations

laggers: total factory payrolls; ninety-day time money rates.

Similar to the Harvard ABC curves, these groups of time series can serve as indicators of past and current economic activities. However, if they are used for forecasting purposes, the same qualifications hold as in the case of the Harvard barometer (cf. Section 1.2.1.1.). Moore (1950) undoubtedly recognized this problem himself, but in the last instance - similar to Persons - he was optimistic that these indicators could be used for predictive purposes:[12]

> *"..., there is some ground for confidence that objective use of these methods will at least reduce the usual lag in recognizing revivals or recessions that have already begun. ... True, this is forecasting of a sort. But it is forecasting with a highly important element of confirmation, which works in two directions. The*

---

[12] *Moore (1950) in Moore (1980), p. 257f. Emphases in original.*

behavior of the roughly coincident series confirms or fails to confirm that over the leading series, and vice versa."

Generally speaking, the hypothesis behind this statement is that forthcoming cyclical turns may be predicted by leading series subject to the confirmation or refutation by the coinciders and the laggers.

Diffusion Index

Another indicator developed by the NBER is the so-called *diffusion index*. This index is closely related to the concept of leading, lagging and coinciding series and goes back to Burns and Mitchell (1946). The concept of this index is rather simple: at any point in time some series out of a specified set may move upward while the rest is moving downward. If the relative number of upward moving time series is greater/less than 0.5, the economy is expanding/contracting.

Burns (1954) and Moore (1954, 1955) adopted this idea systematically to different sets of economic time series and called the proportion of expanding series 'diffusion index'. Burns (1954, p.115) derived a diffusion index from nearly 700 series - including such heterogeneous series as production, prices, interest rates, inventories, etc. - which may serve as an index of general economic activities (cf. Figure 1.2). According to Moore (1954, p.18) *"...this conglomerate is one of the best historical indexes of the cyclical position of our economy that has ever been devised."*

Percentage of Series Undergoing Expansion, 1919-53

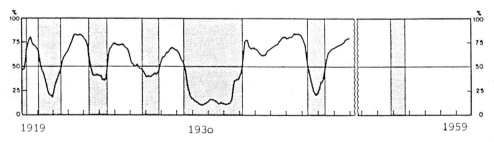

Source: Moore (1954), p.17

Figure 1.2

In Figure 1.3 it is illustrated that the diffusion index truly gives an impression of how the economic activities 'diffuse' over time throughout the economy. The diffusion index in the lower part of this figure is derived in three steps:

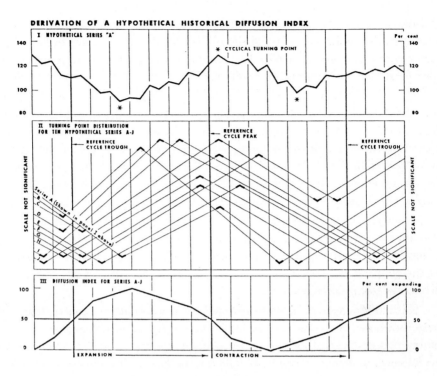

Source: Broida (1955), p.10
Figure 1.3

Step 1: The empirical basis is a collection of some time series; in Figure 1.3 this basis is formed by the ten time series A to J. One of these series, i.e. A, has been plotted in the upper part.

Step 2: For each single time series the lower and upper turning points must be determined, as denoted by asterixes for series A above. These turning points are connected by straight lines, giving an 'ordinal' picture of how a business cycle wanders through the individual series (cf. the middle panel of Figure 1.3).

Step 3: The diffusion index can be calculated by counting the number of upward sloping lines at each point in time in the middle panel and expressing this number as a proportion of the total number of series. This index is plotted in the lower part of the picture above. It reaches its maximum of 100% when all series are moving upwards, and is at its minimum of 0%, when all series are falling.

If the value of the diffusion index is between 50% and 100% (0% and 50%) the economy is on the way to expansion (contraction). This implies that for a value of 100% the economy is in an upswing phase, but has not yet reached its upper turning point, because at that point the value of the diffusion index would have to be 50%. Similar reasoning holds for a value of 0%. The result of these considerations is that the diffusion index must lead any index of aggregate activity.

Indeed, when this method of constructing a diffusion index is applied to historical data, the cyclical turns of the aggregate are preceded by the turns of the diffusion index. Moore (1955, Tab. 8.2) constructed different diffusion indexes for a variety of series, e.g. production series, employment series, wholesale price series, etc., covering the period from 1920 to 1938 for US data. These diffusion indexes showed an average lead at business cycle peaks and troughs, which in most cases ranged between six and twelve months; in no case was there an average lag.

It follows that for analyzing historical business cycles the diffusion index is certainly a helpful tool. It provides information on how many individual series out of a given set are involved by an up- or downswing, and it shows how this number changes over time. Yet the question will nevertheless arise as to how to construct a diffusion index for the current state of economic affairs.

This question cannot be answered easily. The procedure of constructing a diffusion index until now was based on the exact knowledge of past business cycles, i.e., the turning points of each time series are precisely known. However, the identification of current turning points unavoidably involves the forecasting of coming events. A peak or trough comes into existence only by a following decline or rise. To state a current peak or trough is tantamount to declaring that the series in question is - while perhaps not smoothly - unquestionably moving down or up.

This problem is, of course, closely related to the use of diffusion indexes for forecasting purposes. Since the diffusion index leads the turning points, it seems reasonable to use these indexes in forecasting the turning points. However, as noted above, the identification of a current turning point means forecasting. Hence, the construction of a current diffusion index implies forecasting. As Broida (1955, p.12) put it: *"But this would be forecasting for the sake of making a diffusion index - not making a diffusion index for the sake of forecasting."*

These problems involved in constructing diffusion indexes for current affairs were, of course, recognized by Moore (1955). Broida (1955) accordingly differentiated between 'historical' and 'current' diffusion indexes: the former are those which are constructed by hindsight (cf. Figure 1.3); the latter are those for current affairs.

There have been several attempts to construct current diffusion indexes. Particularly, Moore (1955) experimented with different methods. He constructed indexes which recorded the proportion of productive series, employment series, and profit series, respectively, which had arisen from the previous month or quarter. Other indexes were related to moving averages and the directions of change were determined by the centered moving average. In any case, each of these current diffusion indexes behaved much more irregularly than the historical index. Unavoidably, *"(t)he price for obtaining a current diffusion index is greater uncertainty about its cyclical movements."* [13] This dilemma can at best be reduced but not eliminated.

Diffusion Index and the Rate of Change

There has been some discussion to the question (Broida (1955), Moore (1955), Alexander (1958)) whether the diffusion index renders roughly the same information as the rate of change of the respective aggregate. For this question being a meaningful problem, there must first of all exist a sensible aggregation rule for the individual series underlying the diffusion index. Undoubtedly, there hardly exists anything like an equivalent rate of change for the diffusion index of Figure 1.2, because obviously there does not exist anything like a meaningful aggregate of series of production, prices, interest rates, inventories, etc.

In order to clarify the differences between these two measures, the simple aggregation rule of forming weighted averages will be used:

$$x_t = a_1 x_{1,t} + \ldots + a_n x_{n,t}, \quad \sum_{i=1}^{n} a_i = 1, \quad a_i \geq 0. \tag{1.2.1}$$

The diffusion index (DI) for the individual time series of $x_{i,t}$ is:

$$DI = \frac{m}{n}, \quad m - \text{number of positive derivatives} \quad \frac{dx_{i,t}}{dt}. \tag{1.2.2}$$

The rate-of-change index (RC)[14] of the aggregate is

$$RC = \frac{dx_t}{dt} = a_1 \frac{dx_{1,t}}{dt} + \ldots + a_n \frac{dx_{n,t}}{dt}. \tag{1.2.3}$$

Obviously, the diffusion index assumes equal importance of all individual series and neglects the absolute amount of change in the individual series. Hence, generally speaking, both measures are quite different but in practice can roughly coincide if special circumstances are met. Our normal expectation would thus be that a rising diffusion index implies a rising rate-of-change index. When an increasing number of series is rising, then the average should rise, too. But, of course, this is not necessarily true. If the

---

[13] *Moore (1954), p.275.*

[14] *Although 'rate of change' often refers to the relative change, e.g. $\frac{dx/dt}{x}$, in this context it denotes the absolute change as represented by dx/dt.*

Subsequent Performance of Three Groups of Indicators Selected and Classified in 1950.

Business Cycle		Average Lead (−) or Lag (+), in Months					
		At Peaks			At Troughs		
Peak (1)	Trough (2)	Leading Group (3)	Roughly Coincident Group (4)	Lagging Group (5)	Leading Group (6)	Roughly Coincident Group (7)	Lagging Group (8)
November 1948		−15	−3	+2			
	October 1949				−6	−1	0
July 1953		−13	−2	+2			
	May 1954				−4	+1	+2
August		−21	−6	+2			
	April				−2	0	+2
April 1960		−9	−4	+2			
	February 1961				−1	+3	+4
December 1969		−8	−5	+2			
	November 1970				−2	0	+15
November 1973		−6	+6	+11			
	March 1975				0	0	+9

Source: Moore (1980), p. 356
Table 1.2

increasing number of rising series rise by decreasing amounts, whereas the decreasing series decrease by increasing amounts, the two indexes may diverge.

Without discussing all possible circumstances under which the two indexes can diverge, it is an empirical question whether or not they actually diverge in practice. Alexander (1958) compared both indexes for fifteen to twenty-six components of the Federal Reserve Board Index of Industrial Production, covering most of the period from 1919 to 1957. The rate of change index was defined as the first difference of the FRB-Index. This comparison led to the conclusion that *"(t)he choice between a diffusion index and the first difference of the aggregate, therefore, is almost purely one of convenience, so far as predicting turning points is concerned."*[15]

Applications and Revisions

Out of all the applications of the NBER indicators, just two should be mentioned which give an impressive illustration of how these indicators work in practice. Moore (1980) applied the 21 indicators selected in 1950[16] to the respective time series from 1948 to 1975, resp. 1978. Table 1.2 shows the results of this investigation. The leading and lagging groups behave as expected. Only the coincident groups tend to show some deviation from expected performance.

A somewhat similar information is contained in Figure 1.4. The three groups of indicators have been set up by methods used by the Department of Commerce. As Moore (1980) states, *"(t)he indexes move down during each recession, up during each*

---

[15] *Alexander (1958), p. 634.*

[16] *Compare p. 15 above.*

expansion. The sequences among their turning points ... are with rare exceptions in accordance with the patterns expected when the selection of indicators was made in 1950...". [17]

Since 1938 the development of economic indicators in the USA has been improved particularly by the NBER itself, the U.S. Bureau of Census, the Department of Commerce and by many other agencies. The list of indicators, originally assembled in 1938, was revised in 1950, 1960, 1966, and 1975.

The improvements and augmentations in constructing these indicators can neatly be demonstrated by a comparison of the list of leading, lagging and coinciding indicators in 1950 and 1975, cf. Table 1.3.

Many of the series contained in both lists of this table are basically equivalent. Indeed, with only one exception all of the series belonging to the leading group in 1950 are essentially also in this group in 1975. The revisions which took place in the meantime refer to details such as substituting one series for another, splitting one series in two, using monthly series instead of quarterly series etc. Thus, while the revisions have improved the instrument of NBER indicators they have not changed the concept.

1.2.1.3. Indicators in Germany

Both the Harvard barometer and the NBER studies received international attentions and the idea of constructing economic indicators consequently became widespread. Out of all the attempts to develop indicators, only two methods which were conceived in Germany are to be mentioned here. The first one has its direct roots in the Harvard barometer. Although this barometer had been widely criticized (Stähle (1928), Gater (1931)) because of its lack of theoretical foundations and empirical relevance, the Institute for Business Cycle Research ("Deutsches Institut für Konjunkturforschung") in Berlin intended to establish an extended system of indicators. Wagemann (1928), director of the above institute, criticized the Harvard barometer himself,[18] not for theoretical or methodological reasons, but rather for lack of broadness. According to his opinion, only an interrelated system of different barometers could reliably be used for diagnostic purposes.

The barometer system conceived by Wagemann comprised numerous time series which were - preliminarily - condensed to eight barometers. By combining all these barometers it was intended to provide a regionally and temporally differentiated picture of current economic affairs. Indeed, in the last instance it was hoped to use this barometer system for predicting purposes - similar to the case of the Harvard barometer.

---

[17] *Moore (1980), p. 358.*

[18] *Wagemann (1928), p. 114.*

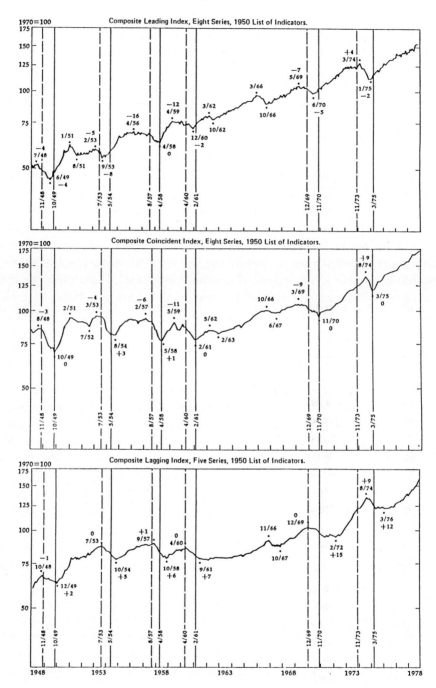

Source: Moore (1980), pp. 359-61

Figure 1.4

Comparison of the 1950 and 1975 Lists of Leading, Coincident, and Lagging Indicators.

BCD No.	Original Series in 1950 List	BCD No.	Corresponding or New Series in 1975 List
	Leading Group		
1.	Average workweek, manufacturing	1.	Same
	* * *	3.	Layoff rate, manufacturing
6.	New orders, durable goods, value	8.	New orders for consumer goods and materials, in 1972 dollars
	* * *	32.	Vendor performance
13.	New incorporations, number	12.	Net business formation
9.	Commercial and industrial building contracts, floor space	20.	Contracts and orders for plant and equipment, in 1972 dollars
n.a.	Residential building contracts, floor space	29.	New building permits, private housing units, number
	* * *	36.	Net change in inventories on hand and on order, in 1972 dollars
n.a.	Wholesale price index, twenty-eight basic commodities	92.	Change in sensitive prices
n.a.	Dow-Jones index of industrial common stock prices	19.	Standard and Poor's index of 500 common stock prices
14.	Liabilities of business failures		* * *
	* * *	104.	Percent change in liquid assets
	* * *	105.	Money supply (M_1), in 1972 dollars
	Roughly Coincident Group		
41.	Employment in nonagricultural establishments	41.	Same
37.	Unemployment, number of persons		* * *
16.	Corporate profits after taxes		* * *
n.a.	Bank debits outside New York	57.	Manufacturing and trade sales, in 1972 dollars
47.	Industrial production index	47.	Same
200.	Gross national product		* * *
335.	Wholesale price index, industrial commodities		* * *
	* * *	51.	Personal income less transfer payments, in 1972 dollars
	Lagging Group		
223.	Personal income, value		* * *
54.	Retail sales, value		* * *
66.	Consumer installment debt, value	95.	Ratio, consumer installment debt to personal income
	* * *	72.	Commercial and industrial loans outstanding
67.	Bank rates on business loans	109.	Prime rate charged by banks
n.a.	Manufacturers' inventories, book value	70.	Manufacturing and trade inventories, in 1972 dollars
	* * *	91.	Average duration of unemployment
		62.	Labor cost per unit of output, manufacturing

Source: Moore (1980), p. 375

Table 1.3

After World War II the idea of constructing a barometer had been picked up by the German "Sachverständigenrat" (Sachverständigenrat (1970)). The council conceived an indicator based on twelve individual time series, ranging from new orders over wages per working hour to the number of unemployed workers. For each of the series, a corridor was perceived that was restricted by a lower and an upper critical value of toleration. Within this corridor a normal value was determined. Consequently, every series was evaluated according to its behavior within the corridor. Figure 1.5 contains this indicator for the period 1959-1970. In later years this indicator was no longer used, apparently due to its lack of practicability and reliability.

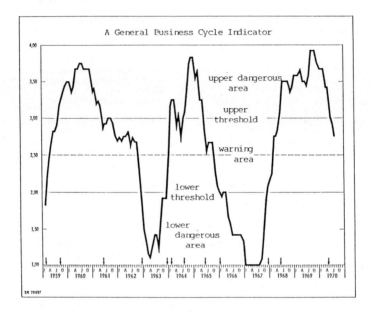

Source: Sachverständigenrat (1970), p.52
Figure 1.5

The IFO-Institute in Munich has developed a somewhat different concept of economic indicators.[19] It regularly asks several thousands of firms about new orders and how they assess the current economic situation. From these results the institute derives an indicator which provides a qualitative assessment of the current economic situation.

---

[19] *An excellent survey of the IFO-Institute's research on economic indicators can be found in Strigel (1977).*

1.2.1.4. Diagnosis and Prognosis by Means of Indicators

Thus far the use of economic indicators has mainly been discussed with respect to providing information on the current or recent state of economic affairs. Only in a few instances has the possibility of using these indicators for predictive purposes been mentioned. Whether this latter use is legitimate or not is a question that has been debated and which is basically a matter of methodological insight. In order to clarify the problem, consider the following definition of what an indicator is supposed to be:

An economic indicator indicates the known state of economic affairs.

While this definition seems to be somewhat vague, it makes clear two decisive points: First, an indicator *indicates* and does not *explain*. Second, it indicates *known* circumstances.

With respect to both aspects, an indicator as defined above can be compared with a barometer.[20] First, this technical instrument *indicates* the level of air pressure and nothing else; particularly, it does not explain why and how this level of air pressure has come about. Secondly, it indicates the *current* or *recent* level of air pressure. The barometer itself does not say anything about future weather conditions. Only by reasonable interpretations of the barometer's indications can a prognosis be ventured. Using the barometer in a different context clarifies that this latter interpretation is essential for the prognosis: if the barometer is used in measuring the altitude while mountain climbing, then only the altitude can be measured due to obvious lack of any other meaningful interpretation.

The same reasoning can be applied to economic indicators. Strictly speaking, such an indicator provides information of past and at best of current economic affairs only. If they are to be used for prognostic purposes, they must be embedded in some kind of economic theory, as unsophisticated as it may be. Koopmans (1947),[21] in reviewing Burns/Mitchell (1946), expressed this view in an even broader context in his famous article on 'Measurement without Theory'. According to him, the indicator concept as developed by Burns/Mitchell generally lacks theoretical foundations. This deficiency particularly refers to economic predictions:

"There is no sign in the book of an awareness of the problems of determining the identifiability of, and measuring, structural equations as a prerequisite to the practically important types of prediction. ... The movements of economic

---

[20] In his essay *"Essai de météorologie économique et sociale"* DeFoville (1888) suggested to introduce barometers, thermometers, hygrometers, etc. to economic observations. Hence, the following notions apply also to hygrometers, thermometers, etc.

[21] Compare also the controversy between Koopmans and Vining. (Koopmans (1949) and Vining (1949 a,b)).

variables are studied as if they were the eruptions of a mysterious volcano
whose boiling caldron can never be penetrated." (Koopmans (1947), p.195)

Basically, one should agree with Koopmans' view. Explanation implies prediction
and (scientific) prediction implies explanation; both are but two sides of one coin. Yet,
explanation means understanding and understanding comes about and expresses itself
by theories. Surely this point of view can methodologically be called into question. As
a discussion of this topic is far beyond the scope of this book, the interested reader is
referred to Popper (1934) for an intensive treatment of this problem.

Aside from the methodological problem which cannot finally be solved here, one
other point deserves attention. The concept of leading, lagging, and coinciding indicators suggests strongly on a more intuitive basis that this concept might be used for
predictive purposes. Indeed, in every-day life as suggested by economic newspapers and
magazines economic indicators are used for predictions. This does not have to be completely senseless in every case, for theoretical insights are *implicitly* involved by correct
interpretations of these indicators.

As a final and less important point the question should shortly be considered
whether indicators are at least able to indicate current turning points. The answer
is, strictly speaking, no, for the problem of prediction is in this case hidden behind
a semantic curtain. Deciding whether a peak or trough prevails implicitly requires
the knowledge of future developments. The statement that a time series currently has
reached a peak or trough unavoidably maintains that it will move downwards or upwards
from now on. This is exactly what an indicator cannot assert by itself.

1.2.2. Capacity Utilization

Measuring business activities using indicators provides the possibility of obtaining a very
differentiated picture of the overall economic situation: output, prices, factor inputs,
employment, bank liabilities, inventories, stock exchange turnovers, profits, and wages
are just a few economic categories which can be condensed and digested into economic
indicators. As long as one only wants to receive a purely descriptive picture of the state
of the economy, this kind of collecting and condensing data might suffice, although
methodological objections can be raised even at this point. For if the hypothesis "the
more the better" were correct, one would end up having to collect virtually *all* economic
data. Regard this matter from the other side: which data should be collected even
in such simple a case as measuring economic activities is to be related to theoretical
considerations which themselves may be inspired by real problems.

Considering the economic development after World War II in the United States
or in Germany may clarify this point. The fact that during business cycles the (un)-
employment rate fluctuates becomes the predominant feature of those cycles. Bearing in

mind the socially detrimental and individually catastrophic consequences of the long en-
during unemployment of up to 25% of the working population during the Great Depression (1929-1931), the unemployment rate and its changes gained increasing attention by
politicians and the public after 1945. The immediate consequence was the Employment
Act of 1946. Its purpose was to maintain high levels of employment and therefore production. The institutional arrangements to secure these goals are the annual 'Economic
Report of the President' and the Council of Economic Advisers. Similar institutional
arrangements, though in a somewhat broader economic context, were set up in West
Germany in 1967 by the so-called "Stability Law".[22] According to this law, a high
employment rate must be one of the economic goals pursued by the government.[23] The
institutions which were established under this law are the "Annual Economic Report of
the Government" (Jahreswirtschaftsbericht der Bundesregierung) and the "Council of
Experts" (Sachverständigenrat).[24] These institutions were conceived as instruments to
assist the government in pursuing these goals.

Now that the public places so much value on a high employment rate, it is no
wonder that the business cycle phenomenon has increasingly been considered with respect to how the employment rate is affected during the business cycle and to what
extend stabilization policy has succeeded in keeping employment at a high level. Thus
(un-)employment itself or closely related economic magnitudes are sometimes used as
a measure of the business cycle.[25] Among the latter magnitudes, the gross national
product (GNP) and its rate of change plays an important role. The interrelationship
between GNP and employment is interpreted mainly in the Keynesian spirit. If capacities are underutilized, a growing (decreasing) GNP must be accompanied by growing
(decreasing) employment. Hence, as long as one stresses the importance of growing
employment during an expansion, it suffices to measure the rate of change of GNP.

This view is in one sense rather narrow-minded. It takes only into account what
actually happened while completely neglecting what *could* have happened. To be more
precise: measuring GNP or its rate of change does not say anything about what GNP
could have been if all productive resources including labor had been fully utilized. This
problem is not at all only of pure academic interest. Consider the 1956/57 recession in
the US, followed by a boom in 1958/59. At the peak of this boom were by no means all
productive resources fully utilized.[26] Although all conventional methods of measuring

---

[22] *Cf. Gesetz zur Förderung der Stabilität und des Wachstums der Wirtschaft.*

[23] *The other goals are: stability of the price level, balanced international trade, and
continuous and adequate economic growth.*

[24] *For a comparison of the Council of Economic Advisers and the 'Sachverständigenrat' see Wallich (1968).*

[25] *Cf. Gordon (1952), pp. 136 ff.*

[26] *Cf. Okun (1970), p. 40.*

business cycles indicated a peak and thus signalled a more or less favorable state of the economy, the underutilized resources would have enabled the economy to produce a substantially higher GNP (cf. Figure 1.6).

Capacity Utilization and Corporate Profits

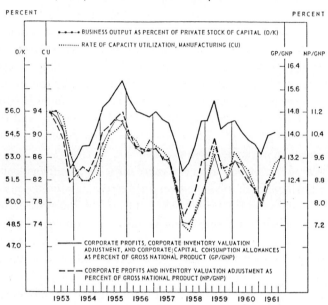

Source: Economic Report of the President (1962), p. 55
Figure 1.6

Following this line of reasoning one arrives at the concept of *potential* GNP which can be produced by *full-employment* of all factors of production, as compared to *actual* GNP being produced by *actual* employment of the factors of production. From here it is only one step to defining the ratio between actual and potential GNP as

$$\lambda(t) = \frac{Y(t)}{Y_p(t)}, \tag{1.2.4}$$

with $Y(t)$ as actual and $Y_p(t)$ as potential GNP. This ratio, respectively its change, may serve as a measure of "general business conditions", *i.e.*, it may serve as a measure for the business cycle.

Since the potential GNP is a theoretical concept, its numerical value will differ as different methods of evaluating its value are applied, and hence different values for the *degree of capacity utilization* $\lambda(t)$ will result. Consequently, important practical issues will be involved. For example, the height of the full-employment budget surplus, the proposed rate of change in the money supply, and the aims of a full-employment policy may depend on the current state of business conditions as expressed by $\lambda(t)$.

1.2.2.1. Concepts Based on Single Factors of Production

The simpler concepts of measuring the rate of capacity utilization explicitly take into account just one production factor. Naturally, this factor is either labor or capital. Both concepts will be discussed briefly.

Labor

Okun (1962) was the first one to develop a concept of measuring potential output as related to labor as a factor of production. In particular, he established a relationship between the extent to which actual output is depressed from its potential level by unemployment in excess of its natural rate. The latter he assumed to be 4 percent. Based on various statistical estimates, Okun ended up with the following relationship between output, potential output, and unemployment:

$$Y_p = Y\left(1 + 0.032(u - 4)\right), \tag{1.2.5}$$

with u as the unemployment rate in percent and Y_p and Y defined as before. This means that when unemployment takes on its natural rate of 4 percent, the actual and potential output coincide. Yet for each percentage point of unemployment in excess of 4%, potential output would be 3.2 % higher than actual output. In other words, one percentage point more in unemployment means 3.2 percent less in GNP.[27]

This relationship between unemployment and the loss in GNP has become famous as *Okun's law*. It had considerable practical impact on viewing the current state of economic affairs. Firstly, it stressed the supply side of the economy. Since the supply capabilities of an economy improve according to increases in the labor force, in investment, and in technology, the demand side should increase at least as much. Otherwise, rising unemployment would result. Hence, record highs in real GNP and income do not necessarily indicate a satisfactory performance of the economy; it might be the case that for lower unemployment the economy would have done even better.

Secondly, the simple judgement of economic performance by rating an expansion as satisfactory and a contraction as unsatisfactory was replaced by the more sophisticated concept of the output gap, *i.e.*, the difference between potential and actual output. As

---

[27] *Actually, one must differentiate between Y_p in percent of Y versus Y in percent of Y_p. But since both concepts yield approximately the same result within this empirically relevant range, the difference can be neglected.*

long as such a gap exists, the economy exhibits underutilized capacities. The apparent need for active economic policy consequently persists. As long as the output gap exists, additional economic actions must be undertaken until it finally disappears.

Capital

While the concept above links potential GNP to the labor force, another concept has been developed which links potential GNP to capital. Mertens (1961) and Krengel (1970) from the German Institute for Economic Research (Deutsches Institut für Wirtschaftsforschung) and later the German Sachverständigenrat (1980) related potential output to the capital stock and its productivity.[28]

First of all, the actual and potential output originating in the rest of the world, in the government sector, and in private households and non-profit institutions are assumed to be identical. With this assumption the Sachverständigenrat follows Rasche/Tatom (1977, p.14). Hence, actual and potential output can diverge only in the private business sector.

The potential product $\tilde{Y}_p(t)$ of this sector is determined as

$$\tilde{Y}_p(t) = k_p(t)K(t), \tag{1.2.6}$$

with $k_p(t)$ as potential capital productivity and $K(t)$ as the actual capital stock. The potential capital productivity is derived in the following way (cf. Figure 1.7).

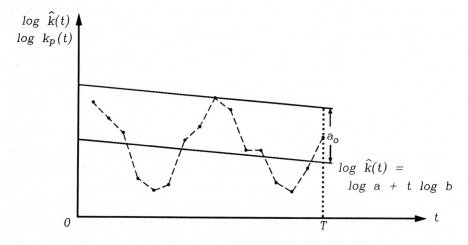

Derivation of Potential Capital Productivity
Figure 1.7

For the reference time period [0, T] the actual capital productivities $k(t)$ are known; hence a logarithmic trend function

$$\log \hat{k}(t) = \log a + t \log b \qquad (1.2.7)$$

can be calculated. Thereafter a parallel to this function is drawn which intersects that actual capital productivity which lies highest above the trend function. This new line indicates the development of potential capital productivity during the reference period. The distance between these two lines is given by $a_0 = \max_t (\log k(t) - \log \hat{k}(t))$, $t \in [0, T]$. Hence, potential capital productivity $k_p(t)$ is determined by

$$\log k_p(t) = a_0 + \log \hat{k}(t), \qquad (1.2.8)$$

for a_0 and t as above. Having determined the trend line of the potential capital productivity in this way, it is easy to derive the trend line of potential GNP by determining the trend line of $\tilde{Y}_p(t)$ and adding the output of the other sectors.

Using this method, the German Sachverständigenrat estimated potential GNPs and the ratio of actual to potential GNP for the period from 1970 to 1987; the results are shown in Figure 1.8.

The upper part of Figure 1.8 is self-explanatory; the lower part deserves some comment. First of all, the ratio of actual to potential GNP is interpreted as the *degree of capacity utilization*. As it is constructed, this measure is bounded from above by 1: since the actual capital productivity can never exceed the potential productivity, actual GNP can never exceed potential GNP. This seems to suggest that *capacity* is a technological category - not in the extreme sense that it implies a maximal "crash production" regardless of economic considerations, which under no circumstances can be surpassed - but rather as a technologically determined maximal production under "normal working conditions", whatever the last qualification may mean in practice.

Secondly, by implicit reasoning, $\lambda(t) = 1$ is interpreted as indicating the highest output which can be produced by utilizing available resources. Yet it may be possible that in the year in which $\lambda(t) = 1$, resources are in fact under-utilized; it is only that in the years before and thereafter resources are utilized even less. Hence, there should be a tendency of this measure to overestimate the "true" rate of capacity utilization.

Finally, it should be mentioned that the above method completely neglects labor as a factor of production. Only if all or at least the most important factors of production are considered in determining the rate of capacity utilization, the results will rest on a sound theoretical basis. In the following discussion, concepts which rely on empirical estimates of aggregate production functions will be presented.

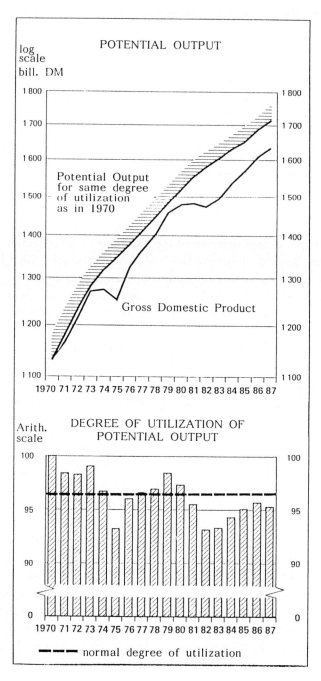

Source: Sachverständigenrat (1988), p. 66

Figure 1.8

1.2.2.2. Concepts Based on Production Functions

Basic Ideas

In the following analysis a macroeconomic production function and therefore the factors of production play an essential role. In the same way that a production function links the actual GNP, $Y(t)$, to the input of actual factors of production $L(t)$ (labor) and $K(t)$ (capital), i.e.,

$$Y(t) = f(L(t), K(t)), \qquad (1.2.9)$$

the potential GNP, $Y_p(t)$, can be linked to the respective potential values $L_p(t)$ and $K_p(t)$ by an equivalent production function

$$Y_p(t) = f_p(L_p(t), K_p(t)). \qquad (1.2.10)$$

Assuming that an econometric estimation $\hat{f}(\cdot)$ of $f(\cdot)$ can be used as a reliable approximation for $f_p(\cdot)$, one can proceed in the following way: potential values of all factors of production, in particular labor and capital, must be estimated. These estimates have to be inserted into the empirical production function yielding the potential output.

By following the procedure just described, the problem of determining potential GNP has been shifted mainly to determining potential values of the factors of production. Additionally, the selection of other factors of production aside from labor and capital and the specifiction of $f(\cdot)$, for example as a Cobb-Douglas or a CES-production function, will affect the resulting potential GNP.

Capital Stock, Labor Force, and Time Trend

Though the notion of *capacity* is a rather old one, the CEA's evaluation of potential output[29] gave rise to further research and contributions in this area. In particular, the idea of using production functions for estimating potential GNP was taken up. Most of these estimates,[30] which take a macroeconomic production function explicitly into account, consider capital, labor, and a time trend (which can be interpreted as technological progress) as factors of production.

Aside from its theoretical advantages this method of estimating potential output gained practical importance in that it was adopted by influential political institutions. In 1973 the German Central Bank (Deutsche Bundesbank)[31] published its estimation

---

[29] *Economic Report of the President (1962), pp. 49 ff.*

[30] *Cf. Kuh (1966), Thurow/Taylor (1966), Black/Russel (1969), Schönfeld (1967).*

[31] *Cf. Deutsche Bundesbank (1973), pp. 28-34.*

of potential GNP based on a Cobb-Douglas production function, and in 1977 the Council of Economic Advisers[32] revised its own old estimate of potential GNP by using a production function. In 1982 the concept was adopted in Austria to estimate potential GNP.[33] In the following discussion the method used by the Deutsche Bundesbank will be outlined.

First, it must be noted that the Deutsche Bundesbank interprets potential output as that output which can be produced with an *average* utilization of factors of production. It thus rejects the concept of measuring potential output according to a *maximum* utilization of capacity during the business cycle. Other economic considerations such as price stability and balanced international trade relations may implicitly enter the concept of potential output in this way. In a similar manner, the CEA defines potential output as[34]

> " ... *the output the economy could produce with the existing technology under assumed conditions of high but sustainable utilization of the factors of production – labor, capital, and natural resources. It does not represent the absolute maximum level of production that could be generated by wartime or other abnormal levels of aggregate demand, but rather that which could be expected from high utilization rates obtainable under more normal circumstances.*"

Taking the "normal circumstances of production" into account, periods of underutilization as well as periods of overutilization can be discerned. Practically, this means that the rate of capacity utilization λ is no longer bounded from above by 1 (as in the last section) but that it may become larger than 1, indicating an overutilization of capacity.

In estimating potential GNP, the Deutsche Bundesbank proceeds in the following way: in a first step it estimates a Cobb-Douglas production function for the period from 1960 to 1972 using the actual values of GNP, labor, and capital. The result is

$$Y(t) = .183 K(t)^{.378} L(t)^{.689} e^{.014t}, \qquad R^2 = .998$$
$$DW = 1.93. \tag{1.2.11}$$

This *actual* production function exhibits slightly increasing returns to scale. $Y(t)$ represents GNP in billion DM, measured in 1962 prices. $K(t)$ represents the actually used capital stock in billion DM (prices of 1962), and $L(t)$ stands for actual labor time, measured in billions of hours.

In the second step, potential GNP has been derived from the production function (1.2.11) by inserting the potential values of the factors of production. Hence, the estimation of potential values of capital and labor is tantamount to the estimation of

---

[32] *Cf. Economic Report of the President (1977), pp. 45-57.*

[33] *Cf. Breuss (1982).*

[34] *Economic Report of the President (1977), p. 52.*

productive capacity of the economy if the production function is given. Since this capacity is considered to apply for "normal circumstances of production", appropriate potential values of the factors of production have to be derived. The Deutsche Bundesbank solved this problem pragmatically by using moving averages of the actual values of capital and labor as the corresponding potential values.

Inserting the potential values of capital and labor into the previously derived production function (1.2.11) one obtains potential GNP. Table 1.4 contains the results of these calculations. Figure 1.9 illustrates the growth of actual and potential GNP as well as the cyclical behavior of the degree of capacity utilization $\lambda(t)$ contained in Table 1.4.

Year	Gross National Product		Degree of Utilization $\lambda(t) = Y(t)/Y_p(t)$
	Actual GNP $Y(t)$	Potential GNP $Y_p(t)$	
	billion DM[†]	billion DM[†]	%
1962	360.9	361.8	99.8
1963	373.3	379.9	98.3
1964	398.5	397.8	100.2
1965	421.0	414.3	101.6
1966	433.0	431.2	100.4
1967	432.1	450.4	95.9
1968	462.9	471.0	98.3
1969	500.9	494.6	101.3
1970	530.6	519.6	102.1
1971	544.4	545.0	99.9
1972	560.4	567.7	98.7

† in prices of 1962

Source: Deutsche Bundesbank (1973), p. 29.
Table 1.4

Energy as an Additional Factor of Production

The concept of potential GNP based on a production function has been improved by Rasche/Tatom (1977), who introduced energy as an additional factor of production into the production function. After the oil price shock in 1973, the supply conditions for energy resources had changed drastically in the US economy as well as in Western Europe

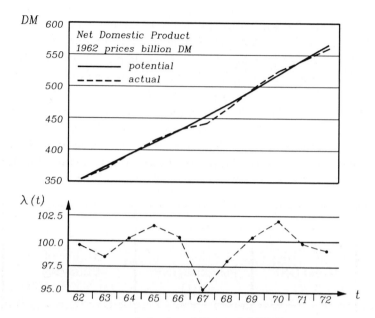

Actual and Potential NDP
Source: Deutsche Bundesbank (1973), p. 33, (upper part); own calculations
(lower part)
Figure 1.9

and the rest of the world. Hence, for the years following 1973 it became unreasonable to
assume that changes in the supply conditions of energy could adequately be captured by
changes in the capital stock. The above authors thus considered energy resources as an
integral part of the production function by using the following Cobb-Douglas function

$$Y(t) = AL(t)^{\alpha} K(t)^{\beta} E(t)^{\gamma} e^{rt}, \quad \alpha + \beta + \gamma = 1, \tag{1.2.12}$$

with A as a scaling factor, $E(t)$ as the flow of energy resources, r as the trend rate
of growth, and the other symbols as used before.[35] In estimating this function the
authors took account of the energy flow in an indirect manner. Due to lack of data,
they assumed that the energy input was governed by profit maximizing behavior, so
that

$$p_E = p\frac{\partial Y}{\partial E} = p\gamma\frac{Y}{E} \tag{1.2.13}$$

must hold with p_E as the price of energy and p as the price of output. From (1.2.12)-

---

[35] *The authors actually differentiated between the private business sector and the rest
of the economy, but for expository purposes we neglect this differentiation.*

(1.2.13) they derived

$$Y(t) = \left(\overline{A}\, L(t)^\alpha\, K(t)^\beta\, (p/p_E)^\gamma\, e^{rt}\right)^{\frac{1}{1-\gamma}}, \quad \overline{A} := A\gamma^\gamma. \tag{1.2.14}$$

This production function was estimated by annual data for the period 1949-75.

The potential values of capital services and labor services are derived from data published by the Federal Reserve Board and the CEA, among others. Substituting these potential values and the price ratio p/p_E into the production function (1.2.14), the coefficient of which has been empirically estimated as described above, yields potential GNP.

The important result derived by the authors is that potential GNP is lower than potential GNP estimated by the CEA method. Hence, the rate of capacity utilization $\lambda(t)$ is higher if energy is taken into account than when is not. Table 1.5 summarizes these findings.

Year	Old CEA		New CEA		Rasche/Tatom		Actual GNP
	$Y_p(t)$	$\lambda(t)$	$Y_p(t)$	$\lambda(t)$	$Y_p(t)$	$\lambda(t)$	$Y_p(t)$
	US $\$^\dagger$	%	US $\$^\dagger$	%	US $\$^\dagger$	%	US $\$^\dagger$
1973	1265.4	97.6	1228.2	100.6	1249.2	98.9	1235.0
1974	1315.9	92.3	1271.7	96.5	1257.8	96.5	1214.0
1975	1368.6	87.1	1316.9	90.5	1283.8	92.8	1191.7
1976	1421.2	89.0	1363.6	92.7	1324.6	95.5	1254.6

† Bill. US $ in prices of 1972

Alternative Measures of Potential GNP and Related Rates of
Capacity Utilization in the United States
Source: Rasche/Tatom (1977), p. 2o and own calculations
Table 1.5

The "Old CEA" measures are those which are derived from Okun's law (cf. eq. (1.2.5)) and the "New CEA" measures are obtained by using a production function yet neglecting energy as a factor of production.

If the different rates of capacity utilization following from the different measures are compared with each other, then both CEA measures indicate a distinctly poorer

performance of the economy than the Rasche/Tatom measure. The consequences for
measuring business cycles and for practical economic policy are obvious: depending on
the theoretical model used for deriving the rate of capacity utilization, the business cycle
may appear as more or less severe. If one accepts, for example, that measure which
indicates a severe recession as the correct one, whereas a more appropriate measure
would indicate only a mild or even no recession, then fighting the alleged recession may
lead to nothing else but additional inflationary pressures. This means that attempts to
reduce a non-existing output gap will not only fail, but will have also adverse effects on
the economy.

The same idea of integrating energy as a factor of production in the production
function has been taken up by the Deutsche Bundesbank (Deutsche Bundesbank (1981)).
Similar to Rasche/Tatom (1977), the Bundesbank uses a Cobb-Douglas production
function

$$Y = AK^\alpha L^\beta E^\gamma e^{rt},$$

with all symbols as before with the exception that the energy input is measured directly
in physical terms. Taking this extension into account, the procedure is basically the
same as in the last subsection. The resulting rates of capacity utilization $\lambda(t)$ are
contained in Figure 1.10.

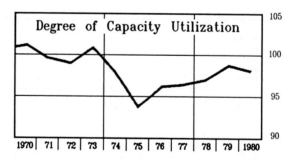

Source: Deutsche Bundesbank (1981), p.33
Figure 1.10

1.2.2.3. Wharton School Index and Surveys

Though concepts of measuring the rate of capacity utilization based on production
functions are theoretically most satisfactory, there exist several other concepts which
have particular merits of their own.

Wharton School Index

This index was developed by Klein (1964) and its main advantage consists in its simplicity. Briefly stated, the last two cyclical peaks of a relevant economic time series are linearly connected (cf. Figure 1.11). For expository purposes, consider GNP as the relevant economic variable in Figure 1.11[36], in which the current point in time is indicated by T and in which the last two peaks are denoted by P_1 and P_2. Hence the line passing through these two points is interpreted as the capacity line. From this interpretation it follows that the ratio between actual and potential GNP as indicated by the capacity line represents the rate of capacity utilization.

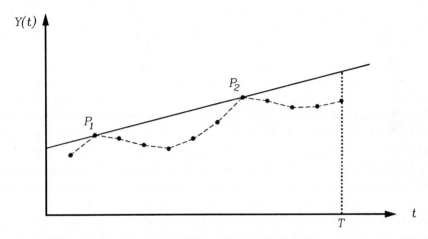

The Derivation of the Capacity Line
Figure 1.11

Though this method is pleasantly simple, some severe objections can be raised against it, as was done, for example, by Phillips (1963). The main objection is that at a cyclical peak the available capacity is not necessarily fully utilized. A cyclical peak is nothing but a local maximum, *e.g.*, in production, and thus leaves the question open whether the economy works with full capacity utilization or not. In fact, as Klein/ Preston(1967, p. 35) mentioned, *"... the general presumption among economists is that the recovery from the 1957-59 recession was incomplete, and the subsequent peaks in many sectors represent points of substantial underutilization of capacity. The Wharton School Index of capacity utilization is therefore thought to be biased upwards since 1958- 59."*

Conclusively, Klein/Preston (1967) developed a production function based concept of capacity much in the spirit of the last section. A comparison of this new measure

---

[36] *Actually, the components of the Federal Reserve Board's index of industrial production were used.*

with the old Wharton School Index confirmed the assumption that the latter is upward biased by and large.

Surveys

Another way of estimating capacity utilization is to survey businesses directly. Christiano (1981) distinguishes between two types of surveys. In the first type a typical question asked is: "At what percentage rate of capacity is your company operating now?" The answers are used to calculate the rate of capacity utilization for a particular industry in a rather straightforward manner. This kind of survey is used by several economic institutions such as the Institut für Wirtschaftsforschung (IFO) in Munich, the U.S. Department of Commerce, and the U.S. Bureau of the Census.

The second survey type estimates only the percentage rate of businesses operating at full capacity. A typical question could be: "Is your company operating at full capacity?" with the two possible answers "Yes" and "No". Clearly, this kind of survey renders less information than the first. Particularly, one receives no information with regard to the actual rate of capacity utilization from those firms with a "No" answer.

Christiano (1981) discusses in detail the advantages and disadvantages of this method. It should only be noted that this method suffers mainly from an insufficient definition of capacity and from the subjective intentions of the respondents. Either the meaning of 'capacity' is not defined at all or its definition is too precise and too complicated. In either case the answer is influenced by the respondants subjective understanding of 'capacity'. Additionally, this subjective and implicit definition may be affected by the respondent's particular situation. For example, in periods of high demand, marginal plants, equipment, and labor may be included in the implicit definition of full or normal capacity, whereas in periods of low demand this is not the case.

Chapter 2

Shock-Dependent Business Cycle Theories

A business cycle model is called *shock-dependent* if, for reasonable values of the parameters, the generation of cycles relies on an impetus which is not explained in itself by the model. Although most of the models in this chapter are able to display steady and explosive oscillations as well, economic reasoning restricts their valid parameter regimes and only damped oscillations around stable equilibria are allowed. In order to exhibit permanent fluctuations these models require the existence of ongoing exogenous forces which disturb the equilibrating tendencies of the model. Only as an exception and for certain parameter constellations can these models generate permanent oscillations with just one initial exogenous disturbance.

The shock-dependent business cycle models will be distinguished according to their mathematical formulation, *i.e.*, whether the models are based on a discrete or continuous time concept. This is done mainly for technical reasons because the mathematical tools used in analyzing a model are quite similar for different economic models of the same kind of time-concept.

This chapter contains the class of multiplier-accelerator models that constitute the "traditional" mathematical business cycle models. Representative for this class of models, the basic approaches of Samuelson and Hicks will be introduced. The presentation of some modifications of these two basic models is followed by Hicks' non-linear ceiling-floor model (basically still a model relying on exogenous forces) and Kalecki's investment delay model.

2.1. Discrete-Time Shock-Dependent Models

A time concept is called discrete if time is conceived as the succession of periods t of finite and equal length. The length of a period is usually defined such that every economic activity can take place once during each period. The adequate mathematical tools in dealing with this discrete time concept are difference equations or systems of difference equations, as opposed to differential equations, which express a continuous time concept (*i.e.*, a concept in which the period length of discrete time models is infinitesimally small and only points of time on a continuous scale are considered). As the mathematics of difference equations are introduced in many macro-textbooks, the reader is supposed to be familiar with the basic ideas of solving these equations. In the following, the important mathematical features are usually only mentioned and not elaborated in detail.[1]

2.1.1. Linear Models of the Cycle

2.1.1.1. The Basic Samuelson Model

In order to construct a dynamic system featuring possible oscillations, Samuelson (1939) considered a simple macroeconomic model that combined the effects of both the multiplier known from today's standard Keynesian income theory and of the acceleration principle.

Let Y_t denote the net national product in period t. Consumption in t is C_t, and I_t denotes net investment.

Assume that consumption C_t in period t depends on the net product of the previous period:

$$C_t = c_0 + cY_{t-1}, \quad c_0 \geq 0, \quad 0 < c < 1. \tag{2.1.1}$$

In the macroeconomic literature, this lag-structure is known as the *Robertson lag* and may be explained in several ways, *e.g.*, by wage payments at the end of a period, adaptive expectations, etc.

---

[1] *Introductions to the mathematics of difference and differential equations can be found in Allen (1965, 1967), Assenmacher (1984), Dernburg/Dernburg (1969), and Baumol (1958), who also elaborate on several of the older models presented here. The more mathematically interested reader is referred to Coddington/Levinson (1955) and Boyce/DiPrima (1977). A complete survey with many economic applications is contained in Gandolfo (1983).*

Investment is assumed to consist of two components, namely induced investment, I_t^{ind}, and autonomous investment, I_t^a. Let autonomous investment be constant over time: $I_t^a = I^a = \text{constant}$.

Induced investment is assumed to behave according to the *acceleration principle*.[2] The essential property of this principle is that investment, *i.e.*, the change in the capital stock, does not depend only on the absolute magnitude of one or several variables (interest rates, capital prices, demand, etc.) but on the *changes* of these variables in the past.

Samuelson proposed a dependence of net investment on the change in consumption demand during the last period:

$$I_t^{\text{ind}} = \beta(C_t - C_{t-1}), \quad \beta > 0, \tag{2.1.2}$$

where the coefficient β is the *accelerator*.[3]

Total net investment is

$$I_t = I^a + \beta(C_t - C_{t-1}). \tag{2.1.3}$$

Equilibrium in the goods market is described by

$$Y_t = C_t + I_t. \tag{2.1.4}$$

The net national product in each period is then determined as

$$Y_t = c_0 + cY_{t-1} + I^a + \beta(C_t - C_{t-1}), \tag{2.1.5}$$

which, after substitution, leads to the second-order, linear, non-homogeneous difference equation

$$Y_t = c_0 + cY_{t-1} + I^a + \beta(c_0 + cY_{t-1} - c_0 - cY_{t-2})$$
$$= c_0 + I^a + c(1 + \beta)Y_{t-1} - c\beta Y_{t-2}$$

or

$$Y_t - c(1 + \beta)Y_{t-1} + c\beta Y_{t-2} = c_0 + I^a. \tag{2.1.6}$$

The particular solution, *i.e.*, the equilibrium value of Y_t, is

$$Y^* = \frac{c_0 + I^a}{1 - c}. \tag{2.1.7}$$

---

[2] *The acceleration principle is due to Clark (1917).*

[3] *Note that investors have to know the consumption function of consumers in order to know the current period's consumption demand in advance. It can alternatively be assumed that the entire consumption demand is effective before investment decisions are made.*

Defining $Y_t = u_t + Y^*$ and substituting into (2.1.6) yields the homogeneous difference equation

$$u_t - c(1 + \beta)u_{t-1} + c\beta u_{t-2} = 0, \tag{2.1.8}$$

which describes the development of the deviation of Y from its equilibrium value over time.

The solution of (2.1.8) has the form[4]

$$u_t = m_1\lambda_1^t + m_2\lambda_2^t, \quad \lambda_1 \neq \lambda_2$$

or   (2.1.9)

$$u_t = (m_1 + tm_2)\lambda^t, \quad \lambda_1 = \lambda_2 = \lambda,$$

with m_1 and m_2 as coefficients still to be determined, and λ_1 and λ_2 as the roots of the characteristic equation

$$\lambda^2 - c(1 + \beta)\lambda + c\beta = 0, \tag{2.1.10}$$

which is derived from substituting the solution trial $u_t = \lambda^t$ into (2.1.8). The solution of (2.1.10) reads

$$\lambda_{1,2} = \frac{c(1 + \beta) \pm \sqrt{\left(c(1 + \beta)\right)^2 - 4c\beta}}{2}. \tag{2.1.11}$$

Finally, the complete solution of (2.1.6) is

$$Y_t = m_1\lambda_1^t + m_2\lambda_2^t + Y^*, \quad \lambda_1 \neq \lambda_2$$

or   (2.1.12)

$$Y_t = (m_1 + tm_2)\lambda^t + Y^*, \quad \lambda_1 = \lambda_2 = \lambda,$$

where m_1 and m_2 are chosen in order to fulfill arbitrary initial values Y_0 and Y_1.

Obviously, the marginal rate of consumption, c, and the accelerator, β, determine the numerical values of the roots $\lambda_{1,2}$ in (2.1.11). Depending on the magnitudes of c and β, the roots of the characteristic equation are real or complex.

First, consider the case

$$\left(c(1 + \beta)\right)^2 \geq 4c\beta$$

or

$$c(1 + \beta)^2 \geq 4\beta, \tag{2.1.13}$$

---

[4] *Cf. Allen (1963), pp. 187 ff.*

i.e., the case of real roots. Suppose firstly that the roots $\lambda_{1,2}$ are not equal. Depending on the dominant root (*i.e.*, the root with the largest absolute value) the system will either be explosive or damped. Inserting the roots in (2.1.9) reveals that the motion will be damped (explosive) if the dominant root is smaller (greater) than unity. In order to examine the relevant parameter regimes of damped and explosive behavior it is not necessary to refer to (2.1.11) directly: from the so-called *Schur criterion*[5] which provides necessary and sufficient conditions for damped monotonic behavior it follows that it is sufficient to examine whether $c(1 + \beta) < 2$. It can easily be shown that this inequality together with the condition for the existence of real roots implies that $\beta < 1$:

$$\left(c(1+\beta)^2 > 4\beta\right) \wedge \left(2 > c(1+\beta)\right) \;\Rightarrow\; 2 > c(1+\beta) > \frac{4\beta}{1+\beta} \;\Rightarrow\; \beta < 1.$$

Thus, damped monotonic behavior occurs for $c \leq 1$ and $\beta < 1$ (cf. Figure 2.1.a). Alternatively, for $c \leq 1$ and $\beta > 1$, the dominant root will be greater than unity and therefore the system will monotonically explode (cf. Figure 2.1.b).

On the margin between damped and explosive monotonic motion, *i.e.*, the stationary case, both roots must be $\lambda_{1,2} = 1$. This can only be the case, however, if $c(1 + \beta)^2 = c\beta$ such that $\lambda_{1,2} = c(1 + \beta)/2$ in (2.1.11). From $c(1 + \beta)^2 = c\beta$ and $c(1 + \beta) = 2$ it follows that $\beta = c = 1$ in the stationary case. The complete solution in this equal roots case is given by $Y_t = (m_1 + tm_2)\lambda^t + Y^*$, implying that $m_2 = 0$ if the solution should be stationary for $\lambda = 1$.

It may happen that equal roots occur having other values than $\lambda = 1$. For example, inserting $\lambda > 1$ into $Y_t = (m_1 + tm_2)\lambda^t + Y^*$ reveals that the term λ^t dominates the term tm_2 such that Y_t is increasing over time.[6] Thus, in the equal roots case the same conclusions concerning the magnitudes of the roots $\lambda_1 = \lambda_2$ can be drawn as those for dominant roots in the previous case.

Second, consider the case

$$c(1 + \beta)^2 < 4\beta, \tag{2.1.14}$$

---

[5] *See, e.g., Dernburg/Dernburg (1969), pp. 216 f. In the case of a second-order polynomial $\lambda^2 + a_1\lambda + a_2 = 0$ the roots are absolutely smaller than one if and only if*

$$1 - a_1 + a_2 > 0$$

$$1 + a_1 + a_2 > 0$$

$$1 - a_2 > 0.$$

With $a_1 = -c(1 + \beta)$ and $a_2 = c\beta$ the first inequality is always fulfilled. From the second and third inequality it follows that $2 > 1 + c\beta > c(1 + \beta)$.

[6] *Cf. Allen (1963), p. 188.*

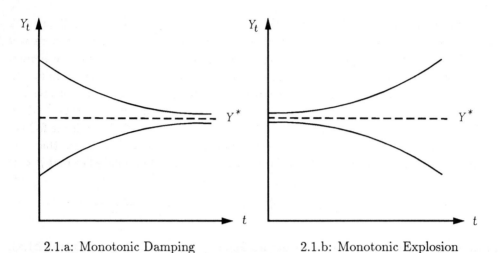

2.1.a: Monotonic Damping   2.1.b: Monotonic Explosion

Figure 2.1

i.e., the case of complex roots. The characteristic roots can be written as

$$\lambda_{1,2} = \frac{c(1+\beta) \pm \sqrt{4c\beta - \left(c(1+\beta)\right)^2}\sqrt{-1}}{2} \tag{2.1.15}$$

or

$$\lambda_{1,2} = a \pm bi$$

with

$$a = \frac{c(1+\beta)}{2}$$

$$b = \frac{\sqrt{4c\beta - \left(c(1+\beta)\right)^2}}{2}$$

$$i = \sqrt{-1}.$$

As complex numbers can be understood as vectors in the $(a-b)$ - plane, the expressions $a \pm bi$ can be re-written as[7]

$$a \pm bi = \text{mod} \ (\cos\theta \pm i\sin\theta) \tag{2.1.16}$$

with mod $= \sqrt{a^2 + b^2}$ as the *modulus*, defined as the Euclidian distance between the origin and the (a, b)- respectively the $(a, -b)$-locus in the plane, and θ as the angle between the distance line and the a-axis (cf. Figure 2.2).

---

[7] *Cf. Dernburg/Dernburg (1969), p. 144f.*

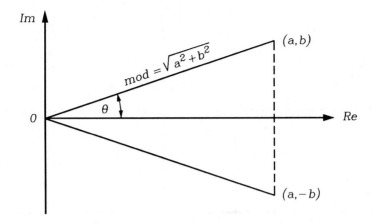

The Modulus of Complex Roots
Figure 2.2

With the help of *DeMoivre's theorem*[8], the solution $u_t = m_1 \lambda_1^t + m_2 \lambda_2^t$ can be written as

$$
\begin{aligned}
u_t &= m_1 \lambda_1^t + m_2 \lambda_2^t \\
&= m_1 \left(\text{mod} \left(\cos \theta + i \sin \theta\right)\right)^t + m_2 \left(\text{mod} \left(\cos \theta - i \sin \theta\right)\right)^t \\
&= \text{mod}^t \left(m_1(\cos \theta t + i \sin \theta t) + m_2(\cos \theta t - i \sin \theta t)\right) \\
&= \text{mod}^t \left((m_1 + m_2) \cos \theta t + (m_1 - m_2)i \sin \theta t\right),
\end{aligned}
\tag{2.1.17}
$$

or, since $(m_1 + m_2)$ and $(m_1 - m_2)i$ are constants which depend on the initial values,

$$
u_t = \text{mod}^t (n_1 \cos \theta t + n_2 \sin \theta t).
\tag{2.1.18}
$$

The term in brackets represents a trigonometric wave motion with a frequency of one complete cycle per interval of length $360^0/\theta$.

Obviously, the modulus serves as a variable that controls the amplitude of the oscillation: for mod $= 1$, a harmonic oscillation around the particular solution Y^* will occur. For mod < 1, the oscillations will be damped (cf. Figure 2.3.a); for mod > 1, they will be increasing (cf. Figure 2.3.b).

As mod $= \sqrt{a^2 + b^2}$, the margin between the two different regimes is determined

---

[8] *DeMoivre's theorem states that* $\left(r(\cos \theta + i \sin \theta)\right)^n = r^n(\cos n\theta + i \sin n\theta)$. *See, e.g., Goldberg (1958), p. 139.*

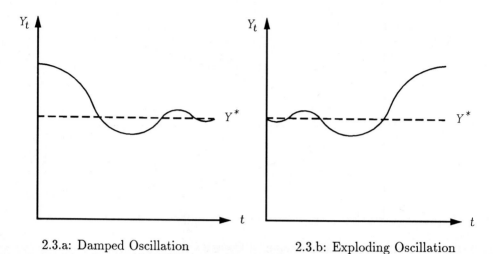

2.3.a: Damped Oscillation   2.3.b: Exploding Oscillation

Figure 2.3

by

$$1 = \frac{\left(c(1+\beta)\right)^2}{4} + \frac{4c\beta - \left(c(1+\beta)\right)^2}{4} \tag{2.1.19}$$

$$= c\beta.$$

Thus, depending on $1/c \gtreqless \beta$, the system's oscillations will either be explosive, constant, or damped.

Summarizing, the parameter constellations and their effects on the dynamic behavior are listed in Table 2.1. The different regimes are diagrammed in Figure 2.4.

Real Roots $c(1+\beta)^2 \geq 4\beta$	Complex Roots $c(1+\beta)^2 < 4\beta$
$c \leq 1 \quad \beta < 1,$ I. Monotonic Damping	$1/c < \beta$ IV. Explosive Oscillation
$c = 1, \quad \beta = 1$ II. Stationarity	$1/c = \beta$ V. Harmonic Oscillations
$c \leq 1, \quad \beta > 1,$ III. Monotonic Explosion	$1/c > \beta$ VI. Damped Oscillation

Table 2.1

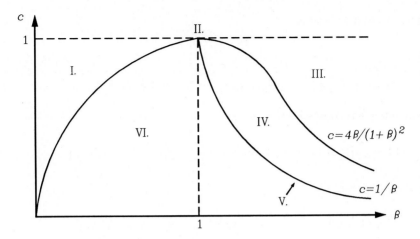

Parameter Regimes in the Samuelson Model
Figure 2.4

2.1.1.2. Hicks' Linear Accelerator

A slight modification in the formal structure of the basic Samuelson model was introduced by Hicks (1950). Instead of (2.1.1), Hicks assumed that

$$I_t^{\text{ind}} = \beta(Y_{t-1} - Y_{t-2}),\qquad(2.1.20)$$

i.e., investment does not only depend on the change in consumption but on the change
in total demand.

Although this is only a minor qualitative change, the additional presentation of
the Hicks model can be justified because it uncovers the sensitivity of linear dynamic
models to the exact structural specification of the model and because it suggests a
slightly different technique in analyzing the parameter regimes.

Following the same procedure as in the preceding section, the Hicks model leads to
the second-order difference equation

$$Y_t - (c+\beta)Y_{t-1} + \beta Y_{t-2} = c_0 + I^a.\qquad(2.1.21)$$

The characteristic equation of the homogeneous part of (2.1.21) is

$$\lambda^2 - (c+\beta)\lambda + \beta = 0\qquad(2.1.22)$$

with the roots

$$\lambda_{1,2} = \frac{(c+\beta) \pm \sqrt{(c+\beta)^2 - 4\beta}}{2}.\qquad(2.1.23)$$

The roots are real as long as

$$(c + \beta)^2 \geq 4\beta \tag{2.1.24}$$

or

$$(c + \beta) \geq \sqrt{4\beta} \quad \text{respectively} \quad 1 - 2\sqrt{\beta} + \beta \geq 1 - c. \tag{2.1.25}$$

As the inequality is fulfilled for

$$(1 - \sqrt{\beta})^2 > (1 - c) \quad \text{as well as for} \quad (\sqrt{\beta} - 1)^2 > (1 - c), \tag{2.1.26}$$

the roots are real for

$$\beta < (1 - \sqrt{1 - c})^2 \quad \text{respectively} \quad \beta > (1 + \sqrt{1 - c})^2. \tag{2.1.27}$$

To limit the possible range of the characteristic roots, consider the function $f(\lambda) = \lambda^2 - (c + \beta)\lambda + \beta$, whose zero roots are the characteristic roots (2.1.23). The extremum of this parabolic function $f(\lambda)$ is given by

$$\frac{df(\lambda)}{d\lambda} = 2\lambda - (c + \beta) = 0$$
$$\Rightarrow \lambda_{\min} = (c + \beta)/2 > 0. \tag{2.1.28}$$

Further, evaluate the function $f(\lambda)$ at the values $\lambda = 0, 1$, and ∞.

λ :	0	1	∞
$f(\lambda)$:	β	$1 - c$	∞

Table 2.2

The function $f(\lambda)$ can cross the abscissa only if its minimum is a negative value. As $f(\lambda)$ is positive for the critical values shown above, it follows that either both roots lie between 0 and 1 or between 1 and ∞.[9] Specifically, if $\lambda_{\min}$ lies between 0 and 1, it follows for the roots $\lambda_{1,2}$ that $0 < \lambda_{1,2} < 1$. Equivalently, for $1 < \lambda_{\min} < \infty \Rightarrow 1 < \lambda_{1,2} < \infty$.

Consider the two possible cases mentioned in (2.1.27), *i.e.*,

$$\beta < (1 - \sqrt{1 - c})^2 \quad \text{and} \quad \beta > (1 + \sqrt{1 - c})^2. \tag{2.1.29}$$

---

[9] *The case $\lambda_1 < 1$ and $\lambda_2 > 1$ is impossible because $f(\lambda)$ must be negative for all $\lambda_1 < \lambda < \lambda_2$. But $f(1)$ was shown to be positive.*

In the case $\beta < (1 - \sqrt{1-c})^2$, substituting $\beta = (1 - \sqrt{1-c})^2$ for β in (2.1.28) yields the extremum

$$\lambda_{\min} = \frac{c + (1 - \sqrt{1-c})^2}{2} = \frac{c + 1 - 2\sqrt{1-c} + 1 - c}{2} = 1 - \sqrt{1-c} < 1. \qquad (2.1.30)$$

Thus, the range of both roots is $0 < \lambda_{1,2} < 1$ with the consequence that the system will exhibit a damped monotonic behavior.

Alternatively, $\beta > (1 + \sqrt{1-c})^2$ implies

$$\lambda_{\min} = 1 + \sqrt{1-c} > 1 \;\Rightarrow\; 1 < \lambda_{1,2} < \infty \quad \Longleftrightarrow \quad \text{explosive behavior.}$$

Stationarity requires $\lambda_1 = \lambda_2 = 1$, and the parabola $f(\lambda)$ must be tangent with the abscissa at $\lambda_{\min}$. From Table 2.2 it follows that $f(1) = 1 - c$, implying that $c = 1$ in order to fulfill $f(1) = 0$. Finally, $c = 1$ implies $\beta = 1$ because $c(1 + \beta)/2 = 1$ at $\lambda_{\min}$. The stationary case therefore prevails if $c = 1$ and $\beta = 1$.

In the case of complex roots, the regimes of increasing and damped oscillations are distinguished according to whether

$$\mathrm{mod} = \sqrt{a^2 + b^2} \gtreqless 1, \qquad (2.1.31)$$

with

$$a = \frac{c + \beta}{2},$$

$$b = \frac{\sqrt{4\beta - (c + \beta)^2}}{2}.$$

Simple inspection shows that

$$\mathrm{mod} = \sqrt{\frac{(c + \beta)^2}{4} + \frac{4\beta - (c + \beta)^2}{4}} > 1 \quad \forall\, \beta > 1, \qquad (2.1.32)$$

and

$$\mathrm{mod} \leq 1 \quad \forall\, \beta \leq 1.$$

The case of harmonic oscillations, *i.e.*, $\mathrm{mod} = 1$, occurs for $\beta = 1$. The marginal propensity to consume must be smaller than 1 in order to guarantee complex roots.

Real Roots $(c+\beta)^2 \geq 4\beta$		**Complex Roots** $(c+\beta)^2 < 4\beta$	
$\beta < (1-\sqrt{1-c})^2$ I. Monotonic Damping		$1 > \beta > (1-\sqrt{1-c})^2$ IV. Damped Oscillation	
$\beta = 1;\ c = 1$ II. Stationarity		$\beta = 1;\ c < 1$ V. Harmonic Oscillation	
$\beta > (1+\sqrt{1-c})^2$ III. Monotonic Explosion		$1 < \beta < (1+\sqrt{1-c})^2$ VI. Explosive Oscillations	

Table 2.3

Summarizing, as the range of complex roots is

$$(1-\sqrt{1-c})^2 < \beta < (1+\sqrt{1-c})^2, \tag{2.1.33}$$

the system exhibits damped oscillations if $(1-\sqrt{1-c})^2 < \beta < 1$ and increasing oscillations if $(1+\sqrt{1-c})^2 > \beta > 1$.

The relevant parameter values are listed in Table 2.3 and are diagrammed in Figure 2.5.

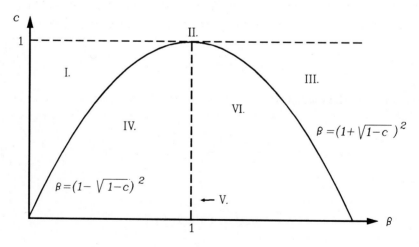

Parameter Regimes in the Hicks Model
Figure 2.5

The main difference between the multiplier-accelerator models of Samuelson and Hicks is that in the Hicks presentation the margin (cases V.) between damped and increasing oscillations depends only on the accelerator β, whereas in the Samuelson model the locus of that margin is influenced by both c and β.

Further extensions of these two basic models of the interaction between the multiplier and the accelerator are easy to perform. Possible variations are, among others, the case of growing autonomous investment, $I_t^a = I_0^a e^{rt}$, $r > 0$, extended consumption lags, e.g., $C_t = c_0 + c_1 Y_{t-1} + c_2 Y_{t-2}$, the introduction of governmental activities, etc.

2.1.1.3. The Influence of Inventories

The models of Samuelson and Hicks are definitely very simple macroeconomic models, as they operate only with consumption and net investment in the capital stock. Specifically, inventories are neglected and expectations are at best implicitly incorporated into the analysis.

Metzler (1941) studied several models that concentrate on the stability effects of different inventory hypotheses and explicit expectations. Among the various models presented by Metzler, the following is the most interesting.

For the sake of simplicity, let the investment in capital be autonomous, $I^a = \text{const.}$ Further, let X_t^C denote the production of goods to meet the expected consumption demand, and let X_t^I denote the production for the inventory stock. The inventory serves as a safety buffer because the firm cannot be sure that the sales expectations are correct.

Assume that the firm attempts to keep the inventory stock B_t^I at a certain level which proportionally depends on the expected sales in the current period:

$$B_t^I = kX_t^C, \quad k > 0. \tag{2.1.34}$$

In the case that expected sales in the current period depend on the realized sales during the previous period, *i.e.*, $X_t^C = C_{t-1}$, and that the consumption function is non-lagged, *i.e.*,

$$C_t = cY_t, \tag{2.1.35}$$

the desired level of stocks will be

$$B_t^I = kX_t^C = kC_{t-1} = kcY_{t-1} \tag{2.1.36}$$

As sales expectations could be incorrect, the actual stock of inventories may have been different from the desired level at the end of the previous period.

The desired level in $t-1$ was

$$B^I_{t-1} = kcY_{t-2} \tag{2.1.37}$$

and expected sales were

$$X^C_{t-1} = cY_{t-2}. \tag{2.1.38}$$

However, because $C_t = cY_t$, actual sales were

$$C_{t-1} = cY_{t-1}. \tag{2.1.39}$$

Thus, a sales discrepancy $C_{t-1} - X^C_{t-1} = c(Y_{t-1} - Y_{t-2})$ may have occurred. As an excess demand decreases the inventory, the actual inventory level at the end of period $t-1$ was

$$B^I_{t-1} - c(Y_{t-1} - Y_{t-2}) = kcY_{t-2} - c(Y_{t-1} - Y_{t-2}) \tag{2.1.40}$$

instead of the planned level B^I_{t-1}.

The production for inventories is the difference between the desired level this period and the actual level at the end of the previous period:

$$X^I_t = B^I_t - (B^I_{t-1} - c(Y_{t-1} - Y_{t-2})) = kcY_{t-1} - kcY_{t-2} + c(Y_{t-1} - Y_{t-2})$$
$$= c(k+1)(Y_{t-1} - Y_{t-2}). \tag{2.1.41}$$

The net income arising from the production of goods and capital investment is

$$Y_t = X^C_t + X^I_t + I^a$$
$$= cY_{t-1} + c(k+1)(Y_{t-1} - Y_{t-2}) + I^a \tag{2.1.42}$$

or

$$Y_t - c(k+2)Y_{t-1} + c(k+1)Y_{t-2} = I^a. \tag{2.1.43}$$

Once again, the model has been reduced to a second-order difference equation with constant coefficients.

Following the procedure in the preceding sections, the characteristic roots are calculated as

$$\lambda_{1,2} = \frac{c(k+2) \pm \sqrt{c^2(k+2)^2 - 4c(k+1)}}{2}. \tag{2.1.44}$$

As (2.1.43) is formally identical with (2.1.21), the presentation will be shortened by a comparison of the different coefficients in both equations.

In (2.1.21) and (2.1.43) the analogous coefficients are

$$c + \beta \cong c(k+2)$$
$$\beta \cong c(k+1), \tag{2.1.45}$$

implying that $\beta \cong c(k+1)$ holds in both cases of (2.1.45).

Real Roots $c^2(k+2)^2 \geq 4c(k+1)$	**Complex Roots** $c^2(k+2)^2 < 4c(k+1)$
$k > 2((1-c) + \sqrt{1-c})\,/\,c$ Monotonic Explosion I.	$k < (1-c)\,/\,c$ Damped Oscillation III.
$k = 2((1-c) + \sqrt{1-c})\,/\,c$ Stationarity II.	$k = (1-c)\,/\,c$ Harmonic Oscillations IV.
	$k > (1-c)\,/\,c$ Explosive Oscillations V.

Table 2.4

In (2.1.21), the real roots case occurs if

$$\beta < (1-\sqrt{1-c})^2 \quad \text{resp.} \quad \beta > (1+\sqrt{1-c})^2. \tag{2.1.46}$$

The equivalent conditions for (2.1.43) are

$$c(k+1) < (1-\sqrt{1-c})^2 \quad \text{resp.} \quad c(k+1) > (1+\sqrt{1-c})^2, \tag{2.1.47}$$

and it follows that

$$k < \frac{(1-\sqrt{1-c})^2}{c} - 1 = \frac{1 - 2\sqrt{1-c} + (1-c) - c}{c}$$
$$= \frac{2((1-c) - \sqrt{1-c})}{c} \tag{2.1.48}$$

for damped monotonicity, and

$$k > \frac{2((1-c) + \sqrt{1-c})}{c} \tag{2.1.49}$$

for increasing monotonic motion. Stationarity prevails for $k = 2((1-c) + \sqrt{1-c})/c$.

However, as $0 < (1 - c) < 1$, it follows that $(1 - c) < \sqrt{1 - c}$, so that the condition for damped monotonic behavior cannot be fulfilled for positive values of k. Therefore, only stationarity or explosive monotonic movements are possible in the real roots case.

In the complex roots case, the characteristic equation (2.1.43) leads directly to the modulus

$$\text{mod} = \sqrt{\frac{c^2(k + 2)^2 + 4c(k + 1) - c^2(k + 2)^2}{4}} = \sqrt{c(k + 1)}. \qquad (2.1.50)$$

The oscillation will thus be damped for $k < 1/c - 1$ and will be explosive for $k > 1/c - 1$.

The parameter regimes are summarized in Table 2.4 and are visualized in Figure 2.6.

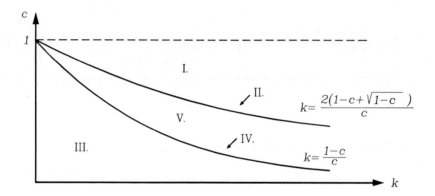

Parameter Regimes in the Metzler Model
Figure 2.6

It has thus been shown that the introduction of inventories in a Keynesian macro-model can imply the same effects as the accelerator-hypothesis. It has often been stressed that inventories play an important role when an economy is fluctuating, and changing inventory stocks may be considered as an indicator of economic activity. Metzler's example shows that inventories do not always have to behave in such a passive manner, but rather that the changing of inventories can constitute the essential dynamic ingredient of a model.

2.1.1.4. Monetary Aspects of the Cycle

In order to construct models which are able to generate cyclic movements it is not necessary to revert to investment accelerators. Rather, it is in general possible to explain oscillations in a whole variety of models featuring certain dynamic lag structures. In the following section a model will be presented that concentrates on monetary aspects of the cycle, *i.e.*, the influence of monetary authorities on the dynamics of the system.

This model, which is based on the trade-off between inflation and the rate of capacity utilization (*i.e.*, a modified Phillips curve) was developed by Laidler (1976).[10]

Let M_t^d denote nominal demand for money, M_t^s nominal supply, and p_t the price level.

The real demand for money is assumed to depend on income:

$$\frac{M_t^d}{p_t} = Y_t^\gamma, \quad \gamma > 0 \tag{2.1.51}$$

with γ as the elasticity of real money demand in response to the real income Y_t. With $M_t^s = \overline{M}_t^s$ exogenously given, the equilibrium condition on the money market is

$$M_t^d = p_t Y_t^\gamma = \overline{M}_t^s. \tag{2.1.52}$$

Further, let Y_t^* denote the exogenously determined full-employment product. Then the ratio

$$y_t = \frac{Y_t}{Y_t^*} \tag{2.1.53}$$

measures the degree of capacity utilization.

The modified Phillips curve mentioned above is derived in the following way: let $g_{p,t}$ be the growth rate of the price level

$$g_{p,t} = \frac{p_t - p_{t-1}}{p_{t-1}} \tag{2.1.54}$$

and let $\hat{g}_{p,t}$ be the growth factor

$$\hat{g}_{p,t} = 1 + g_{p,t} = \frac{p_t}{p_{t-1}}. \tag{2.1.55}$$

Laidler assumed that the growth factor of the price level depends on y_t as well as on the expected growth factor of the price level last period:

$$\hat{g}_{p,t} = y_t^\delta \, \hat{g}_{p,t-1}^e, \quad \delta > 0, \tag{2.1.56}$$

with $\hat{g}_{p,t-1}^e$ as the expected growth factor of the price level.

---

[10] *In Laidler's original contribution all variables are measured in natural logarithms. In order to allow for a direct comparison with previous result, the following presentation is in antilog terms.*

Laidler assumes an adaptive expectation formation process[11] for the logs of the price level which in antilog terms leads to

$$\hat{g}^e_{p,t} = \left(\frac{\hat{g}_{p,t-1}}{\hat{g}^e_{p,t-1}}\right)^\varepsilon \hat{g}^e_{p,t-1}, \quad \varepsilon > 0. \tag{2.1.57}$$

Combining (2.1.56) and (2.1.57) yields

$$
\begin{aligned}
\frac{\hat{g}_{p,t}}{\hat{g}_{p,t-1}} &= \left(\frac{y_t}{y_{t-1}}\right)^\delta \frac{\hat{g}^e_{p,t-1}}{\hat{g}^e_{p,t-2}} \\
&= \left(\frac{y_t}{y_{t-1}}\right)^\delta \left(\frac{\hat{g}^e_{p,t-1}}{\hat{g}^e_{p,t-2}}\right)^\varepsilon \\
&= \left(\frac{y_t}{y_{t-1}}\right)^\delta \left(\frac{(y_{t-1})^\delta \hat{g}^e_{p,t-2}}{\hat{g}^e_{p,t-2}}\right)^\varepsilon \\
&= \left(\frac{y_t}{y_{t-1}}\right)^\delta (y_{t-1})^{\varepsilon\delta}.
\end{aligned}
\tag{2.1.58}
$$

Equation (2.1.58) constitutes Laidler's modified Phillips curve and expresses the well-accepted assumption that the growth rate (or growth factor) of prices increases when production is increasing.

Combining (2.1.51), (2.1.52), and (2.1.53) yields

$$M^d_t = p_t Y^\gamma_t = p_t (y_t Y^*_t)^\gamma = \overline{M}^s_t. \tag{2.1.59}$$

The expression

$$\frac{M^s_t}{M^s_{t-1}} = \frac{p_t}{p_{t-1}} \left(\frac{y_t}{y_{t-1}} \frac{Y^*_t}{Y^*_{t-1}}\right)^\gamma \tag{2.1.60}$$

can be written as

$$\hat{g}_{M^s,t} = \hat{g}_{p,t} \left(\frac{y_t}{y_{t-1}}\right)^\gamma (\hat{g}_{Y^*,t})^\gamma, \tag{2.1.61}$$

and it follows that

$$\frac{\hat{g}_{M^s,t}}{\hat{g}_{M^s,t-1}} = \frac{\hat{g}_{p,t} \left(\frac{y_t}{y_{t-1}}\right)^\gamma (\hat{g}_{Y^*,t})^\gamma}{\hat{g}_{p,t-1} \left(\frac{y_{t-1}}{y_{t-2}}\right)^\gamma (\hat{g}_{Y^*,t-1})^\gamma}. \tag{2.1.62}$$

Substituting for $\hat{g}_{p,t}/\hat{g}_{p,t-1}$ from (2.1.58) and re-arranging yields

$$y_t \, y_{t-1}^{\frac{\delta\varepsilon-\gamma}{\delta+\gamma}-1} \, y_{t-2}^{\frac{\gamma}{\delta+\gamma}} = \left(\frac{\hat{g}_{M^s,t}}{\hat{g}_{M^s,t-1}} \Big/ \left(\frac{\hat{g}_{Y^*,t}}{\hat{g}_{Y^*,t-1}}\right)^\gamma\right)^{\frac{1}{\delta+\gamma}}. \tag{2.1.63}$$

---

[11] *Compare Section 3.3.1.*

Assume that both $\hat{g}_{M^s,t}$ and $\hat{g}_{Y^*,t}$ remain constant over time. Thus, the right hand side of (2.1.63) will take on the value 1. The logarithmic form of (2.1.63) is:

$$\ln y_t - \left(1 + \frac{\gamma - \delta\varepsilon}{\gamma + \delta}\right)\ln y_{t-1} + \frac{\gamma}{\gamma + \delta}\ln y_{t-2} = 0. \qquad (2.1.64)$$

Equation (2.1.64) is again a linear second-order difference equation with constant coefficients. As the procedure to analyse (2.1.64) is the same as, e.g., that for (2.1.21), only the relevant parameter regimes are listed below.

Complex roots arise for

$$\left(1 + \frac{\gamma - \delta\varepsilon}{\gamma + \delta}\right)^2 < \frac{4\gamma}{\gamma + \delta}. \qquad (2.1.65)$$

The modulus is

$$\text{mod} = \frac{\sqrt{\left(1 + \frac{\gamma - \delta\varepsilon}{\gamma + \delta}\right)^2 + \frac{4\gamma}{\gamma + \delta} - \left(1 + \frac{\gamma - \delta\varepsilon}{\gamma + \delta}\right)^2}}{2} \qquad (2.1.66)$$

$$= \sqrt{\frac{\gamma}{\gamma + \delta}}.$$

Increasing oscillations, i.e., mod > 1, would occur if $\sqrt{\gamma/\gamma + \delta} > 1$. However, this implies that $\delta < 0$. The model is therefore able to explain only damped oscillations.

As this result was obtained under the assumption of constant growth rates of the full-employment product Y^* and of the money supply M^s, it confirms the well-known monetaristic statement that an exogenous shock to the system in the form of, e.g., a rise in the absolute level of the money supply, has no long-run effects on the actual level of the national product as long as the growth rate of the money supply is constant. However, the adjustment process after an initial shock may be characterized by damped oscillations.

2.1.2. Non-Linear Multiplier-Accelerator Models

The multiplier-accelerator models discussed in the preceding sections are linear models. A single set of linear difference equations is valid over the entire range of permissable values of the involved variables. In the following, two multiplier-accelerator models will be presented in which bounds to the motion of a single system or different sets of equations for specific situations are introduced. Though the separate elements of these models are linearily structured, the overall systems are non-linear.

2.1.2.1. Ceiling and Floor in the Hicks Model

The investment functions used in the Samuelson and Hicks multiplier-accelerator models are functions that are valid over the full range of a cycle. Desired and actual investment coincide such that the possibility of positive or negative excess capacities is excluded. If the desired amount of investment is expressed by the investment function (2.1.20), it will always be possible for the investing firm to install the additional amount of capital, and - more importantly - the firm will be able to get rid of superfluous capital in the case of excess capacities. The actual capital stock decrease, ΔK_t, equals the amount of induced investment, I_t^{ind}, in this case, i.e.,

$$I_t = \Delta K_t = I_t^{ind}, \tag{2.1.67}$$

with I_t as net investment. In the standard definition $I_t = I_t^{gross} - D$, the amount of depreciation, $D > 0$, is therefore absolutely identical with the actual capital stock decrease, i.e., $D = -\Delta K_t$, when gross investment equals zero. With this assumption being implicitly made in the multiplier-accelerator models above, installation costs and break-up costs are neglected. As soon as a maximal depreciation (due to technical or calculatory reasons) is introduced in such a cycle model, it may be that the value of net investment according to the investment function is absolutely larger than this maximal depreciation. It follows that the investment behavior can be asymmetric in the different stages of the cycle because during a downswing investment is determined by this amount of depreciation and not by an investment function like (2.1.20).

Hicks (1950) modified the uniform multiplier-accelerator analysis in the spirit of the above remark. Specifically, he considered the following extensions of his basic linear model:

- In addition to induced investment according to (2.1.20), autonomous investment I^a is introduced, which is supposed to grow at a constant rate r.[12] The Hicks model therefore turns into a growth cycle model.

- Motivated basically by empirical considerations, the numerical value of the accelerator is chosen such that the linear model generates explosive oscillations. This implies that upper and lower bounds must be introduced if the model still should make sense economically. While the upper bound ("*ceiling*") is defined as the maximal growth path, which is sustainable with the available resources, the lower bound ("*floor*") is the growth path which is possible if only autonomous investment is carried out.

---

[12] *In order to avoid confusion, it is useful to assume that I^a is exogenous government investment.*

- Depreciation is assumed to be exogenously given and constant. Together with the assumption of explosive oscillation this implies that (negative) induced net investment according to (2.1.20) will start to be absolutely larger than depreciation somewhere during a recession. Actual net investment is therefore determined as

$$I^n = \max\bigl(\beta(Y_{t-1} - Y_{t-2}) + I^a, \ I^a - D\bigr); \quad D = \text{constant}, \tag{2.1.68}$$

during a downswing, and as $I^n = \beta(Y_{t-1} - Y_{t-2}) + I^a$ during an upswing of the economy. The accelerator is therefore working only during an upswing and the upper parts of a downswing.

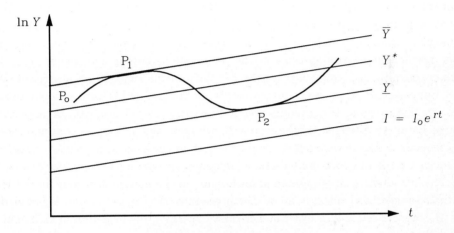

Hicks' Non-Linear Accelerator
Figure 2.7

Figure 2.7 illustrates the working of the process over a complete cycle. As autonomous investment grows exponentially at the exogenously given rate r, the system features a moving equilibrium Y^* determined by the same rate r. The path $\overline{Y}$ describes the development of the ceiling due to resource limitations, *i.e.*, the maximal growth path. An actual trajectory starting at point P_0 is described in the following way: as autonomous investment is rising, the income level will rise, too. Via the acceleration principle, the rise is explosively amplified by induced investment. Actual income therefore rises with a higher growth rate than autonomous investment. At P_1 the ceiling is reached where the growth rate of income is limited by that of the resource capacity. As induced investment depends on the change of income (the change of income is constant and equivalent to the equilibrium growth rate at the ceiling $\overline{Y}$) investment also gradually falls to its equilibrium growth rate. However, the growth of investment at the equilibrium growth rate is not able to support the ceiling level $\overline{Y}$ of income anymore, but rather only the equilibrium level Y^*. Thus, income gradually falls in absolute terms and excess capacities result. The motion will be amplified by the accelerator for a while and net investment will eventually be determined only by depreciation and autonomous investment according to (2.1.68). Thus, only the multiplier works during the downswing movement. As the equilibrium growth path Y^* requires positive induced investment, the actual path crosses the equilibrium path and approaches the lower floor $\underline{Y}$ which is characterized by zero induced investment and an income determined only by autonomous investment and depreciation.[13] However, moving along that lower floor for a while gives an incentive for positive induced investment because the economy features positive growth rates of income. A new cycle starts.

The preceding model is non-linear in the sense that the induced investment function is not valid over the full range of a cycle.[14] Although the Hicks model has the advantage that it is no longer necessary to precisely specify the parameter values which lead to harmonic oscillations, it relies on the assumption of an exogenously given growth rate of the resource capacities, growing at the same rate as autonomous investment. Furthermore, growing autonomous investment is the impetus which keeps a series of cycles alive. Suppose that autonomous investment is not growing but is fixed at some constant level. In this case the Hicks model is able to explain only $1\frac{1}{2}$ cycles, because at the floor no incentive will exist for the system to swing up again. Thus, a continuous series of exogenous shocks were necessary to let the system oscillate permanently, contrary to the linear models in which oscillations - damped or not damped - exist for $t \to \infty$.

The introduction of upper and lower bounds to the motion of income in the Hicks multiplier-accelerator model is an *ad hoc* procedure. The upper bound is not derived from the model itself and its exact numerical value can hardly be determined. The Hicks model therefore possesses an undesirable degree of freedom because different growth rates imply different amplitudes of the cycles. The following section sketches a non-linear multiplier-accelerator model that does not rely on the introduction of these arbitrarily assumed bounds.

---

[13] *As was mentioned by Hicks (1950, p.102, footnote), the assumption of constant depreciation actually does not permit to draw the path $\underline{Y}$ as a parallel straight line in Figure 2.7. Hicks assumed that this influence of a constant amount of depreciation can be neglected, however.*

[14] *For a discussion of this type of non-linearities see Baumol (1958), pp. 281 ff.*

2.1.2.2. The Influence of Ratchet Effects

As is well-known from macroeconomic textbooks, several attempts were made in the 1950s and 1960s to modify the standard Keynesian consumption function. One of the more important modifications was made by Duesenberry and Modigliani who introduced so-called *ratchet effects*: consumption does not only depend on current income but also on the maximum income in the past. Let $Y_t^{\max}$ be this maximum income up to the current period t, i.e., [15]

$$Y_t^{\max} = \max (Y_1, Y_2, \ldots, Y_t). \tag{2.1.69}$$

Consumption C_t in period t is determined by

$$C_t = c_0 + c_1 Y_t + c_2 Y_t^{\max}. \tag{2.1.70}$$

If the current income Y_t is identical with $Y_t^{\max}$, i.e., if it is the highest income which has ever been realized, (2.1.70) becomes

$$C_t = c_0 + (c_1 + c_2)Y_t, \tag{2.1.71}$$

which has the same form as a standard Keynesian consumption function.

As long as $Y_t < Y_t^{\max}$, the maximal value serves as a constant in (2.1.70). In that case the marginal propensity to consume out of current income is lower than in the case (2.1.71), i.e., when $Y_t^{\max} = Y_t$. Consumption therefore does not decrease as much as in the standard Keynesian case when the current income decreases. Consumers' decisions are assumed to be influenced by the maximum income level because they consider the decrease in current income as temporary.

One of the most prominent theoretical applications of this hypothesis can be found in a business cycle model of Smithies (1957) who also introduced ratchet effects in the investment function in addition to those mentioned above. Smithies' purpose was to construct a model which could simultaneously explain fluctuations and a growth trend. The main argument is as follows. Assume that an economy initially experiences rising income levels such that ratchet effects are ineffective. Assume further that the structure of the model economy and the particular parameter constellation imply damped oscillations of the income level. When income has passed its upper turning point, consumers and investors maintain parts of their maximum demand levels, i.e., demand does not decrease as much as would be the case if the downswing were treated symmetrically to the upswing. The downswing phase of the model economy is therefore described by

---

[15] *It is not necessary to include the current income Y_t in (2.1.69); alternatively, $Y_t^{\max}$ can be defined as the maximum value of income up to period $t-1$. The notation will be slightly different in models employing this concept.*

a different set of equations. If the structure of this second set of equations allows for explosive oscillations with unchanged parameters, income will eventually start rising again and will pass the previous maximum income level. If income is higher than that maximum level, the first set of equations without ratchet effects will be activated again until a new and higher upper turning point is reached, and so forth, with the maximal income level increasing from one cycle to another. The motion of income in such a two-stage model is therefore characterized by fluctuations around a growth trend with increasing or decreasing amplitude depending on the particular parameter constellation.

While the idea of simultaneously explaining a growth trend and oscillations in a single model is attractive, the assumptions on the different oscillation properties in the two stages of the Smithies model is rather problematic. Ratchet effects potentially dampen a decrease in income such that it is not immediately obvious why the oscillations in the second stage can be explosive.[16] Kromphardt/Dörfner (1974) demonstrated that it is impossible to find a parameter constellation in the specific model investigated by Smithies which implies damped oscillations in the first stage and explosive oscillations in the second stage. It follows that the original Smithies model is unable to endogenously explain growth cycles. In addition, Smithies' assumptions on ratchet effects in the investment function are rather unconvincing.[17] Hence, in spite of its conceptual merits, the Smithies model cannot be regarded as a standard business cycle model.

While ratchet effects are not suited for explaining endogenous growth cycles, their presence can imply interesting consequences in other business cycle models in which a growth trend is exogenously determined. As a very simple example, recall the linear Hicks multiplier-accelerator model outlined in Section 2.1.1.2. Assume that a ratchet effect is present in the consumption function such that the model becomes

$$
\begin{aligned}
Y_t &= C_t + I_t \\
C_t &= c_0 + c_1 Y_{t-1} + c_2 Y_{t-1}^{\max} \\
I_t &= \beta(Y_{t-1} - Y_{t-2}) + I_0 r^t \\
Y_t^{\max} &= \max{(Y_1, Y_2, \ldots, Y_t)}
\end{aligned}
\tag{2.1.72}
$$

---

[16] *It should be noted, however, that ratchet effects do not generally exclude the possibility of explosive oscillations in the second stage. Though both sets of dynamic equations use the same parameter set, the conditions for damped or explosive oscillations are, of course, different.*

[17] *For example, Smithies assumes that investment increases if full capacity output is lower than the maximal income level in the past. However, full capacity output is lower than this maximal value because investment decreased in the past because of overcapacities and decreasing income. If this ratchet effect in the investment function is abandoned, the Smithies model is unable to generate oscillations at all.*

or

$$Y_t = (c_1 + \beta)Y_{t-1} - \beta Y_{t-2} + c_2 Y_{t-1}^{\max} + c_0 + I_0 r^t$$
$$Y_t^{\max} = \max (Y_1, Y_2, \ldots, Y_t) \tag{2.1.73}$$

with the usual meaning of the symbols. In contrast to the ratchet effect in (2.1.70), consumption in period t is influenced by the maximum income in the past up to the previous period because the Hicks model assumes that individuals can only observe realized values of the variables in the past.

As long as the economy is growing, *i.e.*, if $Y_{t-1} = Y_{t-1}^{\max}$, income develops according to

$$Y_t = (c_1 + c_2 + \beta)Y_{t-1} - \beta Y_{t-2} + c_0 + I_0 r^t. \tag{2.1.74}$$

The particular solution, *i.e.*, the equilibrium level of income, is

$$Y^* = \frac{c_0 + I_0 r^t}{1 - c_1 - c_2}. \tag{2.1.75}$$

As long as $Y_{t-1} \leq Y_{t-1}^{\max}$, income develops according to

$$Y_t = (c_1 + \beta)Y_{t-1} - \beta Y_{t-2} + c_2 Y_{t-1}^{\max} + c_0 + I_0 r^t. \tag{2.1.76}$$

The particular solution of (2.1.76) is

$$Y^* = \frac{c_0 + I_0 r^t + c_2 Y_{t-1}^{\max}}{1 - c_1}, \tag{2.1.77}$$

i.e., the stationary level of income in the second stage increases with the maximum value of Y_t realized in the past.

Equation (2.1.76) is formally identical with equation (2.1.21) of the linear Hicks model (with $c \cong c_1$ and a different amount of autonomous expenditure). The dynamic properties of (2.1.21) for different parameter constellations therefore apply for this equation as well (cf. Table 2.3), and the different parameter regimes of (2.1.76) can be depicted in a diagram like Figure 2.5. Figure 2.8 contains the different parameter regimes for (2.1.76) in the $(\beta - c_1)$ - space. The solid line separates the regions of monotonic and oscillatory behavior. The different regimes are denoted by the superscripts (2) and coincide with the regimes in Figure 2.5.

The parameter regimes of (2.1.74) can be depicted in the same figure. The boundaries between the regimes I. and IV. and between the regimes III. and VI. are obtained by shifting the boundaries of the linear model downwards in the $(\beta - c_1)$ - diagram. This can immediately be seen by writing the functions of the boundaries, *i.e.*, $\beta = (1 - \sqrt{1 - c_1 - c_2})^2$ and $\beta = (1 + \sqrt{1 - c_1 - c_2})^2$, as $c_1 = 2\sqrt{\beta} - \beta - c_2$. The last equation is valid for both boundaries. The dashed line in Figure 2.8 represents the boundaries between the regimes of monotonic damping and damped oscillations, and between the regimes of monotonic explosion and increasing oscillations, respectively. The parameter constellation for a stationary solution is located at the turning point of the dashed line. Harmonic oscillations can again occur for $\beta = 1$. The different regimes of this submodel are denoted by superscripts (1).

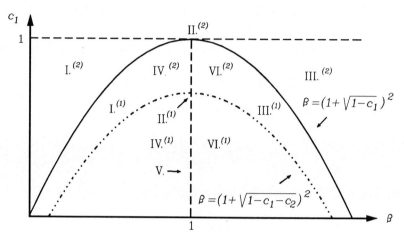

Parameter Regimes in a Hicks Model with Ratchet Effects
Figure 2.8

Figure 2.8 reveals that it is possible to encounter different stability properties in the two systems for a given parameter constellation. For example, all parameter values in region VI.$^{(2)}$ of the second stage model correspond to increasing oscillations while this set is divided into regions of monotonic explosion (III.$^{(1)}$) and increasing oscillation (VI.$^{(1)}$) in the first stage model.

The interesting aspect of the model consists in the fact that the motion of the compound system

$$Y_t = \begin{cases} (c_1 + c_2 + \beta)Y_{t-1} - \beta Y_{t-2} + c_0 + I_0 r^t & \text{if } Y_{t-1} = Y_{t-1}^{\max}; \\ (c_1 + \beta)Y_{t-1} - \beta Y_{t-2} + c_2 Y_{t-1}^{\max} + c_0 + I_0 r^t & \text{if } Y_{t-1} \le Y_{t-1}^{\max}; \end{cases}$$

$$Y_t^{\max} = \max(Y_1, Y_2, \ldots, Y_t)$$

(2.1.78)

differs from a motion obtained by juxtaposing isolated motions of both subsystems. If the first stage model is superseded by the second stage model, the last two realized income values of the first stage model determine the behavior in the second stage. Depending on the precise numerical values of income in the last two periods, the lower turning point of the first cycle in the second stage model can increase or decrease as

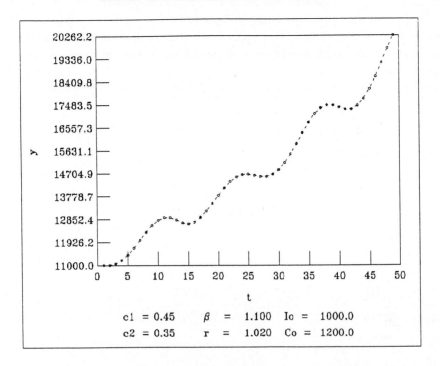

Growth Cycles in the Hicks Model with Ratchet Effects
Figure 2.9

compared with the turning point of the first stage cycle. If the parameter constellation implies explosive oscillations in both stages, the compound model might generate explosive oscillations around an increasing average even when the exogenous growth trend is assumed to be zero.

When a positive growth trend is assumed, the compound model possesses an interesting property. A standard multiplier-accelerator model can generate damped or explosive cycles around a growth trend, but the oscillation is either dying out (when the motion is damped), or negative growth rates emerge during a downswing (when the motion is exploding). When ratchet effects are present, cycles with nonnegative or only slightly negative growth rates can be observed for a considerable time interval before the motion explodes.

Figure 2.9 shows the results of a numerical simulation of the dynamical behavior of the compound model for slightly explosive behavior in both stages. The assumed parameter values can be found in the legend of the plot. In the first two periods, income is assumed to be equal to its equilibrium value Y^* for $r = 1.02$. When a positive growth trend is assumed, the equilibrium level of income gradually increases, and actual income starts moving according to (2.1.78). The growth cycles in Figure 2.9 can be observed for several linear combinations of c_1 and c_2 for a given β, provided that

$c_1 + c_2$ =constant. and $c_2 > 0$. Qualitatively similar results can be obtained for larger growth factors r and larger accelerators. For very high values of β the system explodes monotonically.

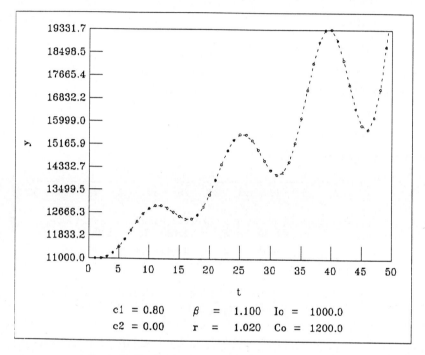

c1	= 0.80	β	= 1.100	Io	= 1000.0
c2	= 0.00	r	= 1.020	Co	= 1200.0

Growth Cycles in the Original Hicks Model
Figure 2.10

Figure 2.10 demonstrates the dynamical behavior of the standard Hicks model with $c = c_1 + c_2$ and identical remaining parameters. As can be expected, the amplitudes of the cycles are permanently increasing and strong recessions occur after a few periods. The presence of ratchet effects in Figure 2.9 therefore implies a damping of the explosive oscillations.

While the original Smithies model fails to explain endogenous growth cycles, ratchet effects can imply interesting properties in other models. However, as the compound model is a non-linear model because of the interaction of two linear submodels, it can be argued that it is theoretically easier and more elegant to construct models that are purely non-linear over the entire parameter range and the domain of the variables. Appropriate models will be discussed in Chapter 4.

2.2. Continuous-Time Shock-Dependent Models

While the multiplier-accelerator models of Section 2.1. are based on a discrete time concept (mathematically implying difference equations or systems of difference equations), it is of course also possible to construct business cycle models which rely on a continuous time concept.

An early example of a continuous-time business cycle model is that by Phillips (1954), which implies results similar to the Samuelson-Hicks-type models.

Let the consumption function be

$$C(t) = cY(t). \tag{2.2.1}$$

The desired capital stock $K^d(t)$ depends linearily on net income $Y(t)$:

$$K^d(t) = vY(t), \quad v > 0. \tag{2.2.2}$$

It is assumed that the firm changes the capital stock as soon as the actual stock differs from the desired one:

$$I(t) = \beta\big(K^d(t) - K(t)\big) = \beta\big(vY(t) - K(t)\big), \quad \beta > 0. \tag{2.2.3}$$

The coefficient β is an adjustment parameter and expresses the reaction speed of investment in response to a discrepancy between actual and desired capital stock.

Let $A(t)$ be an exogenously determined autonomous demand. As total demand is the sum $C(t) + I(t) + A(t)$, and as total supply is $Y(t)$, excess demand in each period is $C(t) + I(t) + A(t) - Y(t)$.

Assume that total supply changes linearly with excess demand:

$$\frac{dY(t)}{dt} = \dot{Y}(t) = \alpha\big(C(t) + I(t) + A(t) - Y(t)\big), \quad \alpha > 0. \tag{2.2.4}$$

Again, the coefficient α is an adjustment parameter.[18] Differentiating (2.2.4) with respect to time yields

$$\ddot{Y}(t) = \alpha\big(-(1-c)\dot{Y}(t) + \dot{I}(t) + \dot{A}(t)\big), \tag{2.2.5}$$

which after substituting for $\dot{I}(t)$ from the differentiated form of (2.2.3), i.e.,

$$\frac{dI(t)}{dt} = \dot{I}(t) = \beta\big(v\dot{Y}(t) - I(t)\big), \tag{2.2.6}$$

---

[18] *Note that the dynamics of the model rely conceptually on disequilibria, whereas the models of Samuelson and Hicks are equilibrium business cycle models.*

turns into

$$\ddot{Y}(t) = \alpha\left(-(1-c)\dot{Y}(t) + \beta\left[v\dot{Y}(t) - (\frac{\dot{Y}(t)}{\alpha} + (1-c)Y(t) - A(t))\right] + \dot{A}(t)\right)$$

or

$$\ddot{Y}(t) + \left(\alpha(1-c) + \beta - \alpha\beta v\right)\dot{Y}(t) + \alpha\beta(1-c)Y(t) = \alpha\beta A(t) + \alpha\dot{A}. \qquad (2.2.7)$$

For simplicity, let $\dot{A}(t) = 0 \,\forall\, t$.

The solution of the second-order differential equation (2.2.7) is quite similar to that of a linear second-order difference equation, namely

$$Y(t) = Y^* + u_1 e^{\lambda_1 t} + u_2 e^{\lambda_2 t} \qquad (2.2.8)$$

with Y^* as the particular solution and $\lambda_{1,2}$ as the roots of the characteristic equation

$$\lambda^2 + \left(\alpha(1-c) + \beta - \alpha\beta v\right)\lambda + \alpha\beta(1-c) = 0. \qquad (2.2.9)$$

The roots are

$$\lambda_{1,2} = -\frac{\alpha(1-c) + \beta - \alpha\beta v}{2} \pm \frac{\sqrt{\left(\alpha(1-c) + \beta - \alpha\beta v\right)^2 - 4\alpha\beta(1-c)}}{2}. \qquad (2.2.10)$$

Multiplication yields

$$\lambda_1 \lambda_2 = \alpha\beta(1-c) > 0 \qquad (2.2.11)$$

such that the roots are either both positive or both negative.

The roots are real as long as

$$\left(\alpha(1-c) + \beta - \alpha\beta v\right)^2 \geq 4\alpha\beta(1-c). \qquad (2.2.12)$$

Because the solution of a differential equation converges to the particular solution Y^* as long as the real parts of the characteristic roots are negative, it follows as a condition for damped monotonic behavior that[19]

$$0 > -\left(\alpha(1-c) + \beta - \alpha\beta v\right) \quad \Longrightarrow \quad v\alpha\beta < \alpha(1-c) + \beta,$$

provided that the roots are real. Alternatively, as long as $v\alpha\beta > \alpha(1-c) + \beta$ and the roots are real, the system will monotonically move away from the stationary equilibrium.

---

[19] *See, e.g., Samuelson (1947), Math. App. B.*

In the complex roots case, *i.e.*, $\left(\alpha(1-c)+\beta-\alpha\beta v\right)^2 < 4\alpha\beta(1-c)$, a damped oscillation occurs as long as the real parts of the roots are negative, *i.e.*,

$$v\alpha\beta < \alpha(1-c)+\beta. \tag{2.2.13}$$

Increasing oscillations will occur if

$$v\alpha\beta > \alpha(1-c)+\beta. \tag{2.2.14}$$

This can also be seen by inspecting the following alternative formulation of the solution (2.2.8) in the complex roots case:[20]

$$Y(t) = Be^{at}\cos(bt-\varepsilon)+Y^*, \quad \varepsilon > 0 \tag{2.2.15}$$

with

$$a = -\frac{\alpha(1-c)+\beta-\alpha\beta v}{2}$$
$$b = \sqrt{4\alpha\beta(1-c)-\left(\alpha(1-c)+\beta-\alpha\beta v\right)^2}.$$

The term B depends on the initial values and ε is a positive constant that expresses the phase of the cycle. Obviously, as long as $a < 0$, the oscillations will be damped and the system converges toward Y^* for $t \to \infty$. Harmonic oscillations around Y^* occur only incidentally for $a = 0$.

2.3. The Kalecki Model and Mixed Difference-Differential Equations

One of the very first mathematical business cycle models was introduced by Kalecki in 1935, which was later elaborated in a series of papers (1937, 1939, 1943).[21] While the first model is basically designed as a linear system (which can be expressed as a mixed difference-differential equation) the later versions (*e.g.*, the 1937- and 1939- models) are non-linear models which lack a simple algebraic treatment. However, the basic economic ideas are the same in both kinds of models.

While the multiplier-accelerator models introduce the necessary time lags by suitable assumptions on consumption or investment decisions, *i.e.*, on individual behavior, the early Kalecki model incorporated technical restrictions in the investment process.

---

[20] *See, e.g., Allen (1967), p. 331 and Goldberg (1958), pp. 141f.*

[21] *The following presentation of the 1935-model is basically adopted from Allen (1967), pp. 369 ff.*

Contrary to the later developed accelerator models, Kalecki assumed that a lag exists between the definitive decision to invest and the installation of the new equipment.

Assume that a definite investment decision takes place at time t, and denote the corresponding amount by $I^D(t)$. If the production of the investment good requires the fixed time interval θ, then the capital stock will be affected at $t + \theta$:

$$\dot{K}(t + \theta) = I^D(t) \quad \text{or} \quad \dot{K}(t) = I^D(t - \theta). \tag{2.3.1}$$

In contrast to the unlagged models, this change in the capital stock is not identical to investment I. As the Kalecki model is an equilibrium model, the value of the production of investment goods at each point in time must be equal to that amount of income which is not consumed, or, loosely speaking, the production has to be financed such that investment I is introduced as an advance payment. The value of the undelivered investment goods at time t is

$$W(t) = \int_{t-\theta}^{t} I^D(\tau) \; d\tau \tag{2.3.2}$$

and accordingly, the average production value of the investment goods industry per unit of time is $A = W/\theta$:

$$A(t) = \frac{1}{\theta} \int_{t-\theta}^{t} I^D(\tau) \; d\tau = I(t). \tag{2.3.3}$$

Formally, (2.3.3) is a uniformly distributed lag.

From (2.3.1) and (2.3.3) it follows

$$
\begin{aligned}
I(t) &= \frac{1}{\theta} \int_{t-\theta}^{t} \frac{dK(\tau + \theta)}{d\tau} \; d\tau \\
&= \frac{1}{\theta} [K(\tau + \theta)]_{t-\theta}^{t} \\
&= \frac{1}{\theta} [K(t + \theta) - K(t)].
\end{aligned} \tag{2.3.4}
$$

Thus, investment is the average change of capital per unit of time.

The determinants of the investment decision $I^D(t)$ are the level of income and the existing capital stock at t:

$$I^D(t) = \Phi\big(Y(t), K(t)\big). \tag{2.3.5}$$

The 1935-model assumes a linear relation

$$I^D(t) = asY(t) - kK(t) + \varepsilon, \tag{2.3.6}$$

with s as the marginal savings rate, a and k as constant coefficients, and ε as a trend term, which will be neglected in the following discussion. Therefore, no accelerator is involved. Combining (2.3.6), (2.3.4), (2.3.1), and $Y = C + I$ yields together with $C(t) = (1 - s)Y(t)$:

$$Y(t) = I(t)/s = \frac{1}{s}\frac{1}{\theta}\big(K(t + \theta) - K(t)\big)$$

$$\Longrightarrow I^D(t) = \dot{K}(t + \theta) = a\frac{1}{\theta}\big(K(t + \theta) - K(t)\big) - kK(t)$$

$$= \frac{a}{\theta}K(t + \theta) - (k + \frac{a}{\theta})K(t)$$

or

$$\dot{K}(t) = \frac{a}{\theta}K(t) - (k + \frac{a}{\theta})K(t - \theta). \tag{2.3.7}$$

Equation (2.3.7) is a mixed difference-differential equation, *i.e.*, a differential equation with a fixed finite delay. The solution of (2.3.7) is again similar to that of a second-order difference equation. With $\theta = 1$ by normalization, a solution of

$$\dot{K}(t) = aK(t) - (k + a)K(t - 1) \tag{2.3.8}$$

is $K(t) = K_0 e^{\rho t}$. Substitution in (2.3.8) leads to

$$\rho = a - be^{-\rho}, \quad b = k + a. \tag{2.3.9}$$

Complex roots occur if $a - \log b < 1$.[22] In that case the solution can be written as

$$K(t) = K_0 e^{\alpha t}\cos(\beta t + \psi), \quad \psi = \text{const.} \tag{2.3.10}$$

with $\rho = \alpha \pm \beta i$. The values of α and β cannot be directly determined in the general case. However, a relation between the two magnitudes can be established. Substitution of $\rho = \alpha \pm \beta i$ in (2.3.9) yields

$$\alpha \pm \beta i = a - be^{-\alpha}e^{\pm \beta i}$$

$$= a - be^{-\alpha}(\cos \beta \pm i \sin \beta)$$

$$= (a - be^{-\alpha}\cos \beta) \pm ibe^{-\alpha}\sin \beta.$$

Identifying real and complex parts on both sides leads to

$$\alpha = a - be^{-\alpha}\cos \beta \tag{2.3.11}$$

$$\beta = be^{-\alpha}\sin \beta \quad \Longrightarrow \quad \alpha = \log b + \log(\frac{\sin \beta}{\beta}). \tag{2.3.12}$$

---

[22] *Compare Allen (1963), p. 255 f.*

Thus, α and β are negatively related. By combining (2.3.11) and (2.3.12), β is determined implicitly by[23]

$$\frac{\beta}{\tan \beta} + \log \frac{\sin \beta}{\beta} = a - \log b < 0,$$

which is negative by the assumption above. Depending on the magnitude of $b = k+a$, the
real part α is positive, zero, or negative. Only by chance does the coefficient k of (2.3.6)
have a value such that $\alpha = 0$, which via (2.3.10) would imply the existence of harmonic
oscillations. All other magnitudes of k lead to damped or increasing oscillations provided
that no real roots occur.

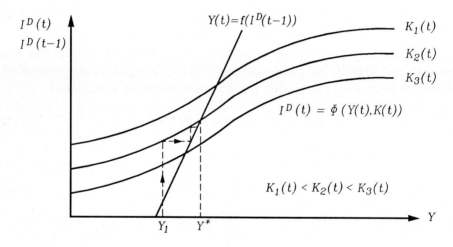

The Non-Linear Kalecki Model
Figure 2.11

The linear version of the Kalecki model therefore exhibits a very similar dynamic
behavior as the multiplier-accelerator models. Because explosive oscillations should be
excluded from the consideration and because steady oscillations occur only for exactly
one numerical value of k, the typical dynamic behavior of the model is characterized
by damped oscillations in the complex roots case. As with the accelerator models, the
linear Kalecki model requires accidental exogenous shocks in order to exhibit permanent
oscillations.

The foregoing algebraic treatment is, of course, valid only for the linear form of
(2.3.5). The 1937-model and subsequent models deal with a non-linear form of (2.3.5),
which is assumed to be S-shaped and in which I^D depends negatively on $K(t)$ (cf.
Figure 2.11).

---

[23] *See Allen (1963), pp. 256 ff. for details on the calculations.*

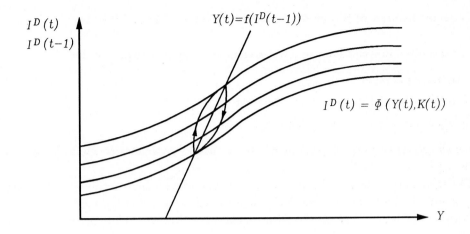

Cycles in the Non-Linear Kalecki Model
Figure 2.12

Suppose that $\theta = 1$, and let $Y(t) = f\big(I(t)\big)$ represent the short-run equilibria of the economy depending on the amount of investment. As was shown above, investment in t is determined by past investment decisions, such that $f\big(I(t)\big) = f\big(I^D(t-1)\big)$ for $\theta = 1$. For simplicity, assume that $Y(t) = f\big(I^D(t-1)\big)$ is a linear function. Putting both functions together yields Figure 2.11, in which the intersection of the curves determines the long-run equilibrium Y^*. In Figure 2.11 it is assumed that the long-run equilibrium Y^* is stable. Provided that income deviates from equilibrium for whatever reason, then an adjustment process towards Y^* is initiated if the equilibrium is stable and if capital is constant. However, at Y_1 investment is very small and capital decreases, leading to an upward shifting of the investment decision curve with eventually increasing investment. The process will come to an end when investment is larger than the long-run equilibrium level, resp. the fixed amount of depreciation. Subsequently, the process will be reversed: capital increases and leads to a downward shift of $\Phi(Y, K)$. It is easy to imagine that a complete cycle will be generated (cf. Figure 2.12).

While this cyclic behavior seems to be intuitively evident, the non-linear version lacks a rigorous mathematical treatment. As the long-run equilibrium is assumed to be stable, the maintenance of cycles requires certain assumptions about the magnitudes of the involved parameters. The Kalecki model assumes that the shifting of the investment decision curve Φ is sufficiently strong. Otherwise, a monotonic return to the long-run equilibrium would occur if the system were exogenously disturbed. Thus, the Kalecki model can generate cycles only in certain cases.

2.4. The Relevance of Shock-Dependent Business Cycle Theories

The linear models described above have in common that they exhibit either

- stationary paths, or
- damped or increasing monotonic behavior, or
- damped, harmonic, or increasing oscillations,

of the endogenous variables depending on the particular parameter constellation of the models.

The stationary as well as the monotonic behavior of a model is certainly interesting for a stability analysis of equilibria, but is irrelevant from the point of view of business cycle theory which deals exclusively with oscillations. However, while increasing oscillations with no endogenous limits to the trajectories are of no economic importance and would provide no empirical meaning, only harmonic and damped oscillations bear any kind of significance. Abstracting from the theoretical fact that harmonic oscillations are possible only for particular parameter constellation in each model, this kind of oscillation must be rejected on empirical grounds because actual time paths of relevant variables (like the national product or the unemployment rate) obviously cannot be described as harmonic fluctuations. Thus, only damped oscillations may have some relevance for business cycle theory. Because the oscillations, initiated by an exogenous disturbance, gradually disappear in case of damped oscillations, a series of exogenous shocks to the system is required in order to keep the economy fluctuating for a longer time interval. In this way, actual empirical fluctuations are explained as superpositions of different sequential cycles. The need for exogenous forces is also evident in Hicks' non-linear model, because in the absence of continuous exogenous shocks (*i.e.*, a constant positive growth rate of autonomous investment) the model can only explain the length of $1\frac{1}{2}$ cycles.

This attribute of shock-dependence can be considered as being unsatisfactory from a theoretical point of view. The problem of explaining more or less regularly appearing business cycles is displaced to the problem of explaining the regular occurrence of exogenous shocks. As exogenous influences like discretionary government spending or autonomous investment are of major importance in these business cycle theories, they ought to be connected with the structure of the models in a reverse causal way, *i.e.*, they should loose their exogenous character and should be made dependent on the state of the economy as well.

Thus, it is either necessary to give up the shock-dependent approach and to concentrate on models that are able to generate cycles endogenously (*i.e.*, without any restrictions on initial states or on parameter ranges), or to roll back the impetus of a cycle even more and to consider the origins of exogenous shocks. Several approaches to the last alternative will be presented in the next chapter.

Chapter 3

Business Cycle Theory and Exogenous Shocks

As was just pointed out, the shock-dependent business cycle models of Chapter 2 require exogenous disturbances in order to generate *persistent* fluctuations in the face of otherwise damped oscillations. There are basically two ways of treating the occurrence of exogenous shocks:

1) Exogenous shocks are beyond the scope of abstractive economic reasoning and are thus considered as influences from a world outside of economics which cannot be analyzed by economists. While this attitude may be appropriate in many cases of economic theorizing, it is definitely unsatisfactory in business cycle theory because of the *essential* importance of exogenous influences in linear models. Nevertheless, it may be useful to investigate the dynamic behavior of shock-dependent business cycle models under certain assumptions about the occurrence (or anticipation) of exogenous shocks over time. Although the majority of the popular Rational Expectations *business cycle* models do not differ from the multiplier-accelerator models in their dynamic structure, it is the consideration of these exogenous shocks in the individual expectation formation process that constitutes a real innovation in business cycle theory. This special way of dealing with exogenous influences is the main reason why a single section (cf. Section 3.3.) is devoted to Rational Expectations business cycle models instead of describing those models in the appropriate Chapter 2. Exogenous influences, however, do not only have interesting consequences in

shock-dependent models. If exogenous shocks are understood as a series of pure random numbers, then it may be possible that a series displays cyclical behavior when particular statistical filters are applied to the series (cf. Section 3.2.1.). Furthermore, the anticipation of probability distributions may influence individual behavior such that fluctuations are generated (cf. Section 3.2.2.). As the stochastic aspect of the exogenous forces plays an essential role in these explanations of business cycles, it is appropriate to term these models *stochastic business cycle models*.

2) While the exogenous forces driving the system are given and unexplained in a model per definition, it may be that economic theory can provide explanations of these forces using other approaches. This idea of partial theorizing, which is standard in economics, may also be applied to business cycle theory and can be justified in the face of the high complexity of an attempted general and comprehensive approach. For example, the so-called political business cycle models investigate the behavior of a government whose aim is to exploit economically given constraints for re-election purposes. While these models basically provide autonomous explanations of the fluctuating of otherwise stationary economies, they can be interpreted as explanations of exogenous forces in the shock-dependent models above. The presentation of these political business cycle models may also be useful because it forcefully demonstrates the difficulties in modelling comprehensive approaches which integrate economic, political, or social aspects of business cycles.

Naturally, the models which are subsumed in these two categories do not represent a complete list but are considered as examples of the theory of exogenous shocks, respectively of interpretations of other theoretical results as exogenous shocks in business cycle theory.

3.1. The Political Business Cycle

Since the introduction of Keynesian macroeconomics and its implicit postulate of the potential influence of governmental activity on the development of an economy, the following basic attitude toward governmental behavior has not only dominated the macroeconomic textbook literature but also the evaluation of the public sector's performance in the eyes of the electorate: if it is possible to manipulate an economy into the desired direction by means of governmental activities, then the government must have an interest - if not a legal commitment - to reduce the unemployment rate and the inflation rate, for example. Popular policy recipes like, e.g., deficit spending, derived from simple Keynesian income-theoretical models, implicitly suggest that no conflicting goals exist, neither in the economic nor in the political sense. The governmental sector is usually supposed to have to follow these prescribed economic rules, because otherwise the incumbent party would be held responsible for the failure to manage an economy and would reduce its re-election chances in the next election. Thus, incumbent political parties are believed to behave counter-cyclically in this theoretical framework in order to diminish business fluctuations.

The actual and theoretical scenario looks more difficult if it is taken into account that in most cases the alternatives for governmental behavior do not consist of gradual manipulations of just one endogenous variable, but rather of a menu of immanently connected and possibly conflicting variables. The well-known "magic triangle" of inflation, unemployment and trade balances expresses the opinion that it is to a large extent impossible to improve the target value of one variable without deteriorating the other ones, measured in terms of social welfare or similar concepts. Provided that no legal prescription for governmental behavior in face of conflicting goals exists, the administration obviously encounters the dilemma of not knowing *a priori* where the emphasis of political activity should be placed. The question arises whether a government can circumvent this dilemma by an appropriate timing of its interventions. If the public is completely informed about the inevitable trade-offs between the involved variables and if it is indifferent between the possible variations on a trade-off curve, there is obviously no room for a political intervention. Otherwise, two cases have to be distinguished. Suppose the economy is fluctuating due to endogenous forces. If the government is aware of the development of the variables in the future and if the public evaluates some goals more positively than others, then it may be appropriate for the administration to influence the more preferred variables in order to receive a good reputation in the eyes of the public. As long as the immanent dynamics of the economy are not known for sure, such an optimization calculus looses its ground or at least becomes ambiguous. Suppose, on the contrary, that the economy is stuck in a resting position away from a long-run, optimal general equilibrium and that no immanent economic forces exist which could alter the economic situation. Provided that the public expects that the administration is doing something to improve the economic situation, it may be asked whether an optimal policy for the incumbent party exists, such that the trade-off is exploited in order to perform best in the public opinion. This last question has been attempted to be answered by the works on the so-called *political business cycle*.

Basically, all political business cycle models establish the existence of a politically induced cycle. While this text is mainly interested in economically-induced cycles, *i.e.*, in the first case mentioned or at least in the case of genuinely connected political and economic sectors, these political cycles may serve as an explanation of the persistence of otherwise flattening cycles in, *e.g.*, linear multiplier-accelerator models. The first section is devoted to the renowned paper by Nordhaus (1975), while the second section presents alternatives to or improvements on the basic approach, and a critique.

3.1.1. Governmental Behavior as the Cause of Business Cycles

One of the first attempts to investigate the influence of governmental behavior on business cycles was undertaken in a paper by Nordhaus (1975), which is also the standard
reference on that subject.[1] The model will be presented in some detail in order to
demonstrate the general ideas which underly nearly all similar approaches.

Suppose that a model-economy is characterized by a macroeconomic trade-off between the inflation rate $\pi(t)$ at time t and the unemployment rate $u(t)$. The expecta-
tions-augmented Phillips curve in continuous time is

$$\pi(t) = f\big(u(t)\big) + \lambda\pi^e(t), \quad \lambda > 0, \tag{3.1.1}$$

with $f'(u) < 0$ and $\pi^e(t)$ as the expected rate of inflation. Expectations on price
inflations are formed according to the adaptive expectations hypothesis[2], *i.e.*,

$$\dot{\pi}^e(t) = \gamma\big(\pi(t) - \pi^e(t)\big), \quad \gamma > 0. \tag{3.1.2}$$

It is essential in this model that no further specifications of the economic structure are
assumed. The economy is completely described by the inflation rate and the unemployment rate $u(t)$, which do not vary endogenously. In case of self-fulfilling expectations,
i.e., $\pi(t) = \pi^e(t)$, the system is stuck somewhere on a fixed Phillips curve. No endogenous force to move the system in the (u, π) - space is involved.

The question arises whether the political parties can exploit this exogenously given
trade-off. Assume that the government is able to move the economy to every point
on the Phillips curve by an appropriately chosen menu of policy instruments. If the
re-election of the incumbent party is solely determined by its ability to manipulate the
economy satisfactorily in the public's opinion, then the incumbent will have an interest
in choosing a policy that increases the probability of being re-elected, provided that the
incumbent is not influenced by other ideological goals. Thus, it is advantageous for the
government to get an idea of voters' preferences between different states of the economy
on the Phillips curve.

Suppose that the preferences of a representative individual (voter) are described by
a utility function $U = U(z_1, ..., z_n)$ with the usual continuity and convexity properties.
Let $z_1 = -\pi$ and $z_2 = -u$ be the inflation rate and the unemployment rate, respectively,
and drop the arguments z_i $(i \neq 1, 2)$, e.g., consumption goods. Individuals are assumed
to be unaware of the macroeconomic trade-off between inflation and unemployment,
but to have positive marginal utilities for a decrease in inflation and unemployment.

---

[1] *Earlier models are developed in Frey/Lau (1968) and Frey/Garbers (1972). Compare also Downs (1959) for a general treatment of political economics.*

[2] *Compare Section 3.3.1.*

Suppose that individuals view the incumbent as being responsible for the state of the economy and that they use a reference standard when they evaluate the incumbent. Let $\hat{\pi}(t)$ and $\hat{u}(t)$ denote these standards which are assumed to be constant over time.[3] Individuals will be content with the incumbent if the utility of the actual inflation and unemployment rates is greater than that of the standard values. The individual voting function is

$$V^i(t) = g_i\big(\pi(t), u(t)\big) = \begin{cases} 1 & \text{if} \quad \dfrac{U^i\big(\pi(t), u(t)\big)}{U^i\big(\hat{\pi}(t), \hat{u}(t)\big)} > 1 \\[2ex] 0 & \text{if} \quad \dfrac{U^i\big(\pi(t), u(t)\big)}{U^i\big(\hat{\pi}(t), \hat{u}(t)\big)} = 1 \\[2ex] -1 & \text{if} \quad \dfrac{U^i\big(\pi(t), u(t)\big)}{U^i\big(\hat{\pi}(t), \hat{u}(t)\big)} < 1 \end{cases} \qquad (3.1.3)$$

i.e., the indivudal votes for the incumbent if $V^i(t) = 1$. Aggregating over all individuals yields $V(t) = g = \sum_i V^i(t)$, and it can be seen that at each point in time the incumbent will be re-elected if $V(t) > 0$. Elections, however, take place only in finite intervals. If the individuals evaluate only the incumbent's past performance, then the appraisal of the government's behavior during the last election period can be expressed by some kind of averaging of the voting functions at each point in time during the period. Assume that the voters have a decreasing memory of past events, i.e., they evaluate the current state of the economy stronger than that of the beginning of the election period. Forward looking, the voting function for the election period is expressed by

$$\tilde{V}(\theta) = \int_0^\theta g\big(\pi(t), u(t)\big) e^{\mu t} dt, \qquad \mu > 0 \qquad (3.1.4)$$

with θ as the election date and μ as the 'decay' rate due to vanishing memory. Suppose that the incumbent party is completely informed about this voting function of the electorate. In order to maximize the number of votes, the incumbent obviously considers the voting function (3.1.4) as the objective that has to be maximized under the constraint of the Phillips curve and the expectations hypothesis:

$$\max \tilde{V}(\theta) = \int_0^\theta g\big(\pi(t), u(t)\big) e^{\mu t} \, dt$$

$$s.t. \quad \pi(t) = f\big(u(t)\big) + \lambda \pi^e(t)$$
$$\dot{\pi}^e(t) = \gamma\big(\pi(t) - \pi^e(t)\big). \qquad (3.1.5)$$

---

[3] Nordhaus starts with the general assumption of a varied adaptive expectations hypothesis. Calculatory difficulties lead to the static case, however.

Formally, the maximization problem is a control problem with $u(t)$ as the control variable.[4]

Nordhaus assumes simple algebraic forms of the involved functions in order to receive a definite result. Let

$$g(\pi, u) = -u^2 - \beta\pi, \quad \beta > 0$$
$$f(u) = \alpha_0 - \alpha_1 u. \tag{3.1.6}$$

In this case the maximization problem simplifies algebraically to

$$\max \tilde{V}_\theta = \int_0^\theta (-\beta\alpha_0 - u^2 + \beta\alpha_1 u - \beta\lambda\pi^e)e^{\mu t} dt \tag{3.1.7}$$

$$s.t. \quad \dot{\pi}^e = \gamma(\alpha_0 - \alpha_1 u - (1 - \lambda)\pi^e)$$

The current-value Hamiltonian is

$$H = (-\beta\alpha_0 - u^2 + \beta\alpha_1 u - \beta\lambda\pi^e) + \psi\gamma(\alpha_0 - \alpha_1 u - (1 - \lambda)\pi^e) \tag{3.1.8}$$

with ψ as the co-state variable, i.e., the shadow price of inflation. The necessary conditions for a maximum are[5]

$$0 = \frac{\partial H}{\partial u}$$
$$\dot{\psi} = -\mu\psi - \frac{\partial H}{\partial \pi^e} \tag{3.1.9}$$
$$\dot{\pi}_e = \frac{\partial H}{\partial \psi}.$$

It follows that

$$\frac{\partial H}{\partial u} = 0 = \beta\alpha_1 - 2u - \psi\gamma\alpha_1 \quad \Longrightarrow \quad u = \alpha_1(\beta - \psi\gamma)/2 \tag{3.1.10}$$

and

$$\dot{\psi} = (\gamma(1 - \lambda) - \mu)\psi + \beta\lambda. \tag{3.1.11}$$

---

[4] In the following, time indexes are suppressed whenever this does not lead to confusion.

[5] See Takayama (1974), ch.8 or Intriligator (1971), ch.14 for an overview of optimal control techniques. Nordhaus originally used a present-value Hamiltonian. The use of a current-value Hamiltonian is analytically more convenient and leads to identical results in this case.

Combining (3.1.10) and (3.1.11) yields[6]

$$\dot{u} = Au + B, \quad A = \gamma(1-\lambda) - \mu, \quad B = -1/2\alpha_1\beta(\gamma - \mu) \tag{3.1.12}$$

At the election day $t = \theta$, the shadow price ψ of future inflation becomes zero because individual voters are assumed to ignore future happenings. From (3.1.10) it follows that $u_\theta = \alpha_1\beta/2$. Substituting μ_θ in (3.1.12) yields

$$\dot{u}_\theta = -\gamma\lambda u_\theta < 0. \tag{3.1.13}$$

As (3.1.12) is a linear differential equation (defined for exactly one election period) only monotonic movements of $u(t)$ can occur in every period. Thus, $\dot{u}(t) < 0$ and $u(t) > 0 \; \forall \, t \in (0, \theta]$ imply that the coefficients A and B have to fulfill $B < -Au$ for consistency.

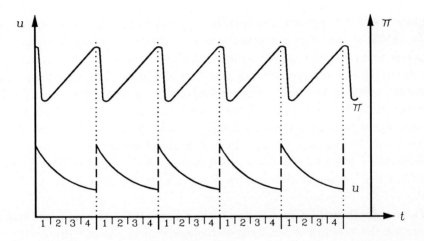

Inflation and Unemployment in the Political Business Cycle
Figure 3.1

    With a monotonic decrease in the optimal unemployment rate according to the optimization program, the optimal policy is defined in the following way: as the unemployment rate can not be decreased forever[7] and as the unemployment rate has to take

---

[6] *Differentiate (3.1.10) with respect to time and substitute for ψ and $\dot{\psi}$ from (3.1.10) and (3.1.11).*

[7] *The foregoing program assumes a linear Phillips curve and the statement is, of course, true. The case of non-linear curves is less obvious and requires separate optimization procedures for each case.*

on its minimal value during the election period exactly at the end of the period, *i.e.*, $u_\theta = \alpha_1 \beta / 2$, the incumbent will maximize the number of votes if the unemployment rate is raised at the beginning of the term and is gradually lowered in the course. This scenario is illustrated in Figure 3.1.

While the unemployment rate optimally follows a strict sawtooth pattern, the dynamic part of the inflation rate is slightly smoothed. This is essentially due to the shifting effect of the inflation expectations in the Phillips curve.

Provided that the government is indeed able to manipulate the unemployment rate to the desired degree, it has thus been shown that a government can generate cyclic motion in an economy which would be characterized by stationary states if no governmental activity took place.

3.1.2. Implications of the Political Business Cycle

The basic Nordhaus-approach has been modified and extended in a number of ways. MacRae (1977) showed that the abandonment of the purely myoptic, ex-post oriented time perspective of the electorate may lead to strategic voting. If the incumbent extends the future to the next election day only and if the electorate "learns by doing" about the government behavior, then the voters are supposed to express a preference for deflation in the elections. As a consequence, the incumbent's policy will tend towards a long-run optimal and stationary point on the long-run Phillips curve.[8] Other models were developed, *e.g.*, by Lindbeck (1976), who took international influences into account, and Frey/Schneider (1978 a,b) who also studied the empirical evidence of the theory for the US and the UK.[9] A recent elaborate work on political business cycles is Kirchgässner (1984).

The empirical work of Frey/Schneider and Frey (1978) showed that there is clear evidence for the assumed dependence of the government's popularity on the state of the economy.[10] Nordhaus (1975) concludes his own analysis with an examination of unemployment rates before and after elections and finds that the theoretical results can not be rejected statistically. While in general it can be argued that the actual cycles are essentially economically generated cycles, which only incidently coincide with election dates, the strong correlation between election dates and immediately following increases in the unemployment rate in different countries with different election dates

---

[8] *See Frey/Kirchgässner (1977) on the neglection of the influence of expectations in MacRae's model.*

[9] *See also Ploeg (1985a), who develops a model in which parties with different political attitudes are involved in the optimal re-election policy in an open economy.*

[10] *See, however, Minford/Peel (1983), who find that Frey/Schneider's (1976) results are not statistically robust.*

at least suggests a loose connection between governmental activities and actual time series.

There seem to exist two basic objections against the political business cycle approach from the economist's point of view.[11] While arguing immanently against the Keynesian stabilization dogma, the political business cycle models assume the same kind of economic manœuvrability as the usual Keynesian macro-theory. Furthermore, the models postulate that interventions have immediate economic consequences. However, recent developments in macroeconomics, especially the Rational Expectations approach,[12] strongly deny the ability of governmental activities to manipulate an economy at all. Without referring to this approach extensively, it has to be kept in mind that a government intending to manipulate unemployment rates and inflation rates has to apply instruments such as tax rate variations, direct government spending, etc., which most likely influence the voters' preferences. A more comprehensive approach, which takes more feedback processes into account, would probably weaken the strong and more or less unambiguous results of existing political business cycle models. Even if it is possible to manipulate the economy to the desired degree, the probably involved time-lags render an exact timing of the outcome of governmental activities difficult.

The more important objection, however, refers to the neglect of endogenous dynamics in the economy. The political business cycle theories postulate throughout that a stable Phillips curve exists (which is not justified by economic reasoning) and assume that in the absence of governmental activity a point on this curve will be realized which is not altered by endogenous forces. Though not characterized by full-employment, the economy is basically stationary. This view of an economy clearly cannot be satisfactory in the light of descriptions or explanations of the business cycle. The historical evidence of business cycles in the absence of governmental activity makes it necessary to embed the analysis of economically-oriented political activity in the context of a fluctuating economy. It can heuristically be presumed that in case of an endogenously fluctuating economy the result of an appropriately specified optimization program will not be a regular intervention advice as in existing models. Rather, it will depend on the actual state of an economy whether or not it is advantageous for the incumbent party to intervene.

On the other hand, the theory of the political business cycle may be utilized to explain exogenous shocks. Since the political business cycle theory states that the incumbents have a vital interest in manipulating an economy for re-election purposes, the governmental behavior may be viewed as providing the necessary exogenous shocks, e.g., in the linear business cycle models of Chapter 2. Depending on the specific form of the incumbent's objective, the underlying constraints in the optimization program,

---

[11] *Politically motivated objections will be ignored. See Frey (1978) for other political views of governmental behavior.*

[12] *Cf. Section 3.3.*

etc., it may be that the government is attempting to manipulate the economy contrary to stabilization policies. When voters expect stabilization policies, activities suited to increase the unemployment rate at the beginning of the election period can be considered as shocks to the economy.

While the political business cycle models described above explain politically-motivated exogenous shocks occurring in regular patterns, an actual economy may be confronted with a variety of exogenous shocks which occur in different patterns and at different points in time. The overall performance of these different shocks can be compared with irregular and random exogenous influences. In the following sections several approaches to these stochastic business cycles will be presented.

3.2. The Theory of Stochastic Business Cycles

The concentration on one or just a few possible causes for the onset of cyclical motions of an economy (which was typical for the classical monocausal explanations of business cycles) is surely unsatisfactory in the face of the complexities of real life phenomena. On the other hand, an attempt to comprehend all existing influencing factors and interrelations is definitely doomed to failure because of mental and algebraic difficulties or impossibilities. Relatively early the idea was uttered that *stochastic* exogenous influences should be considered in the *modelling* of economies (which can be *interpreted* as having taken many complex relations into account and which at the same time are able to display the typical irregular behavior of actual economies). As with exogenous influences, the consideration of stochastics in economics may be justified by two reasons: the introduction of stochastics reflects the fact that some events are indeed purely random (like lottery outcomes), or it expresses the view that some events have deterministic causes which may be explained by other disciplines, but which seem to be random from an economist's point of view. Examples of the second interpretation are crop yields, inventions, and political activities. In any case, the introduction of stochastic exogenous influences not only diminishes the complexity of a complete business cycle model, but it also enriches the theory by taking account of irregularities observable in actual business cycles.

The first section is devoted to Slutzky's experiments with random numbers and Kalecki's augmentations of a deterministic business cycle model by stochastic terms. The second section presents Krelle's outline of a stochastic business cycle model which entirely relies on stochastic influences with respect to the onset as well as the persistence of oscillations.

3.2.1. Business Cycle Models with Stochastic Exogenous Influences

Any economic theory which takes stochastic influences into account has to reflect on the degree to which these exogenous forces may potentially determine the results of a model. The construction of a model, whose results depend crucially on stochastic exogenous forces, can hardly be considered as serious economic theorizing, because in this case endogenous economic interrelations obviously do not explain the essential results. On the other hand, stochastic exogenous influences which are superimposed on known structures without changing the results significantly may be considered as being superfluous. Thus, the introduction of stochastic exogenous influences is a knife-edge-walk between over-emphasis and insignificance.

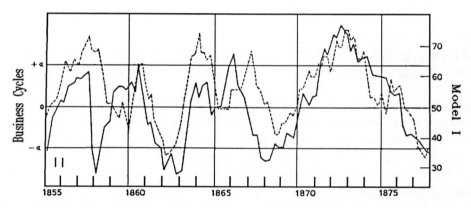

——— An index of English business cycles from 1855 to 1877; scale on the left side.
----- Terms 20 to 145 of Model I; scale on the right side

Source: Slutzky (1937), p. 110
Figure 3.2

An illustrative example of the first type of model was provided by Slutzky (1937) in a statistically oriented study of random causes of cyclical behavior. Without referring to any economic model, he was able to demonstrate that it may indeed be possible to *describe* actually observed business cycles with purely random time series. Out of the drawn numbers of a Russian Government Lottery Loan by the People's Commissariat of Finance (which can surely be claimed as random) he constructed several random number series by using only the last digits, for example. By performing a procedure, which he called "moving summation",[13] Slutzky generated a time series of correlated variables

---

[13] *Compare also Wold (1954).*

although the original numbers were purely random: Let x_t denote the random event at time t and let y_t be a consequence of random events, occurring at t. A consequence at t is assumed to depend not only on x_t but on an average of the random events in the past back to $t - n$:

$$y_t = \sum_{\tau=t-n}^{t} A_\tau x_\tau \qquad (3.2.1)$$

with the A_τ's as the constant weights. While it is not only surprising that the series $\{y_t\}$ features cyclical movements, Slutzky was able to provide a striking example of empirical evidence. Figure 3.2 shows his comparison of a time series obtained by the procedure sketched above and an actual time series of British business cycle indices for the period 1855-1877. Although it has to be kept in mind that the construction of the random series, especially the choice of the values of the weights A_τ, as well as the selection of the time interval of the actual series is arbitrary, the example at least shows that actual business cycles appear to perform in the same way as a stochastic series filtered by a particular procedure. Slutzky's investigation demonstrates that it can be useful to concentrate more intensively on the consideration of stochastic influences. An interpretation of the results as a theoretical explanation of business cycles is inappropriate, however. While it is always possible to identify an actual time series with a somehow constructed stochastic time series, this concept is not suited for predictions and ignores any economic considerations. If one is convinced, however, that stochastic forces indeed play a prominent role in the generation of business cycles, then Slutzky's result can only be interpreted as a 'negative' theory, *i.e.*, that cycles are not predictable within a deterministic context.

The standard procedure in dealing with stochastic exogenous influences dates back to Frisch (1933) and Kalecki (1954) and is still typical in dynamical economics and macroeconometric models. A model which is able to generate regular cyclical behavior is augmented by stochastic terms which act in the same way as arbitrary autonomous shocks. Consider a linear business cycle model of, *e.g.*, the multiplier-accelerator type and assume that the endogenous dynamics of the system are described by a second-order linear difference equation

$$y_t = ay_{t-1} + by_{t-2} + c \qquad (3.2.2)$$

with constant parameters. Assume that the parameters have values such that the oscillations of the system are damped, *i.e.*, after an initial shock the amplitudes of the oscillation steadily decrease. The stochastic influences are introduced by adding a stochastic term μ_t in (3.2.2):

$$y_t = ay_{t-1} + by_{t-2} + c + \mu_t, \qquad (3.2.3)$$

which is either due to the appearance of μ_t in any functional relation that leads to (3.2.3), or which is simply a postulate in order to adapt the dynamics of the system to actual time series. Of course, several hypothesis on the sequence $\{\mu_t\}$ are possible; a normal distribution of μ_t is usually assumed for the sake of simplicity.

The introduction of stochastic random terms u_t in (3.2.3) has important consequences for the dynamic behavior of the system. A linear model like (3.2.2) that shows damped oscillations in the deterministic case generates persistent, non-fading fluctuations in the stochastic case.[14] The amplitude and the frequency of single cycles in time series generated by an equation like (3.2.3) will be different and dependent on the particular stochastic series $\{u_t\}$. Linear models with superimposed stochastic elements are usually called *Frisch-type* models.

An illustrative example of the dynamics generated by these models was provided by Kalecki (1954). A linear approximation of a model with a specific investment lag structure, designed in much the same spirit as the model outlined in Section 3.3., yielded the following equation for the development of net investment:[15]

$$i_t = .634i_{t-1} + .734i_{t-1/2} - .489i_{t-3/2} - .245i_{t-5/2}, \qquad (3.2.4)$$

with i_t as the deviation of net investment from its long-run level in period t. The parameters were estimated on the grounds of US data for the period 1929-1940. Equation (3.2.4) displays damped regular oscillations.

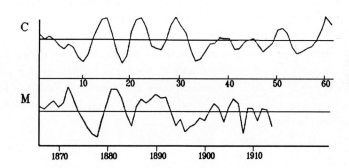

Source: Kalecki (1954), p. 141.

Figure 3.3

---

[14] *In the exceptional case of harmonic oscillations the introduction of stochastic terms implies an average increase of the amplitudes over time. Cf. Samuelson (1947), p. 268f. and Zarnowitz (1985), p. 544f.*

[15] *Different time lags, for example between the investment decision and the actual installation of new capital, imply different dynamic equations.*

The upper curve in Figure 3.3 shows a time series obtained from the equation

$$i_t = .634i_{t-1} + .734i_{t-1/2} - .489i_{t-3/2} - .245i_{t-5/2} + \mu_t, \qquad (3.2.5)$$

with μ_t as normally distributed stochastic terms derived from random sampling numbers. The lower part of Figure 3.3 shows the corresponding actual time series in the US for the period 1866-1914. The cycles in both time series possess nearly identical amplitudes and frequencies. Peaks and troughs roughly coincide in both time series at the beginning of the time interval.

Like Slutzky's example, these generated dynamics of the model fit the actual data more or less satisfactorily. It may be objected that no justification has been provided as to why the stochastic exogenous terms are, for example, normally distributed or why they follow other rules. However, as long as no attempt is made to investigate or to specify the nature of the exogenous influences in greater detail, any special assumption about the kind of stochastics is just as much a postulate as the basic assumption of the entire influence of exogenous forces at all.

3.2.2. A Stochastic Business Cycle Model

As Slutzky's (1937) example is mainly statistically oriented and Frisch (1933) and Kalecki (1954) simply superimposed stochastic influences on a deterministic structure without much economic reasoning, it is desirable to investigate the impacts of a stochastic surrounding on a model economy more intensively.

One of the first steps toward a stochastic theory of business cycles was made by Krelle (1959) in a study of the consequences of stochastic influences in a growing economy. A 'business cycle' in such a context does not consist in positive and negative deviations of major economic variables from an equilibrium level, but rather in fluctuations in the growth rates.

The growth path of an economy is described by

$$Y_t = (1 + a_t)Y_{t-1} \qquad (3.2.6)$$

with a_t as the growth rate. Let $a_0 > 0$ be the equilibrium growth rate and assume that a maximal growth rate $\bar{a}$ exists which is due to rising costs, capacity barriers or liquidity constraints, for example. Without constructing a complete growth model, suppose that the endogenous dynamics of the economy (*i.e.*, those without stochastic exogenous influences) are characterized by the stylized phenomenon that a somehow initiated upswing amplifies itself until it reaches the maximal growth rate, and that the growth rate eventually approaches the equilibrium rate again.

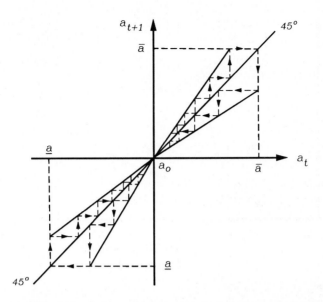

Endogenous Fluctuations in the Growth Rate
Figure 3.4

In formal terms, let the growth rate a_t be a function like $(3.2.7)^{16}$

$$a_t = a_t(a_{t-1}, a_0, \mu_t) \qquad (3.2.7)$$

in which μ_t is normally distributed with zero mean, and suppose that $\partial a_t / \partial \mu_t \geq 0$. In the case of an upswing let the partial derivative of a_t with respect to a_{t-1} be defined piecewisely as

$$\frac{\partial a_t}{\partial a_{t-1}} \quad \begin{cases} \geq 1 & \text{if } (a_{t-1} - a_0) > 0 \quad \text{and} \quad da_{t-1} \geq 0 \\ < 1 & \text{if } (a_{t-1} - a_0) > 0 \quad \text{and} \quad da_{t-1} < 0. \end{cases} \qquad (3.2.8)$$

If the growth rate has increased last period, *i.e.*, $da_{t-1} > 0$, the upswing will be amplified in t. After having reached the maximal growth rate, the decrease will take place in moderate form. Analogous reasoning holds for the case of a recession with $a_t < a_0, \forall t$.

The implications of this postulated growth structure is illustrated in Figure 3.4 for the special case of constant partial derivatives.[17] If there exists an initial deviation of the growth rate from its equilibrium level, a cycle in the growth rate will be generated.

---

[16] *The following formal presentation differs slightly from Krelle (1959).*

[17] *Krelle (1959) assumes absolutely decreasing partial derivatives, which are larger than 1, when the growth rate is moving away from the equilibrium rate.*

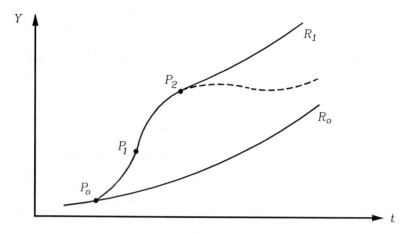

A Stochastic Business Cycle
Figure 3.5

By inspecting the total differential of (3.2.7) in the case of a constant equilibrium growth rate, *i.e.*,

$$da_t = \frac{\partial a_t}{\partial a_{t-1}} da_{t-1} + \frac{\partial a_t}{\partial \mu_t} d\mu_t, \qquad (3.2.9)$$

it can be seen that the overall development of the growth rate depends on the endogenous dynamics of a_t itself as well as on the stochastic influences.

Suppose that initially the economy is on its equilibrium growth path with $a_t = a_{t-1} = a_0 > 0$. If no stochastic exogenous influences were involved, *i.e.*, $\mu_t = 0 \ \forall \ t$, there would be no tendency to move the economy away from that growth path. As μ_t is normally distributed with zero mean, it may be possible that at t_0 a μ_{t_0} occurs which is either positive or negative with the same probability. Assume for example that μ_{t_0} is positive. Because of the bell shape of the probability distribution the occurrence of a small positive value of the random term is more probable than a large one. Let μ_{t_0} indeed be a relatively small number which leads to a deviation of a_{t_0} from a_0 in period t_0. According to (3.2.7) this deviation of a_{t_0} from a_0 will cause a further increase in a_{t_0+1} even if μ_{t_0+1} is equal to zero. If μ_{t_0+1} were positive, then the increase in a_{t_0+1} would be amplified. In face of the normal distribution of μ_t, it is, of course, also possible that $\mu_{t_0+1} < 0$, implying a damping of the increase in a_{t_0+1} or even a reverse in the direction of change. However, once the growth path has started to increase, a negative μ_{t_0+1}, which is absolutely larger than the original positive μ_{t_0}, is required in order to reverse the time path, *i.e.*, $da_{t_0+1} + da_{t_0} < 0$ implies

$$\frac{\partial a_{t_0+1}}{\partial a_{t_0}} da_{t_0} + \frac{\partial a_{t_0+1}}{\partial \mu_{t_0+1}} d\mu_{t_0+1} + \frac{\partial a_{t_0}}{\partial \mu_{t_0}} d\mu_{t_0} < 0$$

$$\frac{\partial a_{t_0+1}}{\partial a_{t_0}}\frac{\partial a_{t_0}}{\partial \mu_{t_0}}d\mu_{t_0} + \frac{\partial a_{t_0+1}}{\partial \mu_{t_0+1}}d\mu_{t_0+1} + \frac{\partial a_{t_0}}{\partial \mu_{t_0}}d\mu_{t_0} < 0,$$

which in case of a constant derivative $\partial a_t/\partial \mu_t$ leads to

$$\frac{\partial a_{t_0+1}}{\partial a_{t_0}} + 1 < -\frac{d\mu_{t_0+1}}{d\mu_{t_0}}. \tag{3.2.10}$$

With $d\mu_t = \mu_t - \mu_{t-1}$ and $\mu_{t_0-1} = 0$, it follows immediately that in the case of an upswing with $\partial a_{t_0+1}/\partial a_{t_0} > 1$ one needs

$$\mu_{t_0+1} < -\mu_{t_0}$$

in order to reverse the growth path. As a large deviation of μ_t from zero is less probable than a small one, it follows that a_t, $t > t_0$, will *probably* be rising.

The business cycle which can be generated by these stochastic influences is illustrated in Figure 3.5. Without stochastic influences, the development of the gross product would be described by the path R_0 with the equilibrium growth rate a_0. Suppose that the function (3.2.7) causes the stylized development of the economy between P_0 and P_2, i.e., after an initial upswing with increasing a_t, the upswing is dampened between P_1 and P_2. At P_2, the former equilibrium growth rate a_0 is reached once again with gross output growing at a higher level.

The closer Y_t is to P_2 the smaller is the necessary stochastic impact which is required to cause a reverse in the development of Y_t. Suppose for simplicity that the growth path R_1 is the maximal attainable growth path of the economy. Thus, at P_2, any positive μ_t can have no influence on the growth rate, at all. However, even an absolutely very small negative μ_t may be able to initiate a downswing of the economy, which would be generated in the same qualitative way as the upswing described above if a minimal growth rate $\underline{a}$ can be defined. An asymmetry may arise here, however, because it may be difficult to explain a lower bound for the development of the gross product. Contrary to the maximal growth path, nothing like lower capacity bounds exist and it may be possible that the downswing continues for a considerable time span. Figure 3.5 assumes the incidental case of a business cycle above the equilibrium growth path, such that there is actually no depression.

The time path between P_0 and P_2 has been drawn smoothly. This does not mean that the immanently generated dynamics with stochastics are actually described by such a smooth curve, but rather should be read as the stylized time path on average. Indeed, at any point in time the stochastic influences may further increase or dampen the development of Y_t. It is also even possible that a very strong negative influence μ_t occurs which immediately causes the growth path to fall to a level below R_0. The smooth curve only indicates the most probable time path of Y_t on average.

It has thus been shown that stochastic influences are able to generate cyclic motions of a model economy. All that is necessary is the assumption of the stylized phenomenon that a deviation from equilibrium amplifies itself for a while until it reaches physical or economical boundaries. It is not necessary to assume a certain dynamic structure, *e.g.*, a two-dimensional dynamic system, which endogenously determines the turning points for purely mathematical reasons. The stochastic exogenous influences are responsible for the onset of a cyclical movement and for the explanations of turning points.

However, the assumed properties of the function (3.2.7) are rather heuristically postulated. While the assumptions may be intuitively reasonable, it is not obvious how the properties can be derived from a standard dynamic model. Nonetheless, the reflections on the influences of stochastic terms in a function like (3.2.7) do enlighten the effects of stochastics in the numerical studies of, *e.g.*, Slutzky and Kalecki (cf. Section 3.2.1.). If a linear business cycle model with damped oscillations is augmented by a stochastic term, it is generally possible to generate time paths with permanent fluctuations which are also irregular. The degree, to which such a time path differs from a non-stochastic path, depends crucially on the numerical magnitude of the stochastic terms.[18]

The relevance of stochastic exogenous influences has been stressed especially by the so-called New Classical Macroeconomics in the context of the expectations formations processes. The Rational Expectations approach to macroeconomics and business cycle theory has made it evident that stochastics can not only be superimposed on existing structural relations and systems, but that they may constitute an essential ingredient in the determinants of individual behavior.

3.3. The Rational Expectations Approach to Business Cycles

Thus far nearly nothing has been said about the role of expectations in the explanation of oscillations in an economy. This may be surprising because the macroeconomic literature in the 1970s and 1980s is dominated by the discussion of the relevance and the implications of the Rational Expectations approach to macroeconomics. The introduction of Rational Expectations by Muth in 1960 has been followed by numerous contributions (which are impossible to be shortly surveyed) and which led to the coinage of that literature as a "revolution" in macroeconomics (Begg (1982)). While the relevance of Rational Expectations for the development of a general theory of expectations formation or for the so-called *policy-ineffectiveness debate* is not called into question, the importance of Rational Expectations in business cycle theory will be interpreted as

---

[18] *Remember that in linear models with damped oscillations, the initial disturbance represents the largest deviation from equilibrium during the entire adjustment process.*

being less significant as is often assumed. It is shown below that the consideration of Rational Expectations as such does not generate cyclical movements and that additional assumptions on the model structure have to be made, which are not essentially different from those described in the previous chapter.

Rational Expectations models rely heavily on the existence of exogenous shocks. This was implicitly the case for the linear multiplier-accelerator type models of Chapter 2 as well. While those models required exogenous shocks in the form of once-and-for-all offsets from time to time, Rational Expectations models typically introduce stochastic exogenous influences in every period. As these stochastic exogenous influences are the essential features in dynamic Rational Expectations models, they are subsumed in this chapter dealing basically with exogenous forces. The Perfect Foresight approach, *i.e.*, Rational Expectations without any stochastic influences, is therefore entirely neglected in the following presentation.

Dynamic Rational Expectations models cannot be understood without a knowledge of the basic approach to the specific expectations formations process. Because there are several good introductory texts on Rational Expectations, only a very short section will be devoted to the portrayal of Rational Expectations and the functioning of the corresponding equilibrium models.

3.3.1. Expectations and Rationality in Economic Theory

The majority of economic classroom models is embedded in a timeless framework for apparently didactic purposes. The standard microeconomic textbook models of individual optimizing behavior – at least at the introductory level – outline a scenario in which agents act as if no past and no future existed which could influence the agents' current decisions.

However, economic life obviously takes place in a dynamic context. Initial environments and endowments, which are determined by past decisions, influence the present decisions. In addition, there are feedback processes with respect to future constellations: current decisions may directly influence future endowments, and reflections about future events may determine current decisions. While there is a common agreement among economists that a meaningful dynamic model should reflect this general intertemporal structure, economic theory has always found it difficult to consider it in the construction of specific models. The abstract thought experiments of the General Equilibrium Analysis (cf. Arrow/Hahn (1971), Debreu (1959)), which assume complete future markets, have even diverted mathematical economists' attention away from the subject. Furthermore, the traditional Walrasian or Marshallian models have essentially been concerned with sequences of the states of an economy in which economic agents basically act unconsciously of time. The time aspect, *i.e.*, the connection of periods, is

introduced merely by an external institution like the auctioneer. This superimposition
of dynamic aspects on a basically static structure is typical for many approaches in
dynamic economic models and also for many theories presented in this book.

Only relatively recently have attempts been made to overcome this shortcoming
in traditional micro- and macroeconomics and to consider individuals who act in a
true dynamic context. The theory of overlapping generations, popularized especially by
Samuelson (1958) and Diamond (1965), has gained prominent attention in dynamical
economics. This theory is easily manageable only in the case of two generations and
has made it evident how difficult it is to satisfactorily depict a dynamic phenomenon.

As soon as an agent is assumed to take future events into account, which may influence his current decision, he has to reflect about something which he *cannot* know for
sure. The individual is forced to speculate about future magnitudes of variables which
he believes to be essential. These speculations or expectations are involved in every
dynamic model that allows for intertemporal individual optimization, either explicitly
stated or implicitly assumed. Despite this fundamental importance of expectations,
economic theory is lacking in investigations of the expectations formation process. As
economics is a science which attempts to describe and to explain real human behavior its
task is to provide abstract pictures of actual expectations formation processes, whether
these expectations are fulfilled or not. Like utility functions, however, expectations are
unobservable, such that it may be impossible to monitor expectations. Basically, there
may be as many different expected values of a certain variable as individuals exist in a
society; thus, the subject of economics in this context can only be the search for roughly
similar patterns and an attempt to categorize them. However, even this seemingly simple task has been doomed to failure when a complete generalization has been attempted.
Rather, dynamical economics has provisionally worked with very few singular forms of
expectations for a long time, during which this provisionary character often has not
been made explicit. While it is possible that they are correct from time to time, the
assumption of, *e.g.*, static, adaptive, or extrapolative expectations are very rough hypotheses which are usually made because of their manageability and not because they
are believed to be correct pictures of individual psychological behavior.

To illustrate the different concepts, consider a variable x_t, whose expected future
value at time $t+1$, formed at t, is denoted by $x^e_{t+1,t}$. *Static* expectations simply assume
that the observed value x_t will prevail in the next period, too:

$$x^e_{t+1,t} = x_t. \tag{3.3.1}$$

Trivially, static expectations are correct only in the case of a stationary equilibrium,
i.e., when the rates of change of each variable are equal to zero. A justification for the
assumption of static expectations can only be given if the individuals have absolutely
no information about future constellations of exogenous forces and about the structure
of the economy. For the purposes of business cycle theory, static expectations are

surely unsuited, because in the case of fluctuating economies individuals with these expectations always lag behind actual developments.

The idea that individuals adjust their expectations in case of discrepancies between previously expected and actual current values of a certain variable is expressed by the hypothesis of *adaptive* expectations (cf. Cagan (1956), Nerlove (1958)). Let $x^e_{t+1,t}$ denote the expected value of x_{t+1} in period t. If the previously expected and the actual values in the current period, i.e., $x^e_{t,t-1}$ and x_t, deviate from one another, expectations about x_{t+1} formed in t will be revised according to

$$x^e_{t+1,t} - x^e_{t,t-1} = \gamma(x_t - x^e_{t,t-1}), \quad 1 > \gamma > 0. \tag{3.3.2}$$

Note that for $\gamma = 1$ equation (3.3.2) is identical to (3.3.1). Furthermore, with adaptive expectations it is impossible to anticipate turning points of a fluctuating economy because the sign of the change of expectations is always the same as that of the current deviation of actual from expected values.

Recursive substitution of the expected values in (3.3.2) and neglecting the influence of the very first expected value in the past yields:

$$x^e_{t+1,t} = \sum_{\tau=0}^{\infty} \gamma(1-\gamma)^\tau x_{t-\tau}, \tag{3.3.3}$$

i.e., the expected value of a variable is an average of all actual values in the past. Thus, adaptive expectations are very similar to *extrapolative* expectations, i.e.,

$$x^e_{t+1,t} = \sum_{\tau=t_0}^{t} \alpha_\tau x_\tau, \quad \alpha_\tau > 0, \tag{3.3.4}$$

with the difference that t_0 may be any point in time in the past.[19]

Adaptive and extrapolative expectations are the most widespread hypotheses on the expectations formation process in dynamical economics. Aside from the fact that these expectations are relatively easy to handle, they also have the advantage that they can constitute the essential dynamic, intertemporal link between periods in economic models. Like any other simplistic hypothesis, adaptive or extrapolative expectations may be correct pictures of actual processes. However, as long as an economy is not characterized by general equilibrium, these expectations may imply that an individual always makes expectational errors. As pointed out above, this is definitely the case if an economy is fluctuating, because turning points can never be anticipated if the adjustment parameter γ is constant over time. It can be argued that individuals ought to

---

[19] *Formally, equations (3.3.3) and (3.3.4) are distributed lags.*

realize these expectational errors and that they attempt to overcome this shortcoming by revising the expectations formation process itself. While this claim of necessary revisions of the thinking process can easily be established, postulating better hypotheses is much more difficult. One proposal which has gained widespread recognition among economists was provided by Muth (1961). As theorists evaluate the different hypotheses on the expectations formation process by means of the specific economic model at hand, it may be useful to assume expectations which basically anticipate the results of exactly that model. Abstracting from stochastic influences for a while, this hypothesis implies that expected and actual values of a variable always coincide. Therefore, these expectations which are always fulfilled are appropriately coined Perfect Foresight. As soon as stochastic influences are considered, the Perfect Foresight approach has to be modified because it can reasonably not be assumed that individuals know the magnitudes of the stochastic variables. However, if individuals are aware that stochastic influences exist and if they know the probability distribution of these stochastic influences, then they do not make *systematic* errors in anticipating actual values. The association of correctness or the absence of systematic errors with rationality led Muth to term these expectations *Rational Expectations*. Rational Expectations models, which differ from Perfect Foresight models only in the respect that actual values of future variables are replaced by current expectations of these variables, are called *certainty equivalence* models (Begg (1982), p. 51f.). The working of Rational Expectations models can best be illustrated in terms of a microeconomic supply and demand framework (cf. Muth (1961))[20]. Let x_t^d be the demand for goods:

$$x_t^d = a - bp_t,$$
(3.3.5)

with p_t as the good's price. Assume that the supply of goods at the beginning of the period depends on the expected price this period

$$x_t^s = c + dp_t^e + \mu_t$$
(3.3.6)

with p_t^e as the expected price for this period and μ_t as a random variable with zero mean.

The equilibrium price of the system, *i.e.*, $p_t = p_{t-1} = p_t^e \, \forall \, t$, is, of course, independent of the specific expectations hypothesis:

$$p^* = \frac{a - c}{b + d}$$
(3.3.7)

or in the random case

$$p_t^* = \frac{a - c}{b + d} - \frac{\mu_t}{b + d}.$$
(3.3.8)

---

[20] *The presentation below follows Carter/Maddock (1984).*

Rational expectations assume that the individuals are able to calculate the equilibrium price and that they expect this equilibrium price to prevail in the current period. Thus, the expected price p_t^e is assumed to be the mathematical expectation of (3.3.8), *i.e.*, $p_t^e = E(p_t^*)$, which is equal to (3.3.7) due to $E(\mu) = 0$. If the expected price p_t^e is substituted in (3.3.6), *i.e.*,

$$x_t^s = c + d\left(\frac{a-c}{b+d}\right) + \mu_t \qquad (3.3.9)$$

the resulting equilibrium price is indeed equal to (3.3.7) plus a random term.

This simple microeconomic model uncovers all the essential features of Rational Expectations. It makes it especially clear that the Rational Expectations hypothesis relies heavily on the assumptions of a permanently equilibrating system. If disequilibria with the consequence of uncertain actual values occurred in a model, individuals would be unable to calculate the expected values. Basically, if actual values are principally undetermined by the model, expectations can also not be formed. From a pragmatic point of view, it is thus quite understandable that Rational Expectations became prominent during the revival of classical economics in the 1970s, because this hypothesis on expectations is the one which fits best with equilibrium macroeconomics.[21]

The very concept of Rational Expectations alone is not able to generate a fluctuating behavior of an economy. A dynamic model, which excludes the possibility of oscillations by its mathematical structure without an exact specification of the expectations hypothesis, cannot be turned into a business cycle model by the introduction of rational expectations. On the other hand, phenomena in dynamic models, which occur for example under adaptive expectations, may be suppressed by rational expectations. The debate over the policy-ineffectiveness has made it evident that the correct anticipation of dynamic policy-rules, for instance steady increases of the money supply, may lead to a failure of these policies. The fact that under Rational Expectations individuals do not lag behind actual developments leads to a damping of potentially oscillatory forces. A business cycle, which was intended to be generated by the policy of incumbent parties (cf. Section 3.1.), would not set in if individuals correctly anticipated the policy rule.

The Rational Expectations business cycle models, *i.e.*, those models which display fluctuations and which are basically compatible with Rational Expectations, are thus models, which deviate from the pure, stylized Rational Expectations models. Either informational shortcomings which cannot be avoided or assumptions about the stochastic process, the propagation of a shock, etc. are necessary to provide the dynamic struc-

---

[21] *Rational Expectations have recently been incorporated in disequilibrium rationing models (cf. Gerard-Varet et al. (1984)). While the appropriate models study the behavior of an economy off the Walrasian general equilibrium, they nevertheless concentrate on the investigation of equilibrium states in the form of temporary or rationing equilibria of an economy.*

ture which allows for oscillatory motions. Thus, it is just the deviation from a world with perfect information which generates cycles in most existing Rational Expectations business cycle models.[22]

All the models which are briefly presented below are equilibrium models in the sense that planned and realized values of a variable coincide, provided that the technical and economic constraints are taken into account, which prevent the system from reaching a Walrasian general equilibrium immediately. While this concentration on equilibrium situations in the New Classical Macroeconomics and in the Rational Expectations business cycle literature has often raised objections - especially because of the treatment of unemployment - it has to be noted that the reference to equilibria is not a characteristic feature of Rational Expectations models.[23]

3.3.2. The New Classical Macroeconomics

One of the main reasons why Rational Expectations models became popular in macroeconomics probably has to do with the importance of the contribution of the New Classical Macroeconomics to the *policy-ineffectiveness debate*. In its simplest form, Rational Expectations macro-models are able to show that demand-oriented policy stimula, which are the essence of Keynesian economic policy, are totally ineffective if individuals know the government's policy-rules and if expectations are formed which take these policy-rules into account.[24] While the basic models have subsequently been modified with qualifying results, the presentation of these simple models is helpful in understanding the working of more sophisticated Rational Expectations business cycle models.[25]

---

[22] *This statement is valid only for the definition of Rational Expectations presented above. Alternatively, Rational Expectations are often defined as the result of an expectations formation process in which all available information has been taken into account. This property cannot be a distinctive feature of Rational Expectations, however, because agents with, e.g., adaptive expectations may have collected all available information as well.*

[23] *Compare also Ramser (1987), pp. 65ff. Aside from the fact that equilibrium models are easier to handle than disequilibrium models, Lucas/Sargent (1979), p. 304 ff. deny that the mere presence of, e.g., inventories and unemployment indicates the occurrence of disequilibria in the sense that actual and planned magnitudes diverge.*

[24] *See McCallum (1980) for an excellent overview of stabilization policies in Rational Expectations models.*

[25] *As a fact, it has turned out that the policy-ineffectiveness-result is valid for a small class of models, only. Compare, e.g., Fischer (1980) who demonstrates "that there is a variety of mechanisms through which even fully anticipated monetary policy can affect the behavior of output." (Fischer (1980), p. 213).*

As Rational Expectations have to refer to equilibrium constellations, the concept
of aggregate demand and supply functions is an appropriate tool in studying macroeconomic relations. While problems may arise with this concept in some interpretations of
Keynesian economics, especially if rationing is involved, a general equilibrium constellation of the entire economy can be illustrated by the intersection of the aggregate supply
function, which represents equilibria in the labor market, and the aggregate demand
function, which reflects simultaneous equilibria in the markets for goods, money, and
bonds.[26] As is generally accepted, the aggregate supply function is usually vertical if the
nominal wage rate is totally flexible. Trivially, demand stimulating policies are ineffective with respect to output and employment and result only in an increase of the price
level. This does not contradict Keynesian theorizing either because demand policies are
concerned with output levels below the general equilibrium level or because the nominal
wage rate is assumed to be inflexible. Obviously, a theoretical prerequisite for a successful demand oriented policy is an upward-sloping aggregate supply function, which can
easily be constructed if the assumption of flexible nominal wages is abandonned. The
other possible way of constructing such a function was proposed by Friedman (1968)
and refers more to individual misperceptions rather than institutional restrictions. Suppose that prices rise as a consequence of a demand stimulus. The *ceteris paribus* decline
of real wages leads entrepreneurs to increase the demand for labor, which eventually
causes a rise in nominal wages such that the initial real wage is restored. This is the
scenario of the vertical aggregate supply function, provided that the lagging of nominal
wages behind prices is not too large. It may be the case, however, that workers transact
sequentially. If they always visit the goods market after having contracted in the labor
market, they may falsely anticipate the goods prices at the moment of drawing up the
contracts in the labor market. Thus, if nominal wages increase as a consequence of
rising prices, workers may nevertheless believe that real wages have risen, provided that
they base their anticipation on last period's prices, *i.e.*, when they have static expectations. A rising demand for labor due to decreasing real wages may thus go hand in
hand with rising supply of labor due to perceived rising real wages. The consequence is
that output and employment may rise and that the aggregate supply function is indeed
upward sloping. As soon as workers realize the higher prices, however, the real wage
rate will correctly be anticipated again and output and employment will return to the
former equilibrium level.

This verbal reasoning can be formalized by the so-called *Lucas-Sargent supply*

---

[26] *See Dornbusch/Fischer (1978), Branson (1979), or Carter/Maddock (1984) for the
concept of aggregate supply and demand functions.*

function:[27]

$$Y_t^s = Y^* + \delta(p_t - p_{t,t-1}^e), \quad \delta > 0. \tag{3.3.10}$$

As long as actual and expected prices coincide, the supply of goods is equal to the general equilibrium level of production Y^*, which, unfortunately, is often called the 'natural' level of production, implying that the corresponding level of employment $N(Y^*)$ is called the 'natural' level of employment.

The policy-ineffectiveness property of some models can easily be demonstrated by the following consideration.[28] Assume that expectations $p_{t,t-1}^e$ in (3.3.10) are formed according to the Rational Expectations hypothesis, *i.e.*, expectations $p_{t,t-1}^e$ are the mathematical expectation $E_{t-1}(p_t^*)$ in $t-1$ of the equilibrium price p_t^* prevailing in period t.

Let the aggregate demand function have a linear form:

$$Y_t^d = \alpha A_t - \beta p_t \quad \alpha, \beta > 0, \tag{3.3.11}$$

in which A_t represents autonomous demand of, *e.g.*, the government and assume that the economy is always in temporary equilibrium such that

$$Y_t^s = Y_t^d. \tag{3.3.12}.$$

Equations (3.3.10), (3.3.11) and (3.3.12) together with the Rational Expectations hypothesis $p_{t,t-1}^e = E_{t-1}(p_t^*)$, constitute a system of 4 equations with 5 unknowns. In order to close the model, assume that A_t is exogenously given. The equilibrium price level p_t^* is obtained by equating supply and demand:

$$p_t^* = \frac{\delta p_{t,t-1}^e + \alpha A_t - Y^*}{\beta + \delta}. \tag{3.3.13}$$

According to the Rational Expectations hypothesis, individual expectations are the mathematical expectations of p_t^*:

$$p_{t,t-1}^e = E_{t-1}(p_t^*) = E_{t-1}\left(\frac{\delta p_{t,t-1}^e + \alpha A_t - Y^*}{\beta + \delta}\right). \tag{3.3.14}$$

Obviously, $E_{t-1}(p_{t,t-1}^e) = p_{t,t-1}^e$, which follows tautologically. As Y^* is a constant and if the individuals perceive it being constant, it follows that $E_{t-1}(Y^*) = Y^*$. If,

---

[27] *It is possible to include a stochastic term in (3.3.10) which reflects exogenous forces other than expectational influences. The results are not altered by these stochastic influences which are therefore neglected below.*

[28] *The presentation below is stimulated by Carter/Maddock (1984).*

furthermore, the coefficients α, β, and δ are correctly anticipated, the expected value of p_t is

$$p^e_{t,t-1} = \frac{\alpha E_{t-1}(A_t) - Y^*}{\beta}. \tag{3.3.15}$$

Combination of (3.3.15), (3.3.13), and (3.3.10) yields

$$Y^s_t = Y^* + \delta \frac{\alpha(A_t - E_{t-1}(A_t))}{\beta + \delta}. \tag{3.3.16}$$

Deviations of Y^s_t from Y^* can only occur if the actual value of A_t differs from its expected value. If expectations are correct up to a stochastic random term, i.e.,

$$E_{t-1}(A_t) = A^e_{t,t-1} = A_t - \mu_t$$

with μ_t as a random variable with, e.g., zero mean, then (3.3.16) becomes

$$Y^s_t = Y^* + \frac{\delta \alpha \mu_t}{\beta + \delta} \tag{3.3.17}$$

and output fluctuates randomly around the natural level Y^*. This result is known as the fundamental policy-ineffectiveness property of Rational Expectations macromodels. If individuals are able to anticipate a demand-stimulating policy correctly, regardless of the magnitude of the intervention, the policy is doomed to failure. The result remains true for diverse policy-rules in this model and the only question which arises is how reasonable it is to assume that individuals have knowledge of the policy-rule. If a standard rule exists which is followed with only minor random disturbances, then it may have happened in the past that individuals underwent a learning process.[29] If no regularity can be uncovered in past policy decisions, it is, of course, difficult to justify the expectations hypothesis. In any case, Rational Expectations are an extreme assumption on the information set available to individuals.

A government that attempts to manipulate the economy by means of demand stimulating policies will succeed only if it intentionally deviates from the fixed rule without announcing this deviation in advance. In other words, demand stimulating policies have to be unanticipated in order to be successful.

The interesting aspect of Rational Expectations with respect to cyclical movements consists of the fact that the policy-ineffectiveness result remains true in this simple model when policy-rules are assumed which are cyclic themselves.[30] Suppose, for example, that the incumbent party's demand policy is cyclical for re-election purposes (cf.

---

[29] *Compare Friedman (1979) for the problem of learning processes in Rational Expectations models.*

[30] *Compare Blinder/Fischer (1981), p. 280.*

Section 3.1.). While this cyclicity of $\{A_t\}$ and hence of $\{Y_t^s\}$ usually cannot be offset by adaptive expectations, Rational Expectations without any informational restrictions indeed straighten the oscillatory forces completely. In this sense, it can be stated that the introduction of Rational Expectations dampens the potential oscillation-initiating influence of exogenous factors, provided that they are not stochastic and thus unpredictable.

Therefore, the Rational Expectations business cycle models which are presented below either have to introduce informational shortcomings in the sense that the individual *cannot* obtain information on relevant magnitudes even if he were to attempt to do so, or dynamic structures of the economy have to be assumed, the effects of which are not substantially influentiable by the expectations hypothesis.[31]

3.3.3. Rational Expectations Business Cycle Models

Rational Expectations business cycle models can be divided into three classes:[32]

i)   The assumed structure of the economy prevents individuals from obtaining information about the potential cyclical forces in the entire economy.

ii)   Expectations are not immediately correct because a learning process has to set in during which expectations are formally identical to adaptive expectations in a broad sense.

iii) Information is complete and expectations are rational but the dynamic structure of the economy will allow for oscillatory motion on its own grounds.[33]

---

[31] *Compare Shiller (1978) and Kydland/Prescott (1980) for the dynamic structure of macroeconomic models.*

[32] *The case, in which exogenous influences are serially correlated, will be ignored in the following.*

[33] *A fourth type of Rational Expectations models that recently has gained much attention is represented by models which allow for so-called sunspot equilibria (cf., e.g., Azariadis/Guesnerie (1986), Cass/Shell (1983), Woodford (1986)). Arbitrary, non-economic events which do not directly influence economic variables are expected to occur by the majority of individuals (Note that this is in contrast with older "sunspot" models which assume a direct dependence of, e.g., crop yields on solar activities). If all individuals believe that economic variables will be affected by these events, their prophecies can be self-fulfilling through their appropriate actions. Historic phenomena like the Dutch tulip mania in the 17th century and the Great Depression may be explained by these self-fulfilling expectations.*
The literature on sunspot expectations concentrates on non-linear dynamic structures of an economy. Most models establish the existence of a period-2 cycle, i.e.,

The first class of models, which encloses the majority of all model presented in this section, is characterized by economic structures which allow for oscillatory motion in the real sector of an economy, and, additionally, by informational shortcomings which cannot be offset by individual efforts. Representative of the models with informational shortcomings is Lucas' 1975-model of equilibrium business cycles, which makes use of Phelps' famous 'island' model of geographically unconnected markets. (Phelps (1969)).[34] Consider an economy, which is divided into different unconnected markets for a macroeconomic good such that an individual on any 'island' (market) does not know precisely what is going on in other markets.[35] At the beginning of each period, individuals randomly search for a market in which they operate for the length of that period. Each island is comparable to a sector of a global economy, in which production and accumulation take place according to the neoclassical growth theory with money. If governmental purchases and - *uno actu* - the money supplied by the government, which administrates the totality of the different markets, are also randomly distributed among the islands, the question arises what kind of information the individuals may possess in such a scenario. The only thing the individual can directly observe is the capital stock on the island he is just visiting, because capital is assumed to be immobile. He neither knows about the beginning-of-the-periods' capital stocks in other markets and thus in the aggregate, nor about the money stocks in those markets. However, he has precise historic knowledge of the economic events in the respective periods in those markets he has visited before. It can be supposed that he has developed a subjective probability distribution of the time paths of capital stocks and governmental purchases. For simplicity, Lucas assumed that the objective probability distribution has settled down to stationary values and that it coincides with the subjective distributions. Individuals have to decide on the amount of next period's capital stock, *i.e.*, additional capital goods have to be produced in the current period, and on the demand for the money stock held at the end of the period. The decision on these magnitudes does not depend on current variables only, but also on expected magnitudes of the next period. The return on money is the expected inflation (deflation) rate, which in the case of uncertainty reads[36]

$$r_{mt} = p_t - \bar{p}^e_{t+1,t} \qquad (3.3.18)$$

with p_t as the actual price level in the market the individual is just visiting, and with

---

an economic variable permanently switches between two possible values. The general case with period-k cycles involves serious technical difficulties (cf. Guesnerie (1986)).

[34] *A similar framework is elaborated in Lucas/Prescott (1974).*

[35] *Note the rather archaic scenario, which totally abstracts from the existence of telecommunications and similar institutional set ups.*

[36] *Lowercase letters indicate that all variables are written in logarithmic form.*

$\bar{p}^e_{t+1,t}$ as the expected *average* price level in the next period, because the individual does not know which market he will visit next period. The return on capital, which is available next period and which will remain in its present location, is defined as the difference between the expected (rental) price next period in the present market $p^e_{t+1,t}$ and the expected average price $\bar{p}^e_{t+1,t}$ again, because the owners will have moved next period:[37]

$$r_{Kt} = p^e_{t+1,t} - \bar{p}^e_{t+1,t}.$$
(3.3.19)

The essential property of this scenario consists of the fact that it is impossible to gain precise information about the exogenous influences even though the probability distributions are known for sure. Therefore, the island model should not be taken to literally. It is just a theoretical example of how incomplete information may occur.

The interesting aspect of the island model in this context is that the informational incompleteness has consequences for the real accumulation process in periods other than the recent one. This intertemporal linkage, however, cannot lead to persistent fluctuations around the stationary values *per se*. As the stochastic influences are serially uncorrelated, the real variables can at best follow a Markov process with a lag of one period behind the stochastic terms.[38] From a formal point of view it is not possible to generate something like sinusoidal movements.[39] If one is willing to accept that a Markov process with its possible abrupt direction changes satisfactorily reflects typical business cycle shapes, then this essentially one-dimensional model may be called a business cycle model. However, endogenous cycles, which were initiated by stochastic exogenous forces, could only be generated if the system were of higher dimension. For this reason, Lucas (1975, p. 202 ff.) stated that it is necessary to modify the internal structure of the model by, *e.g.*, introducing accelerator effects. In that case, a Rational Expectations model would be economically and formally identical to the traditional multiplier-accelerator models with the essential difference that the necessary shocks, which initiate the cyclical behavior, are 'endogenized' in the sense that individual expectations decide whether an exogenous influence acts like a shock or not.

---

[37] *The rental price is actually determined via the marginal productivity of capital. Lucas neglects the possible effects of, e.g., diminishing returns and approximates the rental price by the general price level.*

[38] *Compare Sargent (1979), p. 264, who develops a similar model of the business cycle which incorporates adjustment costs (op.cit.: Ch.16).*

[39] *The coinage of these models as 'business cycle models' depends crucially on the assumed length of the period. A time series of annual data may exhibit a sawtooth pattern while, e.g., weekly data show smoother, sinusoidal time paths. In order to be comparable, it is thus necessary to assume the same period lengths in different models. While the length of exactly one production period has turned out to be the standard reference, the problem remains how long such a period is.*

This necessity of constructing dynamical systems which are formally able to generate permanent fluctuations in Rational Expectations models under the basic assumption of serially uncorrelated stochastic influences in order to be called proper business cycle models can principally lead to the consideration of the whole variety of lags and multiperiod time-linkages that have been presented in Chapter 2. Two approaches have gained prominent interest and will briefly be sketched below.

The investigation of the effects of holding inventories has long been a major focus of research in business cycle theory (cf. Section 2.1.1.3.), because the presence of inventories constitutes one of the most convincing intertemporal linkages. Blinder/Fischer (1981) studied the question of whether the introduction of inventories in a Lucas-supply-function framework alters the basic policy-ineffectiveness result, *i.e.*, whether there are any real and persistent effects of policy interventions. From microeconomic considerations they derive a dynamic equation for the development of the inventory stock, which reads

$$N_{t+1} - N_t = \theta(N_t^* - N_t) - \Phi(p_t - p_{t,t-1}^e), \tag{3.3.20}$$

$$\theta, \Phi = \text{constant}, \ 0 < \theta < 1, \ \Phi \geq 0$$

with N_t as the actual inventory stock at the beginning of t, N_t^* as the desired optimal inventory stock, and p_t and $p_{t,t-1}^e$ as the logs of actual and expected price levels, respectively. The reasoning behind this function is intuitively obvious: if the desired inventory stock is larger than the actual stock, the firm attempts to fill the gap gradually by an amount per period which is smaller than the gap itself. The idea that inventories serve as buffers is expressed by the price-surprise term: if the actual price in the current period has turned out to be higher than the expected price for this period, firms have sold more this period than has been anticipated. *Ceteris paribus*, the inventory stock at the beginning of the next period is therefore smaller than that at the beginning of the current period.

Let $S_t = Y_t - (N_{t+1} - N_t)$ denote actual sales in the market. If the desired and actual inventory stocks deviate and the production of goods is constant, the gap $N_{t+1} - N_t$ can only be filled if sales adjust appropriately. However, it is unrealistic to assume that production will be constant if, *e.g.*, desired inventories exceed actual inventories: the production of goods will probably be increased in order to keep sales on a more or less constant level. Blinder/Fischer (1981) therefore assumed that the amount of produced goods is determined by[40]

$$Y_t = Y_t^* + \gamma(p_t - p_{t,t-1}^e) + \lambda(N_t^* - N_t), \quad \gamma > 0, \quad 0 < \lambda < 1. \tag{3.3.21}$$

Equation (3.3.21) is a modified Lucas-Sargent supply function with Y_t^* as the "natural" output level. The microeconomic considerations of Blinder/Fischer (1981) imply that

---

[40] *An assumed error term in the supply function is dropped once again.*

$\theta > \lambda$ with the consequence that sales are changing if $N_{t+1} - N_t \neq 0$. The model is closed by the introduction of a standard aggregate demand side and by specific assumptions on the determinants of the desired inventory stocks. Blinder/Fischer (1981) were able to show that in the case of a constant desired inventory stock and interest-inelastic money demand, real effects of unanticipated money stock changes occur. A rise in the money stock leads to higher prices and higher sales which decrease inventories initially. This decrease itself leads to higher production and rising inventories in subsequent periods until the original stationary state is reached again. Thus, a part of the business cycle has been explained, i.e., unanticipated changes in the money stock lead to persistent deviations of the real variables from trend, but these changes are unable to initiate a full cycle with permanent up- and downswings. In the case of interest-dependent desired inventories it is possible to get a result only for the special case of perfect foresight: If individuals fully anticipate a change in the level of the money stock at some point in time t, they also anticipate the inflation rate correctly.[41] Provided that the nominal interest rate does not change substantially, a falling inflation rate leads to a rising real interest rate, which implies decreasing desired inventory stocks. For simplicity, Blinder/ Fischer (1981) assumed a linear relation

$$N_t^* = \overline{N} - \delta r_t, \quad \overline{N}, \delta > 0, \tag{3.3.22}$$

in which $\overline{N}$ and δ are constants. Let $t = \tau$ be a point in time when the money stock is changed such that the inflation rate decreases. The time paths of the relevant variables are pictured in Figure 3.6, which illustrates that real effects of anticipated shocks occur before as well as after the effective change of the exogenous variable.[42]

An elaborated model which also investigates the effects of the presence of inventories was developed by Brunner/Cukierman/Meltzer (1983). Brunner et al. assumed that the goods' prices are advertised before the start of the transactions and are kept fixed during the period. An exogenous shock in the form of an unanticipated money stock change influences the real interest rate as well as the inventory stocks. The need to refill the inventories increases the demand for labor, which initiates a rise of the equilibrium real wage rate. An increased real wage rate, however, generates a feedback process because it is now more profitable to produce for inventories than for current sales. The dynamics which occur in this scenario, are again described as persistent but non-oscillating deviations of the real variables from their stationary values.

The second category of models considers a phenomenon in Rational Expectations models which is related to an often raised criticism: The assumption of known probability distributions actually makes sense only if these refer to a unique stationary state.

---

[41] For details, the reader is referred to Blinder/Fischer (1981), appendix.

[42] Blinder/Fischer (1981) also study the effects of an anticipated change in the growth rate of the money stock which leads to slightly different results.

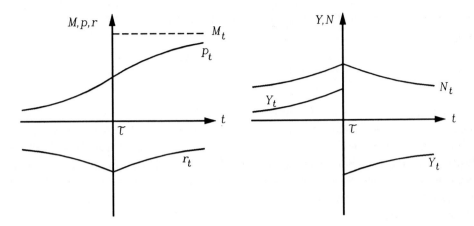

Figure 3.6

If structural parameters of an economy change such that the stationary equilibrium values vary, Rational Expectations imply that individuals are omniscient in the sense that they have to know each informational detail which may potentially influence the equilibrium state. It may be argued that probability distributions are reasonably known only by experience.[43] While these learning processes can be very complicated, Brunner/Cukierman/Meltzer (1980) have pointed out that a further problem may arise in the expectations formation process according to the Rational Expectations hypothesis if it cannot be excluded that variations in exogenous variables will be permanent and thus change the stationary equilibrium state. As soon as the individual faces an unanticipated change in an exogenous variable, it cannot be decided immediately whether the shock is transitory (such that the stationary equilibrium in the future is not affected) or whether it is permanent. Brunner et al. investigated an equilibrium business cycle model with markets for goods, money, and labor, in which individuals know the deterministic as well as the stochastic structure of the economy. However, at time t individuals are unable to decide whether an exogenous shock at t will be transitory or permanent.[44] If individuals know the past values of the exogenous variable $x_t = x_t^p + x_t^t$, with x_t^p as the permanent and x_t^t as the transitory component, then it can be shown that the best estimator for the permanent component of the current shock is a distributed

---

[43] *As mentioned above, this has been assumed, e.g., in Lucas (1975).*

[44] *Ex post, it is even impossible to decide whether the effects of the exogenous shocks are due to the transitory or the permanent components of the shocks in different periods.*

lag of the observed values of the exogenous variable in the past:[45]

$$E(x_t^p) = \lambda \sum_{\tau=0}^{\infty} (1-\lambda)^\tau x_{t-\tau}, \qquad (3.3.23)$$

in which the constant λ is determined by the variances of the probability distributions of x_t^p and x_t^t. A comparison of (3.3.23) with equation (3.3.3) shows that Rational Expectations are formally equivalent to adaptive expectations in this case if the coefficients λ and γ have the same qualitative properties. Consequently, Brunner et al. were able to show that persistent effects of exogenous shocks like productivity decreases exist, which do not rely on accelerator effects or similar phenomena.

While the approaches presented above are usually unable to show the possibility of oscillations, the models of the third category are much more comparable to the traditional business cycle models. Long/Plosser (1983) have shown that it is possible to generate full business cycles in a model which does not have to make use of any of the restrictions mentioned in the models above like incomplete information, adjustment costs, or serial correlation of random terms. Under the assumption of a Robinson-Crusoe-economy without money and with a variety of goods which may also serve as inputs in the production process, Long/Plosser demonstrated that the interaction of intertemporal preferences and production possibilities may lead to cyclical behavior. Consider an economy with n sectors. Every sector produces a single good. The factors of production are labor and the produced goods of all sectors. The economy-wide production function is

$$Y_{t+1} = F(L_t, X_t, \lambda_{t+1}), \qquad (3.3.24)$$

with L_t and Y_{t+1} as n-dimensional vectors denoting labor inputs and outputs, respectively, and X_t as an $n \times n$-matrix of commodity inputs. The n-dimensional vector λ_{t+1} consists of random terms which follow a Markov process and whose actual values will be realized during the production period. While the decision about labor and commodity inputs have to be made at the beginning of the period, the actual output available next period is nevertheless not precisely known at t. For the special case of Cobb-Douglas forms of (3.3.24) and one-periodic utility functions, Long/Plosser (1983) derived a system of difference equations like

$$y_{t+1} = A\,y_t + \eta_{t+1} + k, \qquad (3.3.25)$$

with y_t as an n-dimensional vector of the logs of Y_t, A as an $n \times n$-matrix of input-output coefficients, η_t as the n-dimensional vector of the logs of λ_t, and k as an n-dimensional

---

[45] Compare Brunner et al. (1980), p. 475 and the literatur cited therein for details.

vector of constants.[46] Obviously, the properties of A decide whether cyclical phenomena may occur. It is in principle possible that complex roots occur, implying the generation of permanent oscillations. The combination of those smooth dynamics with randomly distributed exogenous shocks indeed leads to time paths of the real variables, which show striking similarities with actually observed time series.

The Long/Plosser model belongs to the class of so-called *real* business cycle models. Other models relying on the occurrence of direct shocks to real variables can be found, for example, in King/Plosser (1984) and Kydland/Prescott (1982). Real business cycle models have been criticized mainly on two grounds. First, most of these models completely ignore the influence of monetary variables either as original impulses for the onset of oscillations or as a propagation means of a real shock in the economy.[47] Second, it has been doubted that technology shocks occur more or less simultaneously in single industries such that their aggregate effects have a variance sufficiently high to fit actual time series.[48]

The models presented above are all designed in discrete time, which makes the dynamic structure highly transparent and which is a necessary assumption in the presence of uncertainty. For the sake of completeness, a phenomenon will briefly be discussed which arises in continuous-time models with perfect foresight.[49] [50]

Suppose that the dynamic structure of a perfect foresight model can be reduced to a two-dimensional differential equation system

$$\dot{x}_1 = f(x_1, x_2)$$
$$\dot{x}_2 = g(x_1, x_2), \tag{3.3.26}$$

in which x_1 and x_2 may, e.g., express prices and the capital stock. Denote (x_1^*, x_2^*) as the stationary state of the system. Usually, it is desirable that the steady state is globally stable in the asymptotic sense, *i.e.*, whichever initial point is chosen, the trajectories always converge toward the steady state values. Suppose that the system is initially not in this steady state and that individuals have to estimate the initial values of the endogenous variables x_1 and x_2. The assumption of perfect foresight together with the asymptotically stable equilibrium implies that different estimates of

---

[46] *A formally similar equation is derived in Lucas (1973).*

[47] *Of course, this is the case in most business cycle models developed in the postwar era as well.*

[48] *An elaborate discussion of several objections against the relevance of real business cycle models can be found in McCallum (1986). Compare also McCallum (1988) and Zarnowitz (1985).*

[49] *In continuous-time models, perfect foresight and Rational Expectations are equivalent because misperceptions are corrected immediately.*

[50] *See Begg (1982) on the following subject.*

the initial state with consequently different perfect foresight time paths, which all end in the steady state, are all equally 'rational' in the sense that the final state is correctly anticipated. An individual can therefore not discriminate between different estimations of initial states because falsely anticipated time paths nevertheless end in the stationary state. Consequently, the global stability property should not be a feature of perfect foresight models. It has turned out that the special case of saddle-points, which is usually excluded in economic dynamics, is the appropriate dynamic phenomenon, which is compatible with Rational Expectations in continuous-time models (cf. Figure 3.7).[51] If the steady state is a saddle-point, then exactly one trajectory exists, which ends in the steady state. As every other trajectory moves away from equilibrium, perfect foresight implies that the individually estimated initial state has to be on the unique saddle-path in order to talk about a meaningful equilibrium model with perfect foresight.

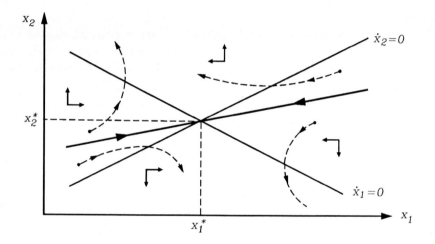

Saddle-point instability
Figure 3.7

In summarizing the Rational Expectations business cycle models presented above, the following features should be mentioned:

- Rational Expectations alone are unable to generate permanent deviations from stationary equilibria or even full business cycles.

- In order to allow for these deviations, scenarios and structures have to be assumed, which either prevent individuals from gaining complete information or which exhibit dynamics of the real sector, the influence of which cannot be eliminated by the introduction of Rational Expectations.

---

[51] *Saddle-points usually occur in markets with financial assets. See Begg (1983).*

- When exogenous influences are stochastic, time series generated in models which allow for oscillations in the deterministic case show striking similarities with actually observed time series. Unlike the linear accelerator-multiplier models, Rational Expectations oscillatory models do not have to refer to the incidental case of the presence of exactly one parameter constellation in order to experience permanent oscillations.

Rational Expectations business cycle models are thus primarily interesting because they treat exogenous influences in a special way. In general, the same objections as those mentioned in Section 2.4. can be raised against these shock-dependent business cycle models. Possible approaches toward shock-independent business cycle models will be presented in the following chapter.

Chapter 4

Shock-Independent Business Cycle Theories

The common feature of all models in Chapter 2 is that they can generate cyclical movements only for special parameter ranges. This may have two consequences for business
cycle theory. Since in most models (at least in those of the linear multiplier-accelerator
type) permanent oscillations occur only for specific parameter constellation, these models should be treated as having a classroom character because usually no empirical
evidence for the existence of these magnitudes can be found.[1] On the other hand, it
is, of course, possible to concentrate on damped oscillations only and to make further
assumptions on the occurrence of exogenous shocks. Aside from the argument that this
does not provide a complete theory of the cycle, it should be noted that, abstracting
from Hicks' nonlinear accelerator, the solutions of all models of Chapter 2 behave in a
sinusoidal manner with equal frequency and amplitude, which definitely does not fit the
empirical facts. Models of the Frisch type appear as better candidates for the *ex-post*
modelling of an economy. While this may be attractive from an empirical point of view,
it is theoretically rather unsatisfactory because it leaves too much room for arbitrary
exogenous shocks. Though it cannot be ignored that shock-dependent models of the
cycle may be useful tools to describe actual cycles from time to time, it is theoretically
desirable to construct models that are capable of generating persistent endogenous cy-

---

[1] *This is, of course, quite natural, because with their simplicity the models are far
from picturing actual economies sufficiently well.*

cles without restrictive assumptions on singular parameter values or specific exogenous shocks. Such endogenous business cycles usually cannot occur in linear dynamical systems. The consequence is that business cycle theory should look for the presence of certain non-linear structures that can be responsible for endogenous cycles.

It can be argued that empirical tests should decide whether time series resulting from linear models with superimposed exogenous influences constitute good approximations of an economy's dynamic behavior. If it can be shown that linear regressions fit the data sufficiently well, there does not seem to exist a convincing reason for a concentration on non-linear approaches. However, Blatt (1979, 1980, 1983) has demonstrated that standard statistical tests can suggest the presence of a linear structure even if the time series has actually been generated by a non-linear model.[2] It can therefore be suspected that the presence of non-linearities has probably been rejected too many times in empirical time series analysis. Empirical tests for non-linearities have to make use of different kinds of numerical tools (cf. Section 5.1.4).

Shock-independent business cycle theory is dominated by non-linear models. However, it is also possible to construct linear models that are able to display persisting oscillations without exogenous shocks. Vicariously for these models, Vogt's linear growth model will be presented. The presentation of the early, well-known quasi-non-linear model by Goodwin with a piecewise-linear investment function will be followed by a discussion of the true non-linear model by Kaldor and by more recent approaches that make use of the Poincaré-Bendixson theorem. Predator-prey interpretations of the cycle and models that make use of the properties of the Liénard-van der Pol equation will be presented as special examples in non-linear dynamics. The chapter concludes with a presentation of the Hopf bifurcation theorem which has turned out to be a fruitful tool in business cycle theory. The continuous-time version and the discrete-time version will be sketched in separate sections.

4.1. A Linear Shock-Independent Growth Cycle Model

Vogt's model (Vogt 1969) represents an attempt to modify the neoclassical vintage growth model in the simplest way in order to obtain cyclical growth. Interestingly from a formal point of view, it leads to an economic example of the *harmonic oscillator* that is popular especially in classical mechanics.

Assume the usual neoclassical framework with perfect competition. The price of consumer goods, p, as well as the nominal wage rate, w, are constant, firms can always realize their demand for labor, and the goods market will always be in equilibrium.

---

[2] *Blatt simulated Hicks' non-linear accelerator model with ceiling and floor. A linear regression of the generated time series yielded an R^2 of $\approx .9$ and a Durbin-Watson value of nearly $Q = 2.0$. Cf. Blatt (1980), pp. 224ff.*

The price of consumer goods is normalized to $p = 1$, such that nominal and real wages coincide.

Let $I_i(\tau)$ denote the capital stock of vintage τ of a representative firm i. The production possibilities are described by the production function[3]

$$Y_i(\tau) = a(\tau)I_i(\tau)^\alpha L_i(\tau)^\beta, \quad \alpha + \beta < 1, \tag{4.1.1}$$

with Y_i as output, L_i as labor input, and $a(\tau)$ as a shifting parameter. Let $r(\tau)$ be the interest rate taken as being constant by the firm. Then the capital value V of an investment $I_i(\tau)$ is given by

$$V = \frac{Y_i(\tau) - wL_i(\tau)}{r(\tau)} - I_i(\tau), \tag{4.1.2}$$

provided that capital goods have an infinite technical durability. In a competitive setting in which the wage rate and the interest rate are considered as given, the necessary optimality condition for the input of capital is clearly

$$\frac{\partial Y_i(\tau)}{\partial I_i(\tau)} = r(\tau) \tag{4.1.3}$$

for the representative firm. As the marginal product of labor equals the real wage

$$\frac{\partial Y_i(\tau)}{\partial L_i(\tau)} = w, \tag{4.1.4}$$

it follows for the additional demand of labor for each investment project

$$L_i^d(\tau) = \left(\frac{\beta a(\tau)}{w}\right)^{1/(1-\beta)} I_i(\tau)^{\alpha/(1-\beta)}. \tag{4.1.5}$$

Carrying out the differentiation in (4.1.3) and substituting for $L_i(\tau)$ yields the investment demand function

$$I_i^d(\tau) = \left(\alpha^{1-\beta}(\frac{\beta}{w})^\beta a(\tau)\right)^{\frac{1}{1-\alpha-\beta}} r(\tau)^{-\frac{1-\beta}{1-\alpha-\beta}}. \tag{4.1.6}$$

While the individual firm encounters decreasing returns to scale in its own production possibility set, the economy as a whole features constant returns to scale. This assumption, which dates back to Marshall and Sraffa, implies that on the aggregate the shifting

---

[3] *In order to receive unambiguous optima, decreasing returns are assumed. The economy as a whole, however, features external economies due to, e.g., better infrastructures during the growth process.*

parameter $a(\tau)$ can be replaced by the expression $a(\tau) = A\big(I(\tau)/z\big)^{1-\alpha-\beta}$, which is deduced from an aggregate production function with constant returns and in which A is a constant, $I(\tau)$ is aggregated actual investment of vintage τ, and z is the number if identical firms.[4] The higher actual investment on the aggregate the better are the production possibilities for each individual firm.[5] Substituting for $a(\tau)$ in (4.1.6) and aggregating over all firms yields the aggregated investment demand:

$$I^d(\tau) = \left(\alpha^{1-\beta}(\frac{\beta}{w})^{\beta}A\right)^{\frac{1}{1-\alpha-\beta}} r(\tau)^{-\frac{1-\beta}{1-\alpha-\beta}} I(\tau). \tag{4.1.7}$$

Write (4.1.7) as

$$I^d(\tau) = \delta I(\tau) r(\tau)^{-\gamma}. \tag{4.1.8}$$

Simple calculation yields

$$\frac{(I^{\dot{d}}/I)}{(I^d/I)} = \frac{\delta(-\gamma) r^{(-\gamma-1)}\frac{dr}{dt}}{\delta r(\tau)^{-\gamma}} = -\gamma\frac{\dot{r}}{r} = -\gamma\hat{r}. \tag{4.1.9}$$

Actual investment $I(t)$, on the other hand, is determined by the consumption and savings decisions of households. With $C(t) = wL(t)$ as workers households' consumption and it follows after some substitutions that[6]

$$C(t) = \beta Y(t), \tag{4.1.10}$$

with $Y(t) = \int_{-\infty}^{t} Y(\tau)d\tau$ as total output of all vintages at period t. Thus

$$I(t) = Y(t) - C(t) = (1-\beta)Y(t). \tag{4.1.11}$$

Suppose the change in the growth rate of the interest rate is described by the function

$$\frac{d\hat{r}}{dt} = \sigma\left(\ln I^d - \ln I\right) = \sigma\ln\left(\frac{I^d}{I}\right), \quad \sigma > 0, \tag{4.1.12}$$

---

[4] *Substituting I/z and L^d/z for I_i and L_i^d in (4.1.1) and aggregating over all firms yields $Y = z^{1-\alpha-\beta}a(\tau)I(\tau)^{\alpha}L^d(\tau)^{\beta}$. If the aggregate production function exhibits constant returns to scale, i.e., $Y(\tau) = AI(\tau)^{1-\beta}L^d(\tau)^{\beta}$, then $a(\tau)$ has the value mentioned above.*

[5] *This dependence of investment demand on actual investment will thus be noticed by the individual firm only through the changing values of the shifting parameter $a(\tau)$.*

[6] *Note that in this competitive framework the production elasticities α and β represent the profit share and the labor-income share, respectively.*

i.e., a positive (negative) excess demand for investment will lead to an increase (decrease) in the growth rate of the interest rate. The hypothesis is an (accelerated) form of the usual absolute value adjustment hypothesis and is not justified qualitatively.

Equations (4.1.9) and (4.1.12) constitute a two-dimensional differential equation system in $\hat{r}$ and I^d/I.

Differentiating (4.1.12) with respect to time and substituting yields the second-order differential equation

$$\ddot{\hat{r}} + \sigma\gamma\hat{r} = 0. \tag{4.1.13}$$

Equation (4.1.13) is a specific form of the so-called *harmonic oscillator*[7]:

$$\ddot{x} + \rho^2 x = 0; \quad \rho > 0, \tag{4.1.14}$$

which has the solution

$$x(t) = b_1 \cos(\rho t - b_2), \quad b_1, b_2 = \text{constant}, \tag{4.1.15}$$

i.e., which displays harmonic oscillations.

Consequently, the solution of (4.1.13) is given by

$$\hat{r}(t) = H_1 \cos\left(t\sqrt{\sigma\gamma} - H_2\right), \quad H_1, H_2 = \text{constant}. \tag{4.1.16}$$

The solution of the other variables can easily be obtained by substituting $\hat{\rho}$ from (4.1.16).

While it can thus be shown that even linear models can behave in cyclical patterns, the differential equation system (4.1.9) and (4.1.12) has a serious disadvantage. As will be discussed more thoroughly in later sections, models that incorporate the harmonic oscillator are *structurally unstable*. Small variations in the structure, for example by adding a numerically irrelevant term $b\dot{x}$ in (4.1.14), can lead to totally different solution forms of the system. While variations in the numerical values of parameters change the stability property of the solution, *e.g.*, in the multiplier-accelerator models of Chapter 2, it is the solution function itself which changes more or less drastically in the case of structural instability. It may thus be argued that business cycle models displaying structural instability cannot be accepted as sound descriptions of reality.

4.2. Goodwin's Quasi-Non-Linear Accelerator

Almost at the same time as Hicks' monograph on non-linear business cycle theory was published, Goodwin (1951) presented a paper that covered several versions of the non-linear accelerator-type models. In contrast to the Hicks model, Goodwin's models were

---

[7] *See Hirsch/Smale (1974), pp. 15, 105f.*

the first quasi-non-linear models[8] which were able to display endogenously generated cycles without any requirements concerning special parameter values. In Hicks' model, it must be assumed that the unconstrained linear multiplier-accelerator model takes on such a value that the system will explode. Goodwin's models, especially the simplest ones, do not have to rely on specific parameter constellations, though they are - in the words of Goodwin - very crude descriptions or explanations of actual cycles. In the following section the simplest version of Goodwin's model will be presented.

Let K be the actual capital stock at time t and let K^d be the desired capital stock.[9] Consumption depends linearily on income Y:

$$C = a + bY \qquad (4.2.1)$$

Income is given by

$$Y = C + I^n = C + \dot{K}, \quad \dot{K} = \frac{dK}{dt} \qquad (4.2.2)$$

with I^n as net investment. The desired capital stock is assumed to depend proportionally on the actual level of income respectively output:

$$K^d = kY, \quad k > 0, \quad k = \text{const.} \qquad (4.2.3)$$

Obviously, this proportional relation is too crude, especially in the context of business cycles, so that it should be viewed only as an example that shows the possibility of cycles in quasi-non-linear theories. As long as the actual and the desired capital stock coincide, net investment, I^n, is zero, and gross investment, I, equals the amount of depreciation D:

$$I^n = \dot{K} = I - D, \quad D = \text{const.} \qquad (4.2.4)$$

Suppose the actual capital stock is lower than the desired capital stock for whatever reason. If no restrictions for investment existed at all, the gap between actual and desired capital stocks would be closed immediately, i.e., $I^n = K^d - K$. Otherwise, the actual stock could only gradually approach the desired level. Goodwin assumed that positive gross investment is limited by the capacity of the investment goods industry to provide these goods. Let the (constant) capacity of this industry at each point in time be $\bar{I}$. Furthermore, it is only possible to produce this amount $\bar{I}$ or nothing in the investment goods industry. This implies that positive gross investment equals $\bar{I}$.

---

[8] *Although it is mathematically superfluous, the term 'quasi-non-linear' is used to distinguish the piecewise-linear dynamic equations below from the pure non-linear models presented in subsequent sections.*

[9] *As the analysis is in continuous time, all time indexes are dropped in the following presentation.*

If the desired capital stock is smaller than the actual stock, *i.e.*, if net investment should be negative, gross investment is zero and the capital stock can only decrease by the amount of depreciation, which is assumed to be constant.

Summarizing, net investment $I^n = \dot{K}$ is given by the piecewisely defined function

$$I^n = \begin{cases} \bar{I} - D & \text{if } K < K^d \\ 0 & \text{if } K = K^d \\ -D & \text{if } K > K^d. \end{cases} \qquad (4.2.5)$$

By combining (4.2.1)-(4.2.5), the desired capital stock as a proportional function of income is given by

$$K^d = \begin{cases} \dfrac{ka}{1-b} + \dfrac{k}{1-b}(\bar{I} - D) & \text{if } K < K^d \\[2mm] \dfrac{ka}{1-b} & \text{if } K = K^d \\[2mm] \dfrac{ka}{1-b} + \dfrac{k}{1-b}(-D) & \text{if } K > K^d. \end{cases} \qquad (4.2.6)$$

As in Hicks' ceiling-floor model it is this piecewisely defined investment function which makes the model quasi-non-linear, in contrast to an investment function which is non-linear for every arbitrarily short interval in the domain.

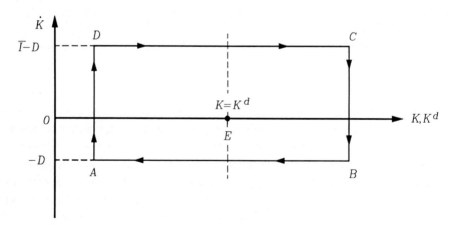

Figure 4.1

Note that in this simple model the capacity output of the investment goods industry as well as the amount of depreciation are constant. This implies that the industry-internal trade cycle of the investment goods industry is described by a bang-bang movement. Note also that the absolutely constant amount of depreciation corresponds to a

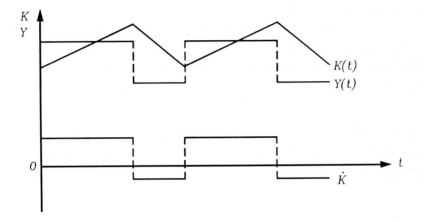

Figure 4.2

form of relatively decreasing depreciation, contrary to the usual proportional depreciation $D = \delta K$, $\delta > 0$ and $\delta =$ constant.

That this simple model can indeed display "cyclical" movements can at best be seen graphically. Suppose that initially the actual and the desired capital stock coincide at point E in Figure 4.1. As long as no disturbances occur the system will remain at the equilibrium position. Now assume a small perturbation $\Delta K > 0$, so that actual and desired capital diverge. In the case $K > K^d$ it will be attempted to fill the gap and negative net investment sets in. However, negative net investment is identical to the constant amount of depreciation $I^n = -D$, implying that desired capital discontinuously switches to

$$K^d = \frac{ka}{1-b} + \frac{k}{1-b}(-D) < \frac{ka}{1-b} \qquad (4.2.7)$$

because of (4.2.6). Thus, net investment is negative as long as the actual capital stock is still larger than the desired stock represented by point A in Figure 4.1. Once A is reached with $K = K^d$, the desired stock switches first to the higher equilibrium level $(ka)/(1-b)$, and because the actual stock in A is smaller than this new desired stock, further to

$$K^d = \frac{ka}{1-b} + \frac{k}{1-b}(\bar{I} - D). \qquad (4.2.8)$$

Thus, net investment discontinuously changes from A to D in Figure 4.1. As long as the capital stock is lower than that represented by point C, net investment will constantly be kept on the level $(\bar{I} - D)$. After having reached C, the same two-step switch in the level of the desired capital stock will occur as that from A to D. At C, $K = K^d$ and it follows that the desired stock switches to $K^d = (ka)/(1-b)$ with the consequence that $K > K^d$ afterwards. Thus, $K^d = (ka)/(1-b) + k/(1-b)(-D)$ and net investment will be negative along the line $\overline{AB}$. The motion of the actual capital stock is shown in

Figure 4.2.

As can be seen, the durations of the boom and of the recession do not have to be of equal length as in the linear models with sinusoidal oscillations, but rather can be modelled arbitrarily by assuming different magnitudes of D and $\bar{I}$.

This model is certainly not a completely satisfactory description of actual business cycles. Nevertheless, by means of a very simple quasi-non-linear investment function it shows the possibility of endogenous "cycles" which are self-sustaining and which do not depend on somehow specified and restricted parameter values. Moreover, it provides a starting point for more sophisticated extensions that are able to avoid the unpleasant discontinuities.

4.3. Non-Linear Theories of the Cycle

4.3.1. Kaldor's Non-Linear Investment and Savings Functions

Kaldor's 1940 business cycle model constitutes one of the first attempts to study the effects of non-linearities in dynamical economics. Stimulated both by Kalecki's work on the trade cycle and by Keynes' income theory, he investigated the interactions between the savings and the investment functions and examined the basic structural requirements for the existence of self-sustaining cycles. Kaldor's model has found interest among many trade cycle theorists until today because of its striking simple elegance.

Suppose investment is a function of real income[10] [11] at each point in time

$$I = I(Y), \quad \frac{dI}{dY} > 0. \tag{4.3.1}$$

Note that this function does not represent the acceleration principle known from Chapter 2. Investment depends on the absolute level of income and not on the change or the rate of change of real income in the past. Further, assume a Keynesian savings function such that

$$S = S(Y), \quad \frac{dS}{dY} > 0. \tag{4.3.2}$$

In order to uncover the necessity of non-linearities in this simple framework - provided that it should serve as the base for business cycle theories - consider first the case of linear savings and investment functions.

---

[10] *Kaldor himself assumes a dependence on "economic activity", correlated somehow to the real income. As he mentions "real income" in the appendix, this expression will be used instead of "activity" throughout this section.*

[11] *Time indices will be omitted throughout this section.*

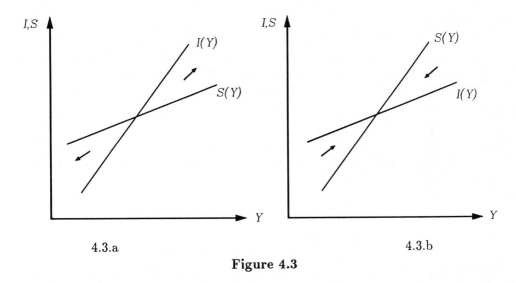

4.3.a   4.3.b

Figure 4.3

Figures 4.3.a and 4.3.b show the two possible situations $dI/dY \gtrless dS/dY$, respectively.

With the usual assumption on the adjustment process in the case of disequilibria, namely that income reacts positively to the excess demand on the goods market, i.e., $\dot{Y} = \alpha(I(Y) - S(Y))$, $\alpha > 0$, the following conclusions can be drawn in these two cases.

i) $dI/dY > dS/dY$: As soon as the equilibrium is disturbed, the system will tend away from equilibrium forever. The system is globally unstable (cf. Figure 4.3.a).

ii) $dI/dY < dS/dY$: The system is globally asymptotically stable (cf. Figure 4.3.b).

Both cases are obviously irrelevant as long as the emphasis lies on business cycles. When cyclic motions are to be studied in this context, the linear structures must be rejected and other forms of the savings function and/or the investment function must be assumed.

Kaldor proposed an S-shaped form of the investment function like that in Figure 4.4. While there is a "normal" level of the investment propensity dI/dY somewhere in the midrange of real income, dI/dY will be relatively small for low as well as for high values of income compared with the normal level. The decreasing slope of the function for decreasing levels of income can be explained by missing profit opportunities in times of low economic activity levels relative to the "normal" midrange level. When income is relatively high, decreasing economies of scale as well as rising financing costs will also lead to a smaller propensity to invest out of real income.

The savings function proposed by Kaldor looks like the mirror-imaged S-shaped curve in Figure 4.5. The explanation of this unusual shape is less convincing than that of the investment function. Suppose again that there is a normal level of the propensity to save dS/dY. If income is high relative to the normal level, the marginal saving

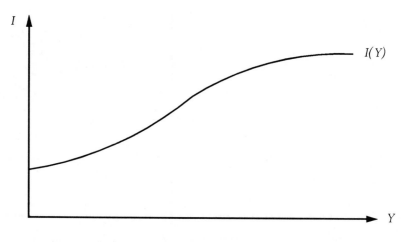

A Non-Linear Investment Function
Figure 4.4

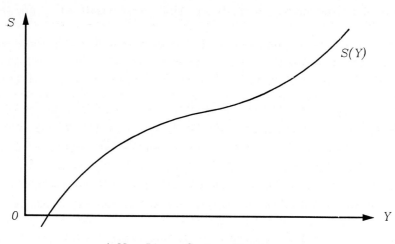

A Non-Linear Savings Function
Figure 4.5

rate will rise, too. This is in accordance with the well-known two-class models in the macroeconomic literature. If income falls below its normal level, a point will be reached where absolute savings will fall drastically. This sharp fall, which of course can lead to negative savings, implies that the marginal savings rate is higher than at the normal level.

There may be several other reasons to justify or to reject the suggested shapes of the savings function as well as the investment function. What is interesting in this context is the fact that these non-linear shapes are a prerequisite for oscillatory motion

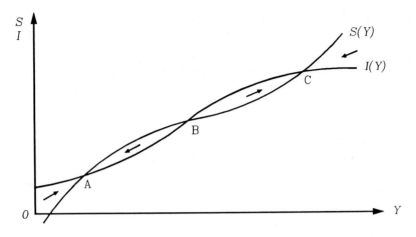

Multiple Equilibria in the Goods Market
Figure 4.6

in this model. Putting both functions together in one diagram, it can be seen that there can be one, two, or three equilibria. Assuming again that income adjusts according to the excess demand in the goods market in case of disequilibria, it is evident that the points A and C in Figure 4.6 are locally asymptotical stable while point B constitutes an unstable equilibrium. Thus, every process starting with an initial income below B will eventually approach the equilibrium at point A. Alternatively, every process with an initial real income higher than that at B will approach the equilibrium at C.

The essential dynamic feature that enables the model to display cyclical behavior is introduced by an assumption about the longer term shifting of the investment as well as the savings function. In the two-dimensional representation of the functions, entities like preferences underlying the consumption function (and hence the savings function), technical progress in the investment function, etc. can be treated as parameters. As the capital stock is directly influenced by the investment decisions, its changing level will probably have a parametric influence on the position of the investment function.

Kaldor assumes that an inverse relation between the capital stock and investment exists: if net investment is high, the capital stock increases. An increasing capital stock lowers the marginal efficiency of capital, implying that investment is lower for each income level. The investment curve is therefore shifting downwards for high capital stock levels. Similar reasoning holds for a low level of the capital stock.

This process of the shifting of the investment curve can also be explained by the following consideration. Suppose the economy has adjusted to an equilibrium with low income at point A. The low investment level at A will eventually lead to a negative net investment $I^n = I(Y) - \delta K < 0$ and the capital stock is therefore decreasing over time. If the system remains at point A, the capital stock will eventually approach zero. Without considering production possibilities explicitly, assume that the economy is characterized by limited factor substitution. It follows that in the case of a decreasing capital stock, output must also decline. In order to support each income level in Figure 4.6 in the case of a low capital stock, investment must be higher for each income level.[12]

While the investment function is shifting upwards for low levels of the capital stock, the savings function will shift downwards due to what can be called an inverse real wealth effect, which is not explained satisfactorily. On the other hand, if the economy is stuck in an equilibrium with a high real income at point C, the capital stock is increasing permanently over time and induces the investment function to shift downwards because of increasing overcapacities. The savings function, on the contrary, shifts upwards due to the same wealth effect.

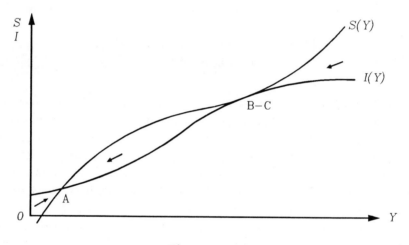

Figure 4.7

These suggested longer-term shiftings of the investment and savings functions can generate cyclic movements of real income and capital. Start with an initial income level arbitrarily close to the right side of point B in Figure 4.6. The income adjustment process will lead the economy to the equilibrium point C more or less rapidly. Point C, however, is characterized by high investment and an increasing capital stock. The investment function consequently starts shifting downwards, while the savings function moves upwards. It can easily be imagined that the points B and C approach each other gradually until the curves become tangent (cf. Figure 4.7). While during the adjustment process to (B-C) the equilibrium at C was stable, an excess supply in the goods market will occur as soon as the curves are tangent at point B-C, because $S > I$ on both sides of

---

[12] *Note that this argument implies a shifting of the whole curve because the capital stock changes only gradually, implying that another income level (and hence investment level) does not lead to an immediate jump in the capital stock.*

the tangential point. Thus, the real income adjustment process lets income move away from (B-C) and toward the stable equilibrium at A. In approaching A or after having reached A, the curves will again shift in opposite directions, finally constituting the picture in Figure 4.8 where the curves are tangent at a low level of income with points A and B coinciding. Note that during this shifting process real income is determined by the intersection of the curves at point A. The tangential point (A-B) constitutes the lower turning point. The investment function shifts upwards again because the capital stock is gradually decreasing at (A-B) while the savings function shifts downward. Thus, a complete cycle of the real income and the capital stock has been described.

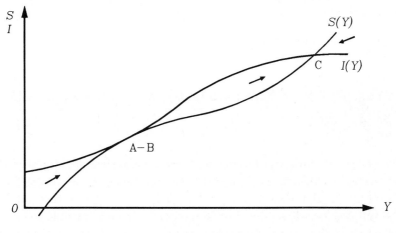

Figure 4.8

The resulting form of the cycle depends on the speed of adjustment in the goods market as well as on the rate of depreciation. Figure 4.9 shows two possible cycles with different α's in the income adjustment equation.[13]

It is noteworthy that this simple model is able to produce permanent cycles in the absence of any initial shock to the system. With the exception of the highly accidental case that the system initially operates exactly at the unstable equilibrium point B, every other initial state originates permanent cycles.

Summarizing in formal terms, the assumptions stated by Kaldor as being necessary to produce cycles are:

i) $\quad I(Y,K) > 0 \, \forall \, Y \geq 0$

---

[13] *Figure 4.9 shows closed orbits of the cycles. Actually, thus far nothing can be said about these orbits in the Kaldor model. As will be made clear in Section 4.3.2.1., however, these orbits indeed exist in some versions of the Kaldor model.*

$$\frac{\partial I}{\partial Y} \geq 0 \,\forall\, Y \geq 0, \quad \exists\, Y_1 \quad \text{such that} \quad \frac{\partial^2 I}{\partial Y^2} > 0 \,\forall\, 0 < Y < Y_1$$

$$\frac{\partial^2 I}{\partial Y^2} \leq 0 \,\forall\, Y_1 \leq Y$$

ii) $S(Y, K) \geq 0 \,\forall\, Y \geq \underline{Y} > 0$

$$\frac{\partial S}{\partial Y} > 0 \,\forall\, Y \geq 0, \quad \exists\, Y_2 \quad \text{such that} \quad \frac{\partial^2 S}{\partial Y^2} < 0 \,\forall\, 0 < Y < Y_2$$

$$\frac{\partial^2 S}{\partial Y^2} \geq 0 \,\forall\, Y_2 \leq Y$$

iii) $\dfrac{\partial I}{\partial K} < 0, \qquad \dfrac{\partial S}{\partial K} > 0$

iv) $\exists\, Y_E \quad \text{such that} \quad S(Y_E, K) = I(Y_E, K) \quad \text{and} \quad I^n = I(Y_E, K) - \delta K = 0,$

$$\frac{\partial I}{\partial Y}\bigg|_{Y_E} > \frac{\partial S}{\partial Y}\bigg|_{Y_E}.$$

As will be shown in subsequent sections, these assumptions fit, together with some modifications and extensions, fairly well the requirements of some advanced mathematical tools. The model probably became so attractive to cycle theorists because it is one of the simplest two-dimensional cycle models. It is even possible to omit the non-linearities either of the savings function or the investment function without destroying the capability of the model to generate endogenous cycles.

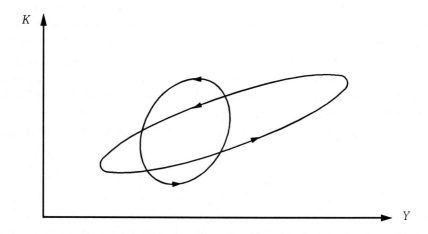

Closed Orbits in the Kaldor Model
Figure 4.9

However, the Kaldor model does not belong to those models which were received without dispute. Indeed, the assumed non-linearities appear to be rather *ad-hoc* and the explanations provided by Kaldor do not seem to be really convincing.[14] Nonetheless, keeping the simplicity of the model in mind, the Kaldor model should be viewed as a demonstration of the influence of non-linearities on the dynamic behavior of an economic model.

Basically, it is assumption iv) that allows the model to be called the first endogenous business cycle model. Though the Kaldor model and especially the investment function is very similar to Kalecki's model (especially the 1939-model), the assumption of an unstable stationary equilibrium leads to a completely different dynamic behavior than that of the Kalecki model. Remember from Section 3.3 that Kalecki assumed explicitly that $\dfrac{\partial S}{\partial Y}_{|Y_E} > \dfrac{\partial I}{\partial Y}_{|Y_E}$, with Y_E as the stationary equilibrium. Thus, the one and only intersection of the curves is stable, and the generation of cycles in the Kalecki model relies on investment delays.

4.3.2. The Poincaré-Bendixson Theorem and the Existence of Limit Cycles

In the preceding sections of this chapter statements about the cyclic behavior of non-linear models could be made either by means of explicit solutions or by means of verbal argumentation. Explicit solutions of dynamical systems, however, are known only for special forms of the underlying differential equations or can only be found accidently.

Fortunately, there are mathematical criteria for the existence of oscillating movements that do not rely on the explicit solution of a dynamical system. While popular in mechanics and electrodynamics for a long time, the *Poincaré-Bendixson theorem* and related theorems have almost recently become attractive to business cycle theorists.

In order to avoid repetition in the following sections, it is useful to give a short overview of the necessary definitions and the most interesting theorems from an application-oriented point of view.[15]

---

[14] *Compare Skott (1985) for a general discussion of the Kaldor model. See also Flaschel (1985) for a critique of the goods market adjustment process.*

[15] *A rigorous textbook presentation of the Poincaré-Bendixson theorem can be found in Hirsch/Smale (1974), Chapter 11, to which the interested reader is strongly referred. Other textbook sections can be found in Boyce/DiPrima (1977), Chapter 9 and Coddington/Levinson (1955), Chapter 16. A comprise overview is Varian (1981).*

Consider the two-dimensional ordinary differential equation system

$$
\begin{aligned}
\dot{x}_1 &= f(x_1, x_2) \\
\dot{x}_2 &= g(x_1, x_2),
\end{aligned}
\tag{4.3.3}
$$

or, in vector notation, $\dot{x} = \phi(x)$, $\big(x = (x_1, x_2)\big)$, defined on an open set $W \subset \mathbf{R}^2$. Let $\Phi_t(x_0)$ be a solution curve (a trajectory) starting at an initial point x_0.[16] A differential equation system like (4.3.3) is often said to describe a *vector field*. A point $\ell \in W$ is a *limit point* of $x_0 \in W$, if a trajectory starting at x_0 approaches ℓ for $t \to \infty$, i.e., $\lim_{t \to \infty} \Phi_t(x_0) = \ell$. The set of all limit points of $x \in W$ is defined as the *limit set* $L(x)$.[17]

Limit sets neither have to be connected nor have to consist of more than one point. Let $x^* = (x_1^*, x_2^*)$ be the unique equilibrium point of (4.3.3). For example, if x^* is asymptotically stable, x^* is the limit set $L(x)$ consisting of a single point.

An example of a limit set which naturally attracts the attention of business cycle theorists is given by a set whose graphical image is a closed orbit. A point x is said to be in a *closed orbit* if there exists $t \neq 0$ such that $\Phi_t(x) = x$, i.e., there exist periodic solutions. Thus, a closed orbit is at least the limit set of every point on it.

The following theorem has turned out to be very useful in the context of two-dimensional differential equation systems:[18]

Theorem 4.1   (Poincaré-Bendixson)

A non-empty compact limit set of a continuously differentiable dynamic system in $\mathbf{R}^2$, which contains no equilibrium point, is a closed orbit.

A limit set that is a closed orbit is called a *limit cycle*. Let Γ denote the set of points constituting a limit cycle (cf. Figure 4.10). It follows from the property of limit sets that either

- $\Phi_t(x)$ is a limit cycle, *i.e.*, $x \in \Gamma$,

or

- for $x \notin \Gamma$, any trajectory $\Phi_t(x)$ approaches the limit cycle: $\lim_{t \to \infty} d\big(\Phi_t(x), \Gamma\big) = 0$ with d as the distance between the trajectory and the limit cycle.

---

[16] *The set of all solution curves starting at different initial points is called the flow of the system.*

[17] *The foregoing definitions ignore complications which may arise from considerations of time reversals. Other definitions of limit sets (e.g., in the form of ω - limit sets and α - limit sets) imply different definitions of other concepts to be mentioned below.*

[18] *Cf. Hirsch/Smale (1974), p. 248 and Coddington/Levinson (1955), p. 390.*

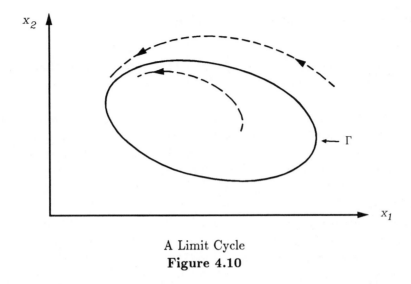

A Limit Cycle
Figure 4.10

A consequence of the Poincaré-Bendixson theorem is the following theorem:[19]

Theorem 4.2

A closed trajectory of a continuously differentiable dynamical system in $\mathbf{R^2}$ must necessarily enclose an equilibrium point with $\dot{x}_1 = \dot{x}_2 = 0$.

In practical applications, limit cycles can be established via the Poincaré-Bendixson theorem in the following 3-step procedure:

Step 1: Examine the local stability properties of the equilibrium point, *i.e.*, whether the eigenvalues have positive or negative real parts. If the equilibrium is unstable it does not belong to the limit set $L(x)$, $x \in W$.

Step 2: Search for a closed subset $D \subset W$ that encloses but does not contain the equilibrium point. Examine whether the vector field described by f and g points into the interior of D.

Step 3: If the equilibrium is unstable and if the vector field points into the interior of D on the boundary of D, a limit cycle exists.

The following theorem is often very useful in excluding the possibility of limit cycles in the system (4.3.3). Let S be a simply connected domain in W.[20]

---

[19] *Cf. Boyce/DiPrima (1977), p. 445 and Hirsch/Smale (1974), p. 252.*

[20] *Cf. Boyce/DiPrima (1977), p. 446. The notion "simply connected" can be read literally: it is a set which consists of one piece (cf. Debreu (1959), p. 15).*

Theorem 4.3   (Bendixson criterion)

Assume the functions f and g in (4.3.3) having continuous first-order derivatives in S. If the sum $(\partial f/\partial x_1 + \partial g/\partial x_2)$ has the same sign throughout S, then there is no periodic solution of (4.3.3) lying entirely in S.

Theorems 4.1-4.3 do not exclude the possibility that more than one closed orbit exists. If there is more than a single cycle, then it follows directly that the outermost and innermost cycles are stable if the stationary equilibrium is unstable and the vector field points inwards the subset $D \subset W$ on the boundary. Further, the closed orbits must be alternatively stable and unstable. If a system is *structurally stable*[21] the number of closed orbits is finite. The assumption that the equilibrium $\dot{x}_1 = \dot{x}_2 = 0$ is locally unstable is not necessary if a neighborhood U of x^* exists, on the boundary of which the vector field of (4.3.3) points inwards to D. In that case, the equilibrium may be locally asymptotically stable, while the boundary of U behaves like the innermost limit cycle.

Obviously, the most serious disadvantage of the Poincaré-Bendixson theorem and the related theorems is the fact that it is restricted to two dimensions. Analogous theorems in higher dimensions do not exist. While this limitation usually restricts the application to highly aggregated model-economies, it - on the other hand - constitutes a powerful tool in the face of complicated two-dimensional dynamical systems which sometimes cannot be described only by means of phase portraits.

4.3.2.1. Chang/Smyth's Reformulation of the Kaldor Model

One of the most interesting examples of the application of the Poincaré-Bendixson theorem in the sense that it uncovers the failure of pure graphical analysis to some degree is given in a paper by Chang/Smyth (1971) who reformulated Kaldor's 1940-business cycle model. It is not only shown that Kaldor's model can principally exhibit limit cycles, but that Kaldor's assumptions described above in Section 4.3.1. are not sufficient to lead to exclusively cyclical behavior.

Recalling the model from Section 4.3.1. and using a net value concept, the dynamic system is given by

$$\dot{Y} = \alpha\big(I(Y,K) - S(Y,K)\big)$$
$$\dot{K} = I(Y,K) \tag{4.3.4}$$

with $I(Y,K)$ as net investment.

---

[21] *Cf. DeBaggis (1952) pp. 43, 53. Simply speaking, a structurally stable system is a system which preserves the form of its solution curves under small perturbations.*

Contrary to Kaldor, Chang/Smyth assume that $\partial S/\partial K < 0$.[22] However, this is not essential to the paper because it is further assumed that $|I_K| > |S_K|$. In order to apply the Poincaré-Bendixson theorem it has to be made sure that the equilibrium $\dot{Y} = \dot{K} = 0$ does not belong to the limit set. Simple calculation shows that for a linear approximation around the equilibrium the product of the characteristic roots is $\alpha(S_K I_Y - S_Y I_K)$, which has to be positive in order to exclude the possibility of a saddle point. By Kaldor's assumption on S_K the expression is definitely positive. Note, however, that the term can be negative if Chang/Smyth's assumption on S_K holds. Furthermore, the sum of the characteristic roots is given by $\alpha(I_Y - S_Y) + I_K$. As $I_K < 0$, the expression is not unambigiously positive or negative. An unstable equilibrium, however, requires that $\alpha(I_Y - S_Y) + I_K$ is strictly positive. Thus, Kaldor's claim that the different slopes S_Y and I_Y alone are sufficient to guarantee an unstable equilibrium is false.[23] Chang/Smyth point out that the slope argument is sufficient to ensure the uniqueness of the stationary state.

As the system (4.3.4) is two-dimensional, its phase space can be pictured in the plane. Consider first the set of points (Y, K) such that the capital stock does not change

$$\dot{K} = 0 = I(Y, K). \qquad (4.3.5)$$

Total differentiation yields

$$\frac{dK}{dY}_{|\dot{K}=0} = -\frac{I_Y}{I_K} > 0. \qquad (4.3.6)$$

Thus, the locus of all points in the set $\{(Y, K) \mid \dot{K} = 0\}$ is an upward sloping curve. Obviously, for all K above the curve $\dot{K} = 0$, investment decreases because of $I_K < 0$, hence $\dot{K} < 0$. In the same way, $\dot{K} > 0$ for all K below the curve for $\dot{K} = 0$.

Secondly, the set of points (Y, K) with $\dot{Y} = 0$ is given by

$$\dot{Y} = 0 = I(Y, K) - S(Y, K). \qquad (4.3.7)$$

It follows that

$$\frac{dK}{dY}_{|\dot{Y}=0} = \frac{S_Y - I_Y}{I_K - S_K}. \qquad (4.3.8)$$

Provided that $(I_K - S_K) < 0$, the sign of (4.3.8) depends on the magnitudes S_Y and I_Y, both being positive by assumption. Recalling Kaldor's assumption, $S_Y - I_Y$ is positive

---

[22] *If the capital stock is considered as wealth by the households, then the negative slope expresses the well-known wealth effect. See, e.g., Patinkin (1965).*

[23] *Kaldor's restriction on the slopes I_Y and S_Y probably stems from the model presentation in an $(Y - I)$-diagram, so that the influence of the capital stock on the stability of the system escaped the author. However, see Kaldor (1971), where he states that Chang/Smyth's condition is a natural assumption in all Keynesian macro-models.*

for low as well as for high levels of income and it is negative for normal levels in the neighborhood of the stationary equilibrium. Hence, the curve for $\dot{Y} = 0$ is negatively sloped for low and for high values of Y and it is positively sloped for normal levels of Y. Furthermore, it follows from the stability analysis above that at the equilibrium position the slope must be positive because of $\alpha(I_Y - S_Y) + I_K > 0$ when the stationary equilibrium is unstable. In order to examine the direction of change of Y for $(Y, K) \notin \{(Y, K) \mid \dot{Y} = 0\}$, divide the plane into regions A, B, and C, characterized by $(S_Y - I_Y) > 0, < 0$, and again > 0, respectively (cf. Figure 4.11). In regions A and C income decreases (increases) for Y to the right (left) of the curve $\dot{Y} = 0$ because of $(S_Y - I_Y) > 0$. For points (Y, K) in B, Y increases (decreases) for Y to the right (left) of the curve $\dot{Y} = 0$.

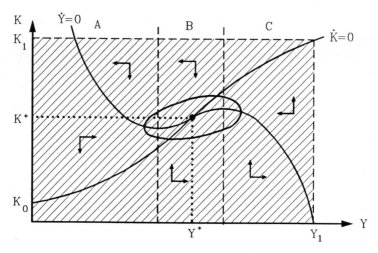

The Phase Portrait of the Kaldor Model
Figure 4.11

Altogether this leads to the phase portrait in Figure 4.11. The curves are drawn such that the locus $\dot{K} = 0$ intersects the ordinate at $K_0 > 0$. The curve $\dot{Y} = 0$ intersects the abscissa at $Y_1 > Y^*$, and approaches the K- axis for $K \to \infty$.
Chang/Smyth (1971) established the following theorem.

Theorem 4.4   (Chang/Smyth)

If the system (4.3.4), defined in the non-negative orthant $\mathbf{R}^2$, has the properties

i) $I_K < S_K < 0, \quad I_Y, S_Y > 0$

ii) at equilibrium Y^* : $\alpha(I_Y - S_Y) + I_K > 0$ and $I_K S_Y < I_Y S_K$

iii) $\dot{K} = 0$ intersects the K-axis for a finite $K_0 > 0$

iv) $\dot{Y} = 0$ intersects the Y - axis for a finite $Y_1 > Y^*$, and $\lim\limits_{Y \to 0} K = \infty$.

v) the system is structurally stable,

then every trajectory starting in $\mathbf{R}^2$ either is a limit cycle or approaches a limit cycle.

The proof is a straightforward application of the Poincaré-Bendixson theorem. With the help of the axis-intersection properties of the $\dot{K} = 0$ and $\dot{Y} = 0$ curves, a subset $D \subset \mathbf{R}^2$ can be constructed: Let K_1 be the capital stock such that $\dot{K} = 0 = I(Y_1, K_1)$. Then D is described as

$$D = \{(Y, K) \mid 0 \leq Y \leq Y_1,\, 0 \leq K \leq K_1\}. \tag{4.3.9}$$

The subset $D \subset \mathbf{R}^2$ is compact, and the vector field of (4.3.4) points inwards the set on the boundary, as can be seen from Figure 4.11. Thus, provided that the equilibrium is locally unstable, the requirements of the Poincaré-Bendixson theorem are fulfilled. The Kaldor model in the Chang/Smyth version has been analytically proved to exhibit limit cycles.

As a by-product, it has been shown that Kaldor's assumptions are neither necessary nor sufficient to guarantee limit cycles. There may exist combinations of α, $(I_Y - S_Y)$, and I_K that violate the instability requirements. Furthermore, even if the equilibrium is locally stable, closed orbits exist in the entire system. This, however, requires that a surrounding U of the equilibrium exists, on the boundary of which the vector field points outwards into D. In any case, it has to assured that the expression $\partial f/\partial Y + \partial g/\partial K = \alpha(I_Y - S_Y) + I_K$ changes its sign somewhere in D. Otherwise no limit cycle exists according to Theorem 4.3.

System (4.3.4) represents a net value concept which differs from Kaldor's original model. Since the depreciation must be financed somehow and $S(Y, K)$ in (4.3.4) has to be net savings, the depreciation can reasonably only be a constant magnitude, financed by a fixed savings amount. However, it is not necessary to study such a net value model in order to detect limit cycles. In Kaldor's original model the capital accumulation is defined as

$$\dot{K} = I(Y, K) - \delta K, \quad \delta > 0. \tag{4.3.10}$$

As the sign of the derivative of $\dot{K}$ with respect to K in Chang/Smyth's model is not affected by this modification, the expression I_K can simply be replaced by $(I_K - \delta) < 0$. Once a distinction between net and gross investment is made, it may happen, however, that negative gross investment occurs formally for $Y \to 0$ on the $\dot{Y} = 0$ - locus because savings is usually negative for low income levels.[24]

---

[24] *Actually, a lower bound for the income level must therefore be introduced in theoretical investigations of the Kaldor model.*

4.3.2.2. The Non-Linear Phillips Curve and the Cycle

In the preceding section the system under investigation was already formulated in the two variables Y and K and allowed an immediate application of the Poincaré-Bendixson theorem. General n-dimensional equilibrium (disequilibrium) models with $n \geq 3$ cannot be analyzed by means of the Poincaré-Bendixson theorem, and it is almost always difficult to construct models even on the macro-level which can be reduced to a two-dimensional differential equation system. In this section, two such attempts of reducing a model to a two-dimensional system are presented, namely the models of Rose (1967) and Wenig (1975)

Rose's paper represents one of the first approaches to business cycle theory which have made use of the Poincaré-Bendixson theorem. By incorporating a non-linear Phillips curve into an essentially neoclassical framework, it was demonstrated that it is indeed possible to construct a two-dimensional system that generates a limit cycle behavior.[25]

Consider a representative firm which produces a net output Y with the homogeneous production function

$$Y = Y(K,N), \quad \text{or} \quad \frac{Y}{K} = f(x), \quad x = \frac{N}{K} \tag{4.3.11}$$

with the usual properties. Assume that the firm faces a conjectural demand function of the form

$$p = A\,u\left(\frac{Y}{B}\right), \quad u' \leq 0, \tag{4.3.12}$$

with $A(t)$ as a function expressing the influence of expectations and $B(t)$ as a growth trend. A ceteris paribus argument leads to the replacement of B by K such that (4.3.12) becomes[26]

$$p = A\,u(\frac{Y}{K}) = A\,u\bigl(f(x)\bigr). \tag{4.3.13}$$

Let w denote the nominal wage rate. The firm maximizes the current period's profit, π, which is a function of x for given expectations, a fixed wage rate during the current period, and a fixed capital stock:

$$\pi = \Bigl(A\,u\bigl(f(x)\bigr)\,f(x) - wx\Bigr)K. \tag{4.3.14}$$

---

[25] *It can be shown that Rose's model is an economically simplified version of a model originally studied by Preiser (1933) (cf. Krelle (1981)).*

[26] *It is assumed that the growth rate of the trend $B(t)$ equals the growth rate of the whole economy if expectations are fulfilled. As the growth rate of the economy is approximated by the growth rate of the capital stock, a linear relation between $B(t)$ and $K(t)$ is established.*

The first order condition for a maximum is

$$\left(1 - \frac{1}{\eta}\right)u\big(f(x)\big)f'(x) = w/A, \qquad (4.3.15)$$

with η as the elasticity of expected demand. By writing (4.3.15) in logarithmic terms and differentiating with respect to time, the following differential equation results:

$$\frac{\dot{x}}{x} = \Phi(x)\left(\frac{\dot{A}}{A} - \frac{\dot{w}}{w}\right) \qquad (4.3.16)$$

with $-1/\Phi(x)$ as the derivation of the log of the left hand side of (4.3.15) with respect to the log of x.

Let planned savings, S, depend on income and capital[27]. The savings function $S = S\big(Y(K, N), K\big)$ is assumed to be linear homogeneous, implying that it can be written as

$$S/K = g(x), \quad g'(x) > 0 \,\forall\, x. \qquad (4.3.17)$$

With the help of (4.3.15) it can be shown that the rate of profit, $\pi/(pK)$, is an increasing function of x. Under the assumption that planned investment will be positively related to real profits π/p, the planned growth rate of the capital stock is given by

$$I/K = k(x), \quad k' > 0. \qquad (4.3.18)$$

The goods market is always in temporary equilibrium. It is assumed that planned savings are always realized. Ex-ante discrepancies between savings and investment end up in buffer stock changes. If buffer stocks are considered as a part of the capital stock, it follows

$$S = \dot{K} \quad \text{respectively} \quad S/K = g(x) = \frac{\dot{K}}{K}, \qquad (4.3.19)$$

i.e., contrary to the usual assumption (i.e., $I = \dot{K}$), actual changes in the capital stock are not determined by planned investment but rather by actual savings. Let n be the growth rate of the labor supply, N^s. Logarithmic differentiation of the ratio $v = N^s/K$ and substituting for $\dot{K}/K$ yields:

$$\frac{\dot{v}}{v} = \frac{\dot{N}^s}{N^s} - \frac{\dot{K}}{K} = n - g(x). \qquad (4.3.20)$$

Equations (4.3.16) and (4.3.20) constitute two equations in the four growth rates $\dot{A}/A$, $\dot{w}/w$, $\dot{x}/x$, and $\dot{v}/v$ and in x. In order to reduce the system to a two-dimensional

---

[27] *Actually, the interest rate has to be mentioned. As it is supposed to be constant, it is suppressed entirely.*

differential equation system, the following hypotheses concerning $\dot{A}/A$ and $\dot{w}/w$ are made: the rate of change of the wage rate is assumed to depend on the employment rate in the well-known Phillips curve manner, *i.e.*,

$$\dot{w}/w = F\left(\frac{N}{N^s}\right) = F\left(\frac{x}{v}\right), \quad F'\left(\frac{x}{v}\right) > 0, \tag{4.3.21}$$

and, additionally, the employment rate x/v is restricted to the interval (a,b) with $0 < a < b \leq 1$.

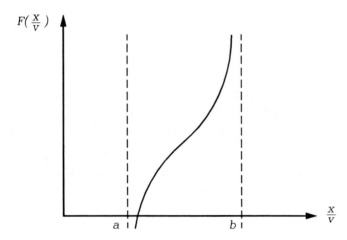

A Non-Linear Phillips Curve
Figure 4.12

The graph of the function $F(x/v)$ is assumed to run as in Figure 4.12. While the rate of change of the nominal wage ratereacts ordinarily in the middle of the interval (a, b), it approaches infinity as soon as the employment rate approaches the upper bound b of the interval (accordingly it approaches $-\infty$ for $x/v \to a$). A satisfying justification for this shape of $F(x/v)$ is not provided. Although the assumption of changing slopes $F'(x/v)$ and fixed bounds is essential in proving the existence of limit cycles, it will be taken for granted in this model economy.

Finally, it is assumed that the rate of change of the expectations A depends on the relative excess demand in the goods market as expressed by the difference $I/K - S/K$:

$$\dot{A}/A = E\left(\frac{I}{K} - \frac{S}{K}\right) = E\big(k(x) - g(x)\big) = H(x) \tag{4.3.22}$$

with $E(0) = 0$ and $E' > 0$. Since $H'(x) = E'(\cdot)(k' - g')$, it follows that sign $H' = $ sign $(k' - g')$. Combining equations (4.3.16), (4.3.21), and (4.3.22) yields

$$\dot{x}/x = \Phi(x)\big(H(x) - F(x/v)\big), \tag{4.3.23}$$

which together with (4.3.20) constitutes the two-dimensional autonomous differential equations system

$$\dot{x}/x = \Phi(x)\big(H(x) - F(x/v)\big)$$
$$\dot{v}/v = n - g(x) \tag{4.3.24}$$

The first step in detecting limit cycles consists once again of an inspection of singular points, *i.e.*, the equilibria of the system. It can be shown that an equilibrium (x^*, v^*) exists and that it is unique. The local stability of the system can be examined by means of a linear expansion of (4.3.24) around the equilibrium leading to the Jacobian matrix[28]

$$M = \begin{pmatrix} \Phi(x^*)\big(x^* H'(x^*) - \frac{x^*}{v^*} F'(\frac{x^*}{v^*})\big) & \Phi(x^*)(\frac{x^*}{v^*})^2 F'(\frac{x^*}{v^*}) \\ -v^* g'(x^*) & 0 \end{pmatrix}. \tag{4.3.25}$$

The assumption about F, g, and Φ guarantee that the determinant is positive. Thus, the equilibrium is not a saddle point. Furthermore, the equilibrium is either stable or unstable if the trace is either negative or positive, respectively. As

$$\operatorname{tr} M = \Phi(x^*)\Big(x^* H'(x^*) - \big(\frac{x^*}{v^*}\big) F'\big(\frac{x^*}{v^*}\big)\Big), \tag{4.3.26}$$

it follows that the equilibrium is unstable if

$$H'(x^*) > \frac{1}{v^*} F'\big(\frac{x^*}{v^*}\big). \tag{4.3.27}$$

In order to assure instability, it is necessary, yet not sufficient, that $H'(x^*) > 0$ and consequently $g'(x^*) < k'(x^*)$, and, furthermore, the employment ratio may not be too high or too low at equilibrium due to the slope of $F(x/v)$. Consider the graphs of the system (4.3.24) for $\dot{x} = 0$ and $\dot{v} = 0$. As $g(x)$ is monotonically increasing, $x = g^{-1}(n)$ is unique and establishes the equilibrium value x^* with $\dot{v} = 0$.

As the function $F(x/v)$ is defined in the interval (a, b), the curve $\dot{x} = 0$ with $H(x) = F(x/v)$ is located in the interior of the cone described by the rays $x = av$ and $x = bv$ in Figure 4.13. In order to construct an unstable equilibrium (x^*, v^*), it follows from (4.3.17) that the graph of $\dot{x} = 0$ must have a negative slope at x^* because of

$$\frac{dx}{dv}\Big|_{\dot{x}=0} = -\frac{\frac{x}{v^2} F'(\frac{x}{v})}{H'(x) - (1/v)F'(\frac{x}{v})} < 0 \quad \text{if} \quad H' > (1/v)F'. \tag{4.3.28}$$

It can easily be shown that v is decreasing (increasing) above (below) the graph $\dot{v} = 0$. In addition, $\dot{x} < 0 (> 0)$ for v to the left (right) of the graph $\dot{x} = 0$. Construct a subset

---

[28] *Note that $H = F$ at equilibrium.*

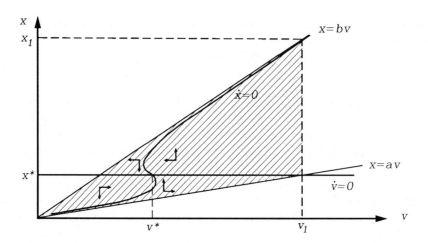

The Phase Portrait of the Rose Model
Figure 4.13

$D \subset \mathbf{R}^2$ with $D = \{(x, v) \mid 0 \le v \le v_1,\ av \le x \le bv\}$ with v_1 as the intersection of $\dot{v} = 0$ and $x/v = a$. It remains to be shown that on the boundary of D the vector field points into the interior of D. The rays $x = av$ and $x = bv$ are the only critical regions. By noting that $F(x/v) \to \infty(-\infty)$ as soon as the boundaries are approached with $\dot{v}$ still being finite, it can be concluded that there exists a compact subset $D \subset \mathbf{R}^2$ that fulfills the requirements of the Poincaré-Bendixson theorem. Hence, a limit cycle exists.

Actually, it cannot be excluded that more than a single closed orbit exists. In that case, the cycles are alternatively stable and unstable. Note that in Rose's model it is possible to make statements at least on the maximal amplitudes of the employment rate. As the function $F(x/v)$ is defined in the interval (a, b), the employment rate cannot fluctuate with amplitudes larger than $b - a$.

The flat portion of the Phillips curve constitutes the essential cycle generating ingredient in this model. For example, suppose that initially the economy is in a state of a low employment rate x/v, represented by a tangential point of the cycle and a ray $x = cv$ with c close to a. Wages are falling, and when the expected demand prices, p, do not fall faster than wages, the real wage rate declines, imlying a rising rate of profit and a rising labor-capital ratio. If the Phillips curve were linear, the rising employment rate would induce proportionally rising wages, leading to a moderation of the increase in x. Both x and v would monotonically approach their equilibrium values. As the Phillips curve possesses a flat portion, however, wages increase less than in the former case, implying that the labor-capital ratio is less moderated. If the curve is sufficiently flat, x will exceed its equilibrium value and a reversal in the labor-capital ratio will occur only for relatively high employment ratios N/N^s. Thus, it is essentially an overshooting of x due to the flat portion of the Phillips curve which prevents the system from reaching its equilibrium value. Analogous reasoning holds for the downswing phase.

It is possible to vary the model in order to allow for cost-push inflation and demand-pull inflation. As has been shown by Rose, the essential properties of the model described above remain unchanged. In contrast, as soon as monetary authorities are able to operate with the money supply as a policy instrument the existence of limit cycles can be excluded, provided that the interest rate fulfills a money market equilibrating condition.

Another model which coincides with Rose's paper in the way of formal argumentation can be found in Wenig (1975). The model allows to make direct statements concerning the change in the income distribution over the cycle. However, it neglects a major variable in business cycle models, namely the capital stock. As was pointed out by Wenig, the implementation of capital accumulation into non-linear models represents a further destabilizing effect. Thus, it may be worthwhile to study the dynamic effects of the struggle for income redistribution as an isolated item. In the following discussion, only a sketch of the model will be presented.

Let $N = h(Y)$ be the inverse of the production function with the usual properties for a given capital stock. Nominal income, pY, is the sum of the wage income, wN, capital income by contracts, R, and profits, π:

$$pY = wN + R + \pi. \tag{4.3.29}$$

Total demand, D, is the sum of consumption demand, $C(Y)$, autonomous investment, I^a, and inventory investment, $I^Y(Y)$:

$$D(Y) = C(Y) + I^a + I^Y(Y), \tag{4.3.30}$$

with $D'(Y) > 0$ and $\lim_{Y \to 0} D(Y) = D_0 > 0$. The profit share in national income is given by π/pY, which can also be interpreted as real average profit per goods unit. Let $s = \pi/pY$ and $d = D/Y$. Assume that the rate of change of production can be described by[29]

$$\dot{Y}/Y = f(d, s) \tag{4.3.31}$$

with the properties

$$\frac{\partial f}{\partial d} > 0, \quad \frac{\partial f}{\partial s} > 0, \quad \exists\, s \text{ such that } f(d, s) = 0 \,\forall\, d > 0$$

i.e., ceteris paribus, production will be increased as soon as the relative demand or the average profit increases. Further, for a given demand there exists a minimal profit which

---

[29] *Originally, a distinction is made between actual and desired change, but for expository purposes it will be omitted.*

leads to a non-decreasing production change. By substituting for s, (4.3.31) becomes

$$\dot{Y}/Y = f\left(d, 1 - \frac{R}{pY} - \frac{w}{p}\frac{h(Y)}{Y}\right). \tag{4.3.32}$$

Assume that R is adjusted all the time such that R/pY is a constant. Following an approach by Solow/Stiglitz (1967), the following hypothesis about the rate of change of the real wage rate is made:

$$\widehat{(w/p)} = G(\ell, w/p), \quad G_\ell > 0, \quad G_{w/p} > 0 \tag{4.3.33}$$

with ℓ as the employment ratio N/N^s between employment and the constant labor supply. Equation (4.3.33) is the result of the assumption of a modified (essentially Phillips-curve-like) relation derived by Solow/Stiglitz. The additional influence of w/p in (4.3.33) is explained by the following consideration. When the Phillips curve is interpreted as the outcome of a bargaining process in the labor market, the labor-supply side can be considered as being more aggressive the worse the economic situation is, expressed by a ceteris paribus lower or higher real wage rate.

Equations (4.3.32) and (4.3.33) constitute a two-dimensional system in $(Y, w/p)$. Without going into further details, the graphs of the $\dot{Y} = 0$ and $(w/p) = 0$ -loci are pictured in Figure 4.14. The vertical line $\overline{Y}$ represents the capacity boundary.

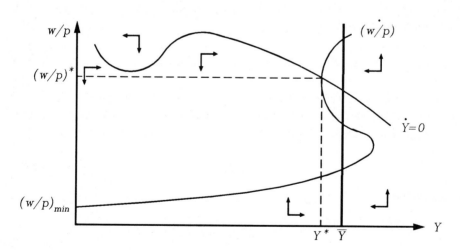

Figure 4.14

It can be shown that for certain parameter constellations the equilibrium is unstable, provided that it is not the full-employment equilibrium. It is possible to construct a compact set D by means of introducing a minimum real wage, some assumptions about the limits of the functions f and G and by means of the capacity boundary $\overline{Y}$. As the vector field points inwards on the boundary of D, the Poincaré-Bendixson theorem can be applied to establish the existence of limit cycles.

4.3.2.3. Non-Walrasian Macroeconomics and the Business Cycle

The non-linear models presented so far are either equilibrium models, or possible disequilibria on the markets have no influence on the actions of individuals at all. The equilibrium models postulate temporary equilibria in all markets at all times. The dynamic forces of these models stem, for example, from specific discrepancies between the actual and the desired capital stock. On the other hand, most of the models presented in previous sections assume that the excess demands in the markets are the main driving force of output, interest rates, and the wage rate, but the possible temporary consequences of discrepancies between supply and demand are left in the dark. Fairly recent work on temporary equilibria with rationing has stressed the importance of two points:[30] i) If there are disequilibria in a market the quantity rationing of the long side can have consequences to the supply or demand on other markets. This is evident in aggregated macro-models in which for fixed prices in the short run a rationing of the labor supply will probably affect the consumption demand. ii) The Keynesian income model can be interpreted as a macro-model with rationing.[31]

It is impossible to present a satisfactory survey of this approach at this place and a very short description must suffice. Consider a very simple macroeconomic framework with households and firms and three goods (consumption goods, labor, and money). Assume that during the relevant time period the prices of all goods are constant. Let p_C, p_ℓ and p_M be the prices of consumption goods, labor and money, respectively. Further, let $z_i^d(p)$ and $z_i^s(p)$, $p = (p_C, p_\ell, p_M)$, denote the demand for and the supply of good i of households or firms, depending on all prices in the usual Walrasian manner. If prices incidently (or after an adjustment process) are general equilibrium prices, then, of course,

$$z_i^d(p) = z_i^s(p) \quad \forall\, i. \tag{4.3.34}$$

However, it cannot be excluded that the constant prices have values such that disequilibria occur in the sense that the Walrasian demand and supply diverge:

$$z_i^d(p) \neq z_i^s(p). \tag{4.3.35}$$

---

[30] *See Benassy (1982) for an introduction to the theory of disequilibria with quantity rationing.*

[31] *It should be stressed, however, that the rationing approach is not the only microeconomic explanation of the Keynesian income theory. See, e.g., Davidson (1984).*

For example, let $z_\ell^s(p)$ be the labor supply of households and $z_\ell^d(p)$ the labor demand of firms and suppose that $z_\ell^s > z_\ell^d$, i.e., there exists an excess supply of labor. Obviously, firms cannot be encouraged to hire more workers than necessary for profit maximization and it follows immediately in this simple context that the actual employment level z_ℓ is given by

$$z_\ell = \min\{z_\ell^d, z_\ell^s\}. \tag{4.3.36}$$

In this case of rationing on the labor market it must further be investigated whether the consumption demand is affected. The Walrasian supply and demand for all goods are derived from a simultaneous optimization process. Consumption demand, z_C^d, was formulated under the assumption that the labor supply could be realized. If there is rationing in the labor market, the consumption demand of the unemployed workers obviously cannot be realized and the consumption demand function must be changed. If credits are not allowed, consumption demand is determined by actual income Y of workers, which is lower than the anticipated Walrasian (utility maximizing) income. It follows that

$$C(Y) \le z_C^d(p). \tag{4.3.37}$$

This consumption function $C(Y)$ is obviously identical with the Keynesian consumption function and was called *effective demand function* by Clower (1965) in contrast to the *notional* Walrasian functions.

The described procedure in investigating the consequences of rationing can of course be applied in all possible rationing constellations, e.g., rationing of firms in the consumption goods market or in the labor market. With money only as a means of transaction, there are exactly four different constellations of excess supply and demand on both markets in addition to the Walrasian equilibrium for different values of the (constant) prices. Malinvaud (1977) has called the four different regimes *Classical Unemployment* (excess supply of labor, excess demand for consumption goods), *Keynesian Unemployment* (excess supply in both markets), *Repressed Inflation* (excess demand in both markets), and *Underconsumption* (excess demand for labor, excess supply of goods), respectively. Figure 4.15 illustrates the different regimes depending on different price-wage-combinations. The standard Keynesian macro-model can be considered as a special case in this scenario, namely as the boundary between the regions of Classical and Keynesian Unemployment with excess supply of labor and equilibrium in the consumption goods market.

While this approach has contributed to a much better understanding of macro-economic phenomena in the short-run, extensions of the basic model which include a variable capital stock, slowly adjusting prices, or other dynamic processes have always turned out to be problematic.[32] One of the very few exceptions is a model by Benassy

---

[32] *This is mainly due to the complicated mathematics of piecewisely defined dynamic systems and discontinuities in some models (cf. Section 5.2.2.).*

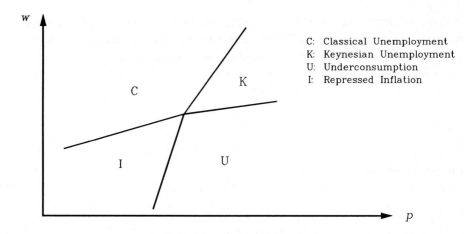

The Regimes in the Malinvaud Model
Figure 4.15

(1984), which provides a synopsis between short-run Keynesian economics, interpreted in the non-Walrasian manner, and mid-term business cycle theory.

Consider a macro-model with a consumption good, labor, money, and bonds. The goods price and the interest rate adjust immediately such that these markets are always in equilibrium. With a fixed nominal wage rate during each period,[33] the system always operates on the boundary between Keynesian and Classical Unemployment in the terminology of Malinvaud (1977). In that case, the demand side of the model can be described by the IS-LM equations

$$Y = C(Y, p) + I(X, r) \tag{4.3.38}$$

$$M^d(Y, r, p) = \overline{M}^s$$

with M^d as the demand for money, $\overline{M}^s$ as the constant money supply, r as the interest rate, p as the price of the consumption good, and X as expected demand. In addition to the usual signs of the partial derivatives, it is assumed that $C_p < 0$ because of a real balance effect, $M_p^d > 0$ because of increasing transaction money demand, and $I_X > 0$ as investment due to expected demand. Equations (4.3.38) can be solved for Y and r with X, p, and $\overline{M}^s$ treated as exogenous variables at this stage. Let $Y = E(X, p)$ be the solution of (4.3.38) in Y for alternative values of X and p.[34] The function $Y = E(X, p)$ describes an *aggregated demand curve* of the system.

---

[33] *As the analysis is in continuous time, the period length is, of course, infinitely small.*

[34] *As $\overline{M}^s$ is constant during the entire time interval, it will be dropped in the following.*

An *aggregated supply curve* is derived in the following way: since competition is assumed, the firm chooses the labor input such that the real wage rate, w/p, equals the marginal product of labor. With a production function

$$Y = F(L) \quad \text{or} \quad L = F^{-1}(Y) \tag{4.3.39}$$

it follows

$$F'(L) = w/p, \tag{4.3.40}$$

and production is

$$Y^0 = F\left(F'^{-1}(w/p)\right). \tag{4.3.41}$$

Y^0 represents the usual neoclassical supply of goods. As the labor input is restricted to be equal to or less than the constant supply of labor $\overline{L}^s$, i.e., the full-employment level, output is the minimum of the neoclassical Y^0 and the full-employment output level $Y_0 = F(\overline{L}^s)$:

$$Y = \min\{F(\overline{L}^s), F(F'^{-1}(w/p))\} = \min\{Y_0, Y^0\}. \tag{4.3.42}$$

Equations (4.3.38) and (4.3.42) constitute a temporary Keynesian equilibrium with a variable goods price. The aggregated demand curve and the supply curve are shown in Figure 4.16. The demand curve will shift upwards for increasing demand expectations, which are reasonably bounded by Y_0, i.e., by $X_3 = Y_0$ in Figure 4.16, and the supply curve will shift downwards for decreasing wage rates. The constellation of the aggregated supply and demand curves in Figure 4.16 represents an underemployment equilibrium which is apparently due to high wages.

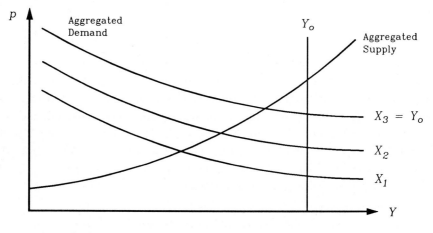

Aggregate Supply and Demand; $X_3 > X_2 > X_1$

Figure 4.16

If $Y < Y^0$, the points of intersection of the aggregated supply and demand curves are described by the solution of the system

$$Y = E(X, p)$$
$$Y = F\big(F'^{-1}(w/p)\big). \tag{4.3.43}$$

Equations (4.3.43) constitute a system of two equations in the two endogenous variables Y and p and in the parameters X and w, and can therefore be solved for Y and p. Let $Y = Z(X, w)$ be the solution of (4.3.43) in Y for different values of X and w. The multipliers are calculated as

$$\frac{dY}{dX} = Z_X > 0$$

$$\frac{dY}{dw} = Z_w < 0. \tag{4.3.44}$$

The function $Y = Z(X, w)$ and the analogue solution in p represent a temporary Keynesian equilibrium with fixed wages and constant expected demand in the investment function.

In order to introduce the dynamic aspects, suppose that the wage rate adjusts according to a usual Phillips curve relation

$$\dot{w} = H(\overline{N} - L), \quad H' < 0, \tag{4.3.45}$$

with $\overline{N}$ as the constant supply of labor.

As labor is the only factor of production, L can be substituted by Y by means of the production function, hence

$$\dot{w} = G(Y), \quad G' > 0. \tag{4.3.46}$$

Assume further that there exists a $\overline{Y} > 0$ such that $\dot{w} = 0$:

$$\dot{w} = G(\overline{Y}) = 0, \quad 0 \le \overline{Y} < Y_0. \tag{4.3.47}$$

Finally, let the demand expectation adjust adaptively to the difference between actual income and expected demand:

$$\dot{X} = \mu(Y - X), \quad \mu > 0. \tag{4.3.48}$$

Equations (4.3.46) and (4.3.48) constitute a two-dimensional autonomous differential equations system.

The set of points $\{(X, w) \mid \dot{w} = 0\}$ is given by $\overline{Y} = Z(X, w)$ because of (4.3.47). The curve is upward sloping because

$$d\overline{Y} = 0 = Z_X dX + Z_w dw \tag{4.3.49}$$

$$\Longrightarrow \frac{dX}{dw} = -\frac{Z_w}{Z_X} > 0.$$

As $\overline{Y} < Y^0$, the curve $\dot{w} = 0$ is located below the curve $Y^0 = Z(X, w)$, which would be the solution of (4.3.43) if the intersection of the aggregate supply and demand curve coincided with the full-employment output level. The wage w will decrease (increase) to the right (left) of the locus $\dot{w} = 0$ because $\dot{w} = G(Z(X, w))$, $G' > 0$, and $Z_w < 0$.

A long-run expectations equilibrium is defined by

$$\dot{X} = 0 = \mu(Y - X) \Longrightarrow X = Y = Z(X, w). \tag{4.3.50}$$

The slope of the $\dot{X} = 0$ - locus is given by

$$\frac{dX}{dw} = \frac{Z_w}{1 - Z_X} \gtrless 0 \quad \text{if} \quad Z_X \gtrless 1. \tag{4.3.51}$$

Thus, the shape of the $\dot{X} = 0$ - locus is not given *a priori* because no assumption has been made so far regarding the magnitude or the constancy of Z_X besides $Z_X > 0$. An examination of the stability properties of the system, however, will uncover that at equilibrium Z_X must be greater than unity in order to guarantee an unstable equilibrium.

A linear approximation of (4.3.46) and (4.3.48) around the long-run equilibrium leads to the exclusion of a saddle point because the determinant of the Jacobian M is positive. Moreover, the trace is given by

$$\text{tr } M = G_Y Z_w + \mu(Z_X - 1) \gtrless 0. \tag{4.3.52}$$

Therefore, as the trace must be positive in the case of local instability of the equilibrium, it follows that, at equilibrium, Z_X must be greater than one.

The locus $\dot{X} = 0$ is defined for $X \leq Y \leq Y_0$, and therefore starts on the full-employment locus $Y_0 = Z(X, w)$, which has a positive slope like the locus $\dot{w} = 0$. Expectations X therefore equal the full-employment output level Y_0 at the intersection of $Y_0 = Z(X, p)$ and the $\dot{X} = 0$ curve.

The expected demand will increase (decrease) for all X to the left (right) of the locus $\dot{X} = 0$ because $d\dot{X}/dw = \mu Z_w < 0$. Figure 4.17 shows a possible configuration of the $\dot{w} = 0$ and $\dot{X} = 0$ - loci which features an unstable long-run equilibrium at

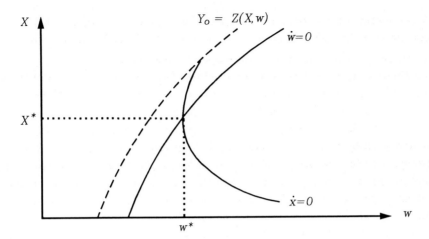

Figure 4.17

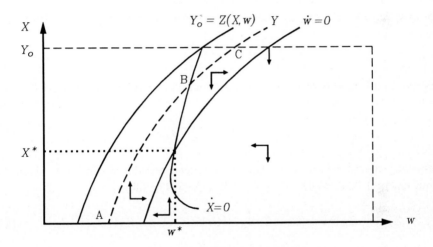

The Phase Portrait in the Benassy Model
Figure 4.18

(w^*, X^*). The graph with $\dot{w} = 0$ intersects the abscissa for $w > 0$ and a corresponding $Y < Y_0$ if the assumptions underlying Figure 4.16 are valid. It further follows from those assumptions that the curve $\dot{X} = 0$ always stays in the positive orthant because there will always be a positive Y which solves equation (4.3.43).

Note that according to Theorem 4.3 a necessary condition for the existence of a closed orbit is that the sign of the expression

$$G_Y Z_w + \mu(Z_X - 1) \tag{4.3.53}$$

changes somewhere in the domain. In case of a constant sign of Z_w, this necessary condition implies that Z_X changes its value such that $Z_X \gtrless 1$ at least once in the domain, implying a changing sign of the slope of the curve $\dot{X} = 0$.

The phase portrait is pictured in Figure 4.18. Once again, the Poincaré-Bendixson theorem will be applied to establish the existence of limit cycles. In order to construct a compact subset $D \subset \mathbf{R}^2$, choose Y_0 as the upper bound for X and choose an upper bound for w such that it is higher than the wage rate which fulfills $\dot{w} = 0$ for $X = Y_0$. The set described by these bounds and the full-employment line $Y_0 = Z(X, w)$ cannot be the desired subset, because at the intersection of the locus $\dot{X} = 0$ and the curve $Y_0 = Z(X, w)$ the vector field does not point inwards the set. Thus the boundary of the subset must lie to the right of that intersection. Consider a point C to the right of the intersection. As C lies on the locus of a definite $\tilde{Y} = Z(X, w)$, it has to be examined whether the vector field points inwards the set D bounded by the line $\tilde{Y} = Z(X, w)$. For the segment BC this is unambigously the case. For segment AB, however, both $\dot{X}$ and $\dot{w}$ are positive. If the vector field implied that the motion of X and w kept the variables on the line AB, i.e., $\tilde{Y} = Z(X, w) = $ constant, then it would be that

$$\dot{Y} = 0 = Z_w \dot{w} + Z_X \dot{X}. \tag{4.3.54}$$

As it is required that the vector field points inwards the subset D, it must be that

$$\dot{Y} < 0 \Longrightarrow \dot{X} < -\frac{Z_w \dot{w}}{Z_X}. \tag{4.3.55}$$

The following consideration shows that it is indeed possible to find a $\tilde{Y}$ which fulfills the requirement $\dot{Y} < 0$. With $(Y - X) < Y_0 \; \forall \; X > 0$ it follows

$$\dot{Y} = Z_X \dot{X} + Z_w \dot{w} = \mu(Y - X)Z_X + G(Y)Z_w < \mu Y_0 Z_X + G(Y)Z_w \tag{4.3.56}$$

which is negative for a $\tilde{Y}$ with $G(\tilde{Y}) > \dfrac{\mu Y_0 Z_X}{Z_w}$. With $\lim\limits_{\tilde{Y} \to Y_0} G(\tilde{Y}) = \infty$, i.e., the wage rate tends to infinity for Y approaching the full-emplyment output level, the existence of a $\tilde{Y} < Y_0$ fulfilling the inequality is assured.

Through the existence of this compact subset D with the desired properties and an unstable long-run equilibrium, the requirements of the Poincaré-Bendixson theorem are fulfilled, and there exists at least one closed orbit in this non-Walrasian model.

While no specific assumption has been made about the shape of the Phillips curve or the investment function $I(Y)$ as in the previous section, the essential requirement of the Benassy model in order to exhibit cyclical behavior is the changing of the magnitude of Z_X over the domain. An inspection of the multiplier reveals that, among others, the partial derivative I_X, i.e., the response of investment to changing demand expectations, can be viewed as being mainly responsible for high or low values of Z_X. It is interesting, however, that all that is needed is a rising I_X abstracting from all shapes and specific non-linearities over the entire domain. It is unclear, however, why I_X should increase near the long-run equilibrium at all. One possible reason for a declining propensity to invest far from equilibrium may be the decreasing prospect to gain profits, which is the same argument delivered by Kaldor in his 1940 model.

Another model that makes use both of an IS-LM-framework and the Poincaré-Bendixson theorem was presented by Schinasi (1982). The essential difficulty in investigating dynamical systems by means of the Poincaré-Bendixson theorem, namely to make sure that the vector field points inwards an appropriately defined subset D, is circumscribed in that model by the *a priori* assumption that such a set exists.

4.3.3. Predator-Prey Interpretations of the Business Cycle

The tools to study dynamical systems used thus far are not specific to economics. Most of the well-known dynamic relations, such as the harmonic oscillator, the van der Pol equation, etc., were introduced during the study of physical phenomena like the movement of a pendulum or the reaction of springs under suspension. However, as will be stressed in Chapter 5, dynamic phenomena play an increasingly important role in other disciplines such as chemistry and biology as well, with a striking similarity of problems and their possible solutions in all these fields.

An early attempt to grasp a biological or an ecological phenomenon by means of mathematical analysis is the work of Lotka (1925) and Volterra (1931). They studied the dynamic relations between two interdependently related species - adriatic fishes, actually - which can be described as predators and preys, respectively. Without going into details, the Lotka/Volterra dynamical system consists of the two-dimensional differential equation system

$$\begin{aligned} \dot{x} &= ax - bxy \\ \dot{y} &= -cy + dxy \end{aligned} \qquad a, b, c, d > 0, \qquad (4.3.57)$$

in which x describes the total prey population and y the population of the predator. The preys are the only food source for the predator. Thus, if $x = 0$, the predator population decreases exponentially at the rate c. If $y = 0$, then the prey population grows exponentially to infinity at the rate a.

The Lotka/Volterra system is of interest in various fields because it has an important property:

Theorem 4.5 (Hirsch/Smale (1974) p. 262)

Every trajectory of the Lotka/Volterra equations (4.3.57) is a closed orbit (except the equilibrium (y^*, x^*) and the coordinate axes).

It follows that the closed orbits cannot be limit cycles. Otherwise, the trajectories which approach a limit cycle are not closed orbits. The initial population at $t = 0$ determines which closed orbits describes the dynamic behavior of (4.3.57) (cf. Figure 4.19).

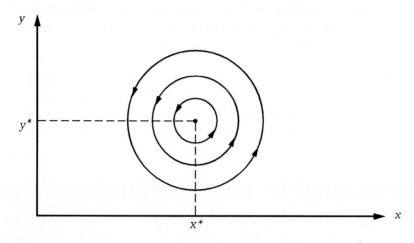

Figure 4.19

Note further that in predator-prey models like (4.3.57) the equilibrium is stable, though not in the asymptotic sense: for a small deviation from equilibrium there is always a neighborhood U around the equilibrium with $(v^* + \Delta v) \in U$, such that $v(t) \in U \; \forall t$, $v = (x, y)$.

This predator-prey relation between biological species motivated Goodwin (1967) to construct a model of the class struggle which essentially leads to the same formal framework.[35]

Consider two households: workers and capitalists. Workers spend all their income wL on consumption, while capitalists save all their income $Y - wL$, with Y as production. The goods price is normalized to unity. Let K denote capital, $a = a_0 e^{\phi t} = Y/L$ denote labor productivity growing at the constant rate ϕ, and $N = N_0 e^{nt}$ denote labor supply growing at the rate n. Finally, let σ be the capital output ratio K/Y.

The wage income share of national income is $wL/Y = w/a$. Hence, the profit share is $1 - w/a$. As savings (which equals profits) is $S = Y - wL = (1 - w/a)Y$, investment is $\dot{K} = S = (1 - w/a)Y$. The growth rate of the capital stock, $\dot{K}/K$, is then given as $\dot{K}/K = (1 - w/a)Y/K = (1 - w/a)/\sigma$. Provided that the capital-output ratio is constant, it follows that $\dot{K}/K = \dot{Y}/Y$. By definition, employment L is given by Y/a, hence

$$\dot{Y}/Y - \dot{L}/L = \phi. \qquad (4.3.58)$$

---

[35] *Cf. Gandolfo (1983), p. 474ff. for a discussion of the Goodwin model that is similar to the one presented below.*

Thus, $\dot{L}/L = (1 - w/a)/\sigma - \phi$. Call the labor bill share $u = w/a$ and the employment rate $v = L/N$. Logarithmic differentiation yields

$$
\begin{aligned}
\dot{v}/v &= \dot{L}/L - \dot{N}/N \\
&= \dot{Y}/Y - \phi - n \\
&= (1 - w/a)/\sigma - (\phi + n) \\
&= \frac{1 - u}{\sigma} - (\phi + n)
\end{aligned}
\tag{4.3.59}
$$

and

$$
\dot{u}/u = \dot{w}/w - \dot{a}/a = \dot{w}/w - \phi.
\tag{4.3.60}
$$

The wage rate is once again assumed to change according to a Phillips curve relation, i.e.,

$$
\dot{w}/w = f(v), \quad \lim_{v \to 1} f(v) = \infty, \quad \lim_{v \to 0} f(v) = \omega < 0, \quad \frac{\partial f}{\partial v} > 0.
\tag{4.3.61}
$$

Approximating (4.3.61) linearily by $\dot{w}/w = -\gamma + \rho v$ yields

$$
\dot{u}/u = -\gamma + \rho v - \phi.
\tag{4.3.62}
$$

Equations (4.3.59) and (4.3.62) constitute a system of two differential equations which together indeed have the same formal structure as the Lotka/Volterra equations (4.3.57):

$$
\begin{aligned}
\dot{v} &= \left(1/\sigma - (\phi + n) - u/\sigma\right)v \\
\dot{u} &= \left(-(\phi + \gamma) + \rho v\right)u.
\end{aligned}
\tag{4.3.63}
$$

The employment rate v serves as the prey while the wage bill share acts like a predator. The relations are intuitively quite reasonable: Let $v \to 0$, i.e., there will be no employment at all. Then, of course, the wage bill tends toward zero, implying that the employment rate will be increased since no relevant labor costs occur.

Fortunately, the dynamics can easily be presented graphically.[36] Eliminate time by dividing both equations:

$$
\frac{dv}{du} = \frac{\left(1/\sigma - (\phi + n) - u/\sigma\right)v}{\left(-(\phi + \gamma) + \rho v\right)u}
$$

$$
\Longrightarrow dv\left(-(\phi + \gamma)/v + \rho\right)vu = du\left((1/\sigma - (\phi + n))/u - 1/\sigma\right)vu
$$

$$
dv\left(-\frac{(\phi + \gamma)}{v} + \rho\right) = du\left(\frac{1/\sigma - (\phi + n)}{u} - 1/\sigma\right).
\tag{4.3.64}
$$

---

[36] *The presentation given here is slightly different from Goodwin's and is adapted from Clark (1976).*

Integrating both sides yields

$$-(\phi + \gamma)\ln v + \rho v = \left(1/\sigma - (\phi + n)\right)\ln u - u/\sigma + c, \tag{4.3.65}$$

where c is a constant. By introducing a dummy variable z, both sides of (4.3.65) can be presented separately, namely

$$z = F(v) = -(\phi + \gamma)\ln v + \rho v \tag{4.3.66}$$

$$\frac{dz}{dv} = -(\phi + \gamma)/v + \rho$$

and

$$z = G(u, c) = \left(1/\sigma - (\phi + n)\right)\ln u - u/\sigma + c \tag{4.3.67}$$

$$\frac{dz}{du} = \left(1/\sigma - (\phi + n)\right)/u - 1/\sigma.$$

As can easily be examined, equations (4.3.66) and (4.3.67) are convex and concave, respectively, with respect to the origin (cf. Figure 4.20).

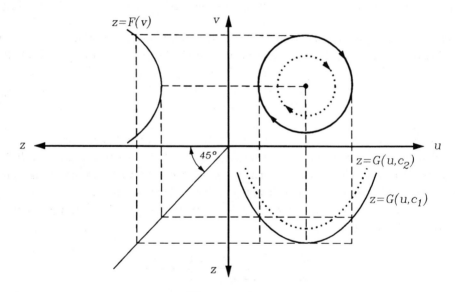

Figure 4.20

By inspecting the slopes of (4.3.66) and (4.3.67) it can be seen that the functions' extrema are exactly at the equilibrium values of (4.3.63). Starting with an arbitrary v in the $v - z$- orthant, the corresponding value of u fulfilling the simultaneous equation system (4.3.63) is found by equating the z-values via the 45^0-line. Either by graphical construction or by means of the theorem stated above it can be checked that the

$u - v$ - combinations which fulfill the equation system (4.3.63) are in a closed orbit. The direction of change in the orbit is clockwise, which is obvious from (4.3.63). The entire constellation of orbits can be constructed by varying the integration constant c in (4.3.65), which corresponds to different initial values of v and u.

Goodwin's approach has gained a favorable reputation among business cycle theorists. Desai (1972) incorporated price dynamics and studied the effects of a variable σ.[37] Velupillai (1979) examined the stability properties of the Goodwin model extensively. Aside from the crucial item of structural instability in that model, Velupillai investigated the abandonment of the linearity of the Phillips curve-relation in Goodwin's original presentation. The conclusion is that the introduction of non-linearities in the function (4.3.61) above, namely $\dot{w}/w = f(v)$, does not change the dynamic behavior of the model.[38] Flaschel (1984) dealt with an extended version of the Goodwin model which allows for variable goods prices and money illusion. It can be shown that the original Goodwin model is a special case - a bifurcation point of a money illusion parameter, actually - of this extended version. Van der Ploeg (1983, 1985b) compared the predator-prey model as an illustration of post-Keynesian growth theory with the standard neoclassical growth theory. A two-sectoral version of the model can be found in Sato (1985). Pohjola (1981) studied a one-dimensional discrete-time version of the Goodwin model and showed that it is possible to generate chaotic time paths in this version of the model.[39]

While the *formal* identity of the Goodwin model with the Lotka/Volterra predator-prey system establishes only a superficial analogy between the class struggle and the struggle of competing species, the Goodwin model with its interaction of the employment rate and the wage bill share (respectively the "profit rate") reminds strongly of the models of classical "political economics". Indeed, the Goodwin model is often called a neo-Marxian model,[40] which (together with the work of other Cambridge economists like, e.g., Sraffa) has initiated a renewed interest in the work of classical economists like Ricardo, Smith, or Marx. From the viewpoint of business cycle theory it is especially the role of dynamics in classical economics which deserves attention. Dumenil/Levy have stressed in a series of papers (e.g., Dumenil/Levy (1985,1986)) that the usual identification of classical economics with the idea of equilibrium is correct only in the sense that the classics postulate a convergence of dynamic processes to equilibria. As

---

[37] *Desai's paper, however, is not free from misconceptions, as it was pointed out by Velupillai (1979). Desai's stability concept refers to asymptotic stability, which is inadequate in the context of the closed orbits above.*

[38] *Compare also Flaschel/Krüger (1984) for the influence of the Phillips curve in the Goodwin model.*

[39] *See Chapter 5 for a presentation of chaotic dynamics.*

[40] *Alternatively, it is sometimes called a neo-Keynesian or post-Keynesian model because of the affinity of some Cambridge economists to Marxian ideas.*

adjustment processes last for longer time periods and as there always exist disturbing forces in real life, actual economies are (according to this interpretation of classical economics) thus characterized more by disequilibria than by equilibrium states.

Furthermore, the formal structure of these models in the classical tradition does not exclude the possibility of cyclic behavior and the postulated convergence to equilibria appears as a special case in a general analysis.[41] This interpretation of classical ideas will probably constitute a major focus of future research in dynamical economics and will be interesting at least with respect to the competing interpretation in the form of the New Classical (equilibrium) Macroeconomics (cf. Chapter 3).

The crucial instability property of the Goodwin model was also discussed by Samuelson (1971, 1972). The original Goodwin model is a so-called *conservative system*, i.e., the system can be thought of as being confronted neither with some kind of friction nor with an energy-like amplification by means of exogenous forces. By introducing diminishing returns to scale, Samuelson transformed the conservative Goodwin model into a *dissipative system*, i.e., a system which collapses to the non-oscillating fixed point if the exogenous driving force tends toward zero.

4.3.4. The Liénard-van der Pol Equation

4.3.4.1. The Uniqueness of Limit Cycles

Aside from the predator-prey model presented in the previos section only a few explicit non-linear dynamical systems exist, for which exact statements concerning their trajectories can be made. One dynamical non-linear system which has gained some interest in physics is the so-called generalized *Liénard equation*[42]

$$\dot{x} = y - f(x)$$
$$\dot{y} = -g(x) \tag{4.3.68}$$

or

$$\ddot{x} + f'(x)\dot{x} + g(x) = 0. \tag{4.3.69}$$

The equation expresses the dynamics of a spring mass system with $g(x)$ as the spring force and $f'(x)\dot{x}$ as a damping factor. A special form of the Liénard equation is the *van der Pol equation* with $g(x) = x$ and $f(x) = (x^3/3 - x)$:

$$\ddot{x} + (x^2 - 1)\dot{x} + x = 0. \tag{4.3.70}$$

---

[41] *Compare also Flaschel/Semmler (1985) and Medio (1980) for other models that elaborate on classical ideas.*

[42] *See Hirsch/Smale (1974), p. 215 and Boyce/DiPrima (1977), p. 447 ff. Compare also Gandolfo (1983), p. 446ff.*

The Liénard equation (4.3.69) is of special interest in dynamical systems theory because it is possible to make statements on the uniqueness of limit cycles. The following result was provided by Levinson/Smith (1942) for equation (4.3.69).[43]

Theorem 4.6   (Levinson/Smith)

Equation (4.3.69) has a unique periodic solution if the following conditions are satisfied.

i) f' and g belong to C^1.

ii) $\exists\, x_1 > 0$ and $x_2 > 0$ such that for $-x_1 < x < x_2 :\quad f'(x) < 0$, and > 0 otherwise.

iii) $xg(x) > 0 \,\forall\, x \neq 0$

iv) $\lim\limits_{x \to \infty} F(x) = \lim\limits_{x \to \infty} G(x) = \infty$ where $F(x) = \int_0^x f'(x)dx$, and $G(x) = \int_0^x g(x)dx$.

v) $G(-x_1) = G(x_2)$

It can be shown that condition v) is fulfilled if $f'(x)$ is even and $g(x)$ is odd.[44]

The theorem seems to require rather artificial properties, but as will be seen below, it is only assumption v) which represents a more or less severe specification of (4.3.69) compared with the previous differential equation systems.

For example, it can easily be seen that the van der Pol equation (4.3.70) fulfills the requirements of the Levinson/Smith theorem:[45]

Corollary   (Hirsch/Smale)

There is one non-trivial periodic solution of the van der Pol equation (4.3.70) and every non-equilibrium solution tends to this periodic solution. Thus, the system oscillates.

The proof consists of a simple examination of conditions i) - v):

i) obvious

ii) Consider the roots of $(x^2 - 1) : x_{1,2} = \pm\sqrt{1}$. Then, $f'(x) < 0 \,\forall\, x \in (-\mid x_1 \mid, \mid x_2 \mid)$

---

[43] Cf. Levinson/Smith (1942), p. 397 f.

[44] A function is even if $f(x) = f(-x)$, e.g., a parabolic function with the origin as the center. A function is odd if $-g(x) = g(-x)$, e.g., a cubic equation.

[45] Cf. Hirsch/Smale (1974), p. 248, who present an own specific proof without resort to Levinson/Smith.

iii) $xg(x) = x^2 > 0 \,\forall\, x \neq 0$

iv) $F(x) = \int_0^x f'(x)dx = x^3/3 - x$ and $G(x) = \int_0^x xdx = x^2/2$. Thus $\lim\limits_{x\to\infty} G(x) = \lim\limits_{x\to\infty} F(x) = \infty$

v) $f'(x) = (x^2 - 1) = f'(-x) = ((-x)^2 - 1), \quad -g(x) = -x = g(-x) = -x$

Figures 4.21.a and 4.21.b show two graphical examples of limit cycles of the van der Pol equation.[46] By letting $f'(x) = \alpha(x^2 - 1)$, it can be seen that for varying α's, e.g., $\alpha_1 < \alpha_2$ in Figs. 4.21.a and 4.21.b, the limit cycles can have shapes which are geometrically quite different from circles.

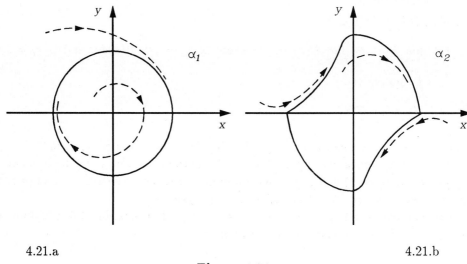

4.21.a   4.21.b

Figure 4.21

4.3.4.2. The Kaldor Model as a Liénard Equation

The Liénard-van der Pol equation has found relatively little attention in business cycle theory. This is probably due to the restrictive symmetry assumptions or properties which are necessary to apply the Levinson/Smith theorem. A very first model that applied the Liénard equation was presented by Ichimura (1955), who examined the most popular business cycle theories of the day, namely the models of Kaldor, Goodwin, and Hicks. Naturally, his conclusion was that a unique limit cycle can neither be detected in one of the models without making further assumptions nor can it be excluded *per se*.

---

[46] *For numerically exact plots see Boyce/DiPrima (1977), p. 448.*

Another model is that of Schinasi (1981) who studied the effects of monetary policies in an IS-LM-framework and who came to the conclusion that a unique cycle exists under certain assumptions.

In order to elucidate the necessary assumptions exemplarily, the Kaldor model will be examined once again. Recall the Chang/Smyth-formulation of the Kaldor model:

$$\dot{Y} = \alpha\big(I(Y, K) - S(Y, K)\big)$$
$$\dot{K} = I(Y, K), \tag{4.3.71}$$

with $I_K < 0$, $S_K > 0$, and the S-shaped (respectively mirror-S-shaped) investment and savings functions in dependence on Y.

Differentiating the goods market adjustment equation with respect to time yields

$$\ddot{Y} = \alpha(I_Y\dot{Y} + I_K\dot{K} - S_Y\dot{Y} - S_K\dot{K}). \tag{4.3.72}$$

Substitution for $\dot{K}$ and rearranging leads to

$$\ddot{Y} - \alpha(I_Y - S_Y)\dot{Y} - \alpha(I_K - S_K)I(Y, K) = 0. \tag{4.3.73}$$

A comparison between (4.3.73) and (4.3.69) reveals that (4.3.73) is not a Liénard equation because the capital stock still appears as a second variable.[47] In order to transform (4.3.73) into a Liénard equation at least two alternatives exist:

i) Investment is independent of the capital stock, i.e., $I = I(Y)$. Consequently, the shifting of the savings function will be the only factor which is responsible for the occurrence of cycles instead of monotonic motions.

ii) Planned investment is treated as usual, but the actual change in the capital stock is determined by savings decisions, i.e., $\dot{K} = S$. In this case savings must also be independent of the capital stock.

Additionally, it has to be assumed in both cases that the expression $(I_K - S_K)$ is independent of the capital stock, i.e., that the functions are linear in K.

In the following, only alternative ii) will be considered.[48] With the described modifications equation (4.3.73) turns into

$$\ddot{Y} - \alpha(I_Y - S_Y)\dot{Y} - \alpha I_K S(Y) = 0. \tag{4.3.74}$$

---

[47] *For this reason the equations studied by Schinasi (1981) (e.g., eq. (15)) do not fulfill the requirements of Liénard equations, though the opposite is claimed by Schinasi.*

[48] *Basically, this is the procedure proposed by Ichimura (1955). Unfortunately, there are some minor errors in his calculations.*

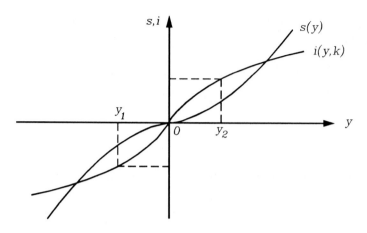

Figure 4.22

Equation (4.3.74) is a Liénard equation with $f'(x) \cong \alpha(S_Y - I_Y)$ and $g(x) \cong -\alpha I_K S(Y)$. In order to examine the conditions of the Levinson/Smith theorem, a change of coordinates will be carried out such that the stationary equilibrium is the origin of the system:

$$\dot{y} = \alpha(i(y, k) - s(y))$$
$$\dot{k} = s(y) \tag{4.3.75}$$

or

$$\ddot{y} - \alpha(i_y - s_y)\dot{y} - \alpha i_k s(y) = 0 \tag{4.3.76}$$

with $y = Y - Y^*, k = K - K^*$, the asterix denoting equilibrium values. Figure 4.22 pictures the transformed system (4.3.75).

Let y_1 and y_2 be the deviations from the stationary equilibrium for which the slopes of the investment and the savings functions coincide.

With condition i) fulfilled by assumption, ii) is fulfilled for $y \in (y_1, y_2) : f'(y) = \alpha(s_y - i_y) < 0$ because of the usual Kaldor-type functions. iii) With $s(y) \gtrless 0$ for $y \gtrless 0$ and $-i_k > 0 \,\forall y$ by assumption, it follows that $g(y)y = -\alpha i_k s(y)y > 0 \,\forall y \neq 0$. iv) $F(y) = \int_0^y \alpha(s_y - i_y)dy = \alpha(s - i)$. Thus, obviously, $\lim_{y \to \infty} F(y) = \infty$. $G(y) = \int_0^y \alpha(-i_k) s \, dy = \alpha(-i_k) \int_0^y s \, dy$. As $s(y)$ is non-decreasing for $y > 0$, $\lim_{y \to \infty} G(y) = \infty$. v) Consider the shape of the difference $(s_y - i_y)$ in Figure 4.23. Obviously, in order to be an even function, $f'(y) = \alpha(s_y - i_y)$ has to be symmetric with respect to $y = 0$. Further, $g(y) = \alpha(-i_k)s(y)$ is odd if $s(y)$ is symmetric in the sense that $s(y) = -s(-y)$. With $f'(y)$ even and $g(y)$ odd, condition v), $G(-y_1) = G(y_2)$, is fulfilled and there exists a unique limit cycle.

While conditions i) to iv) do not require additional assumptions in this modified Kaldor model, condition v) makes it necessary to postulate symmetric shapes of the

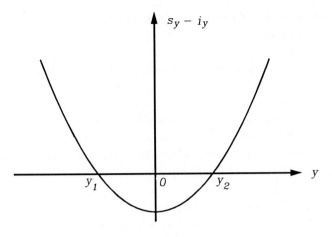

Figure 4.23

investment and savings functions if the Levinson/Smith theorem is to be applied in detecting a unique cycle in the modified Kaldor model. If the graph in Figure 4.23 corresponds with a parabolic function, e.g., $y^2 - a$, it is immediately clear that the Liénard equation (4.3.76) has the special form of the van der Pol equation with

$$\alpha(s_y - i_y) = (y^2 - a)/a = f'(y) \qquad (4.3.77)$$

which has a unique limit cycle as shown above.

The restrictive assumptions which are necessary to assure a unique limit cycle even in this simple Kaldor-type model make it evident that it is usually difficult to exclude a multiplicity of limit cycles in non-linear business cycle models. Thus, in most non-linear models the independence of a motion in (or convergence to) a closed orbit from initial states cannot be established.

4.3.5. The Hopf Bifurcation in Business Cycle Theory

The mathematical tools for investigating the qualitative behavior of dynamical systems described thus far restrict a model's dimension to $n = 2$. The Hopf bifurcation theorem for a continuous-time system is (in principle) suited to establish the existence of closed orbits in the n-dimensional case. As the discrete-time version is defined only for $n = 2$, both versions of the Hopf bifurcation theorem will be presented separately.

The central expression of this section is *bifurcation*. In general, the term bifurcation describes the occurrence of a qualitative change in the solution of a dynamical system when an exogenously determined parameter is changed. Specifically, this section is concerned with bifurcations that imply the emergence of a closed orbit in a system which formerly possessed only a fixed point. To make some ideas more precise,[49] consider the differential equation system[50]

$$\dot{x} = f(x, \mu), \quad x \in \mathbf{A} \subset \mathbf{R}^n, \quad \mu \in \mathbf{R}, \tag{4.3.78}$$

in which x denotes the vector of the state variables and μ is an exogenously given parameter. Let $x(t, x_0, \mu)$ be a solution of (4.3.78). Two solutions $x(t, x_0, \mu_1)$ and $x(t, x_0, \mu_2)$ for different values of the control parameter μ are said to be *topologically equivalent* if their corresponding trajectories stay close together in the case of small differences in μ. If two solutions are topologically equivalent, the system (4.3.78) is said to be *generic* or *structurally stable*.

There may be systems like (4.3.78), which are structurally stable only locally for certain intervals of the parameter μ. Let $\mathbf{S}$ be the subset $\mathbf{S} \subset \mathbf{R}$ of all μ, for which the system (4.3.78) is structurally stable. The complementary set $\mathbf{B} = \mathbf{R} \setminus \mathbf{S}$ is called the *set of bifurcation points*. Summarizing, a value μ_0 in equation (4.3.78) for which the flow of that equation is not structurally stable is a bifurcation value of μ.[51]

As economics can never be sure about the absolute numerical preciseness of the variables and constants in practical applications, it is highly important to know whether small deviations from the assumed values leave the qualitative features of the models unchanged. Thus, in face of a concrete model, it is essential to know whether it is structurally stable for all μ, or – if not – what the bifurcation values are.

4.3.5.1. The Hopf Bifurcation in the Continuous-Time Case

Consider the differential equation system (4.3.78), and assume that for every μ the system posses a unique fixed point x^*, i.e., an equilibrium, such that

$$\dot{x} = 0 = f(x^*, \mu). \tag{4.3.79}$$

It follows by the implicit function theorem that $x^* = x^*(\mu)$, provided that the determinant of the Jacobian does not vanish.

Assume that this fixed point is stable for small values of the parameter μ. The subject of the Hopf bifurcation is the question, whether the corresponding fixed points x^* loose their stability when the parameter μ is changed and what happens when the fixed point has become unstable.

---

[49] *See Cugno/Montrucchio (1984) for an overview of the following concepts.*

[50] *The case of a discrete-time system can be treated analogously.*

[51] *See Guckenheimer/Holmes (1983), p. 119, who also mention the restrictions implied by that definition.*

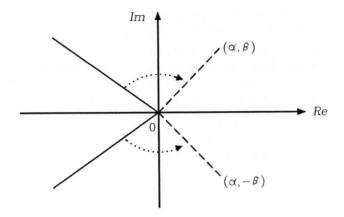

The Eigenvalues in the Hopf Bifurcation
Figure 4.24

There exist several versions of the Hopf bifurcation theorem. The following is a truncated version of Guckenheimer/Holmes (1983), p. 151 ff.[52]

Theorem 4.7   (Hopf)

Suppose that the system (4.3.78) has an equilibrium (x^*, μ_0) at which the following properties are satisfied:

   i) The Jacobian of (4.3.78) has a pair of pure imaginary eigenvalues and no other eigenvalues with zero real parts.

This implies that there is a smooth curve of equilibria $(x^*(\mu), \mu)$ with $x^*(\mu_0) = x^*$. The conjugated complex eigenvalues $\lambda(\mu), \bar{\lambda}(\mu)$ of the Jacobian which are purely imaginary at $\mu = \mu_0$ vary smoothly with μ. If moreover

   ii) $\dfrac{d(\mathrm{Re}\lambda(\mu))}{d\mu} \Big|_{\mu = \mu_0} > 0$

then there exist some periodic solutions bifurcating from $x^*(\mu_0)$ at $\mu = \mu_0$ and the period of the solutions is close to $2\pi/\beta_0$ ($\beta_0 = \lambda(\mu_0)/i$).

By increasing the parameter μ at $\mu = \mu_0$, the formerly stable fixed point looses its stability because the real parts $\mathrm{Re}\,\lambda$ become positive after having crossed the imaginary axis. The movement of the eigenvalues is illustrated in Figure 4.24.

---

[52] *For other versions see, e.g.,   Alexander/Yorke (1978) and Marsden/McCracken (1976).*

Note, however, that the theorem does not imply that for $\mu > \mu_0$ there are indeed *stable* closed orbits. The theorem establishes only the bifurcation of the fixed point into a closed orbit at $\mu = \mu_0$. Indeed, the closed orbit may arise on either side of μ_0.

The case, in which closed orbits arise at $\mu < \mu_0$ is called the *subcritical* case: closed orbits enclose stable fixed points $x^*(\mu)$, implying that the orbit is repelling. Figure 4.25 illustrates this subcritical bifurcation in the two-dimensional case. All points on the μ - axis represent equilibria of the system. For $\mu < \mu_0$, closed orbits enclose the locally stable equilibria. Trajectories starting at initial values in a neighborhood of the closed orbits are repelled from these orbits. For $\mu > \mu_0$, the equilibria become unstable and no orbit exists.

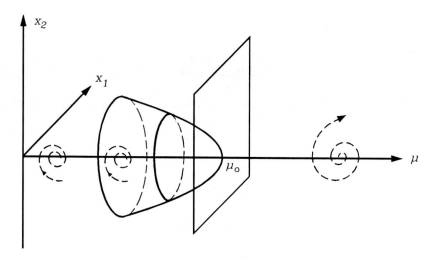

The Subcritical Case
Figure 4.25

The second case is the more important one from an economic point of view.[53] The orbit arises on the side $\mu > \mu_0$, i.e., where the fixed points $x^*(\mu)$ are unstable. Thus, in these *supercritical* bifurcations the orbits are attracting (cf. Figure 4.26).

Which kind of bifurcation actually occurs depends on the coefficients of a specific third-order Taylor expansion of (4.3.78), which are in general not easy to compute and which usually lack an economic interpretation.[54]

In order to establish the *existence* of closed orbits in a concrete system, it is thus sufficient to show that by an increase of the control parameter μ

- complex roots exist or emerge,

---

[53] *See Benhabib/Miyao (1981) for economic interpretations of subcritical bifurcations.*

[54] *See Guckenheimer/Holmes (1983), pp. 144-152.*

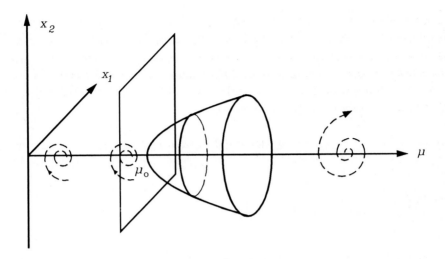

The Supercritical Case
Figure 4.26

- the real parts of a pair of complex conjugate roots are equal to zero at the bifurcation value $\mu = \mu_0$,
- all other real roots differ from zero at $\mu = \mu_0$,
- the real parts differ from zero for $\mu > \mu_0$.

In case of two- or three-dimensional systems the criteria can still be applied by means of simple algebra.

Consider the two-dimensional system

$$\dot{x} = f(x, \mu), \quad x \in \mathbf{R}^2, \quad \mu \in \mathbf{R}. \tag{4.3.80}$$

The characteristic equation reads

$$\lambda^2 + a\lambda + b = 0, \tag{4.3.81}$$

and it can easily be shown that $a = -\text{trace } J$ and $b = \det J$, with J as the Jacobian matrix. With

$$\lambda_{1,2} = -a/2 \pm \sqrt{a^2/4 - b} \tag{4.3.82}$$

the stability conditions can be discussed directly, namely that the fixed point is locally stable if and only if the real parts are negative. As b must be positive ($\det J > 0$) in order to exclude a saddle point, the stability criterion reduces to the condition of a positive coefficient a of (4.3.81), *i.e.*, a negative trace of J. According to Theorem 4.7, a Hopf bifurcation occurs if the conjugate complex roots cross the imaginary axis.

Apparently, the roots are conjugate complex with zero real part if $a = 0$. As there are no other real roots in this two-dimensional example, the consideration is complete if the real parts differ from zero if μ is increased beyond μ_0, *i.e.*, when $a = a(\mu)$ with $da/d\mu > 0$; hence the system undergoes a Hopf bifurcation at $a(\mu_0) = 0$.

The three-dimensional case is slightly more difficult but still analytically computable. The characteristic equation is given as

$$\lambda^3 + a\lambda^2 + b\lambda + c = 0 \tag{4.3.83}$$

with

$a = -\text{tr } J$
$b = \sum \text{principal minors of } J$
$c = -\det J.$

Let $A = a^3/27 - ab/6 + c/2$ and $B = b/3 - a^2/9$. Equation (4.3.83) has one real and two complex conjugate roots if the discriminant of (4.3.83), *i.e.*,

$$D = A^2 + B^3, \tag{4.3.84}$$

is positive.

A very helpful criterion in proving the local stability of a dynamic system is the Routh-Hurwitz criterion.[55] In the three-dimensional case the real parts of the roots are negative if

$$a, b, c > 0 \quad \text{and} \quad ab - c > 0.$$

Making use of the fact that

$$\sum_{i=1}^{3} \lambda_i = -a \quad \text{and} \quad \prod_{i=1}^{3} \lambda_i = -c,$$

it follows that the real parts of the complex conjugate roots are zero and that there is no other real root which equals zero if

$$a, b, c > 0 \quad \text{and} \quad ab - c = 0.$$

The Hopf bifurcation in dynamic systems with $n = 3$ therefore occurs for a μ_0 which fulfills these requirements.

In higher-dimensional systems with $n \geq 4$ the bifurcation values μ_0 can often be calculated only by means of numerical algorithms.

---

[55] *See, e.g., Dernburg/Dernburg (1969), pp. 214 ff.*

The procedure described above can easily be demonstrated with the familiar Kaldor model:

$$\dot{Y} = \alpha\big(I(Y,K) - S(Y)\big)$$
$$\dot{K} = I(Y,K) - \delta K$$

(4.3.85)

with the usual meaning of the symbols (cf. Section 4.3.1).

The Jacobian is

$$J = \begin{pmatrix} \alpha(I_Y - S_Y) & \alpha I_K \\ I_Y & I_K - \delta \end{pmatrix}$$

(4.3.86)

with the determinant

$$\det J = \alpha(I_Y - S_Y)(I_K - \delta) - \alpha I_Y I_K > 0$$

(4.3.87)

and the trace

$$\mathrm{tr}\, J = \alpha(I_Y - S_Y) + (I_K - \delta).$$

(4.3.88)

The fixed points are stable if $a = -\mathrm{tr}\, J > 0 \Longrightarrow \mathrm{tr}\, J < 0$, which is the usual local stability condition in the Kaldor model:

$$\alpha(I_Y - S_Y) + (I_K - \delta) < 0.$$

(4.3.89)

Identify the adjustment coefficient α with the bifurcation parameter μ mentioned above. With $(I_Y - S_Y) > 0$ at the stationary equilibrium and $I_K = \mathrm{const.}$, it can directly be seen that there exists a value $\alpha = \alpha_0$ for which

$$\alpha_0(I_Y - S_Y) + (I_K - \delta) = 0,$$

(4.3.90)

implying that the conjugate complex roots cross the imaginary axis. As, for $\alpha > \alpha_0$, the real parts are positive, the point α_0 is indeed a bifurcation value in the Kaldor model. Provided that the bifurcation is supercritical, a periodic orbit arises for $\alpha > \alpha_0$.

This Hopf bifurcation as a tool for establishing closed orbits in dynamical systems seems to have been originally introduced to economics by Torre (1977), who studied a standard IS-LM model:

$$\dot{Y} = \alpha\big(I(Y,r) - S(Y,r)\big)$$
$$\dot{r} = \beta\big(L(Y,r) - \overline{M}\big)$$

(4.3.91)

with r as the interest rate. As sign $I_Y =$ sign L_Y and sign $I_r =$ sign L_r, the structure of the model is formally similar to the Kaldor model (4.3.85). While no explicit assumption is made by Torre on the form of the investment function, a necessary assumption for the bifurcation in the model is that $\alpha(I_Y - S_Y) > 0$ at equilibrium, which can be achieved either by an S-shaped investment function or an equivalently shaped savings function.

Other applications of the Hopf bifurcation theorem can be found in, *e.g.*, Benhabib/ Nishimura (1979) and Medio (1987), who investigated the cyclic behavior of optimal growth models.

In the two-dimensional case the use of bifurcation theory actually provides no new insights into known models. As can be seen in the demonstration of the Kaldor model, the formally necessary assumptions for the occurrence of closed orbits are indeed identical to those of the Poincaré-Bendixson theorem. In many applications, however, it may be easier to use bifurcation theory because it may be more difficult to find graphically the necessary set on whose boundary the vector field points inwards that set than to calculate the bifurcation values.

The real domains of bifurcation theory are dynamical systems of dimension greater than or equal to three because the Poincaré-Bendixson theorem cannot be applied anymore.

Consider an augmented IS-LM business cycle model:[56]

$$\dot{Y} = \alpha\big(I(Y,K,r) - S(Y,r)\big)$$
$$\dot{r} = \beta\big(L(r,Y) - \overline{M}\big) \qquad (4.3.92)$$
$$\dot{K} = I(Y,K,r) - \delta K$$

with the usual meaning of the symbols. The model essentially constitutes a combination of (4.3.85) and (4.3.91) and seems to be one of the simplest complete business cycle models in the Keynesian tradition.

The Jacobian of the linearized system is

$$J = \begin{pmatrix} \alpha(I_Y - S_Y) & \alpha(I_r - S_r) & \alpha I_K \\ \beta L_Y & \beta L_r & 0 \\ I_Y & I_r & I_K - \delta \end{pmatrix} \qquad (4.3.93)$$

with the characteristic equation

$$\lambda^3 + a\lambda^2 + b\lambda + c = 0 \qquad (4.3.94)$$

and

$$a = -\mathrm{tr}\,J = -\Big(\alpha(I_Y - S_Y) + \beta L_r + (I_K - \delta)\Big)$$
$$b = \beta L_r(I_K - \delta) + \alpha(I_Y - S_Y)(I_K - \delta) - \alpha I_Y I_K \qquad (4.3.95)$$
$$\quad + \alpha\beta(I_Y - S_Y)L_r - \alpha\beta L_Y(I_r - S_r)$$
$$c = -\det J.$$

---

[56] *Compare Boldrin (1984) for a similar model.*

Assume that the discriminant[57] of (4.3.94) is always positive in order to assure that the three roots consist of one real and two complex conjugate roots. Let α be the bifurcation parameter. The Hopf bifurcation occurs at a value $\alpha = \alpha_0$ where

$$a, \ b, \ c > 0 \quad \text{and} \quad ab - c = 0.$$

If the coefficients are positive by assumption, the complex conjugate roots cross the imaginary axis at $\alpha = \alpha_0$, where $ab - c = 0$ is fulfilled. It can be seen that $ab - c = 0$ is a quadratic function in α for the coefficients in (4.3.95). In principle, it is thus possible that two positive values of α occur. If both α_1 and α_2 are positive, other dynamic phenomena than limit cycles have to occur in the range $\alpha_1 < \alpha < \alpha_2$.

As $ab - c$ is decreasing for an increasing α beyond α_0,[58] the real parts are becoming positive such that the fixed points $(Y, K, r)^*_{|\alpha > \alpha_0}$ become unstable. Thus, it has been established that closed orbits emerge at $\alpha = \alpha_0$, with the stability depending on the sub- or supercriticality of the cycle.

An important contribution to applied bifurcation theory in economic dynamics was provided by Benhabib/Miyao (1981), who reexamined the monetary growth model of Tobin, originally formulated in 1965, and who showed that the model can display cyclical behavior. A general version of this model is

$$
\begin{aligned}
\dot{k} &= sf(k) - (1 - s)(\theta - q)m - nk \\
\dot{m} &= m(\theta - p - n) \\
\dot{q} &= Q(p, q) \\
p &= \epsilon\big(m - L(k, q)\big) + q,
\end{aligned}
\tag{4.3.96}
$$

with k, m, q, and p as the capital-labor-ratio, money per capita, expected and actual inflation rates, respectively, and s, θ, ϵ, and n as the savings rate, the rate of monetary expansion, the adjustment speed of the inflation rate, and the population growth rate, respectively. The original Tobin model is characterized by unstable steady states and explosive dynamic behavior, due mainly to the assumption of perfect-foresight short-run expectations q. It can be shown that the generalized model (4.3.96) with adaptive expectations exhibits stable steady states when the adjustment speed of the expectations is sufficiently slow. It is essential to the discussion of the Tobin model that the different versions of the model result alternatively either in stable or unstable modes of the steady state. By performing basically the same procedure as described above, Benhabib/Miyao were able to show that the Tobin model can undergo a Hopf bifurcation if the parameter expressing the expectation adjustment speed is increased. Thus, in addition to the stable

---

[57] *Cf. eq. (4.3.84).*

[58] *This follows immediately from $\partial a / \partial \alpha < 0$, $\partial b / \partial \alpha < 0$, and $\partial c / \partial \alpha > 0$.*

mode there may exist limit cycles such that the generalized Tobin model is characterized by persisting fluctuating growth.

4.3.5.2. The Hopf-Bifurcation in the Discrete-Time Case

The bifurcation of a fixed point into a closed orbit in continuous-time systems as described above was the subject of the original work of E. Hopf in 1942. While continuous-time systems play an essential role in theoretical sciences, the application of computers in the face of complex phenomena makes it necessary to formulate a problem basically in discrete time. Furthermore, economic problems often suggest to design a model in discrete time so that it is useful to have a statement on bifurcations in those systems, too.

The following result is essentially due to Ruelle/Takens (1971):[59]

Theorem 4.8   (Ruelle/Takens)

Let the mapping $x_{t+1} = F(x_t, \mu)$, $x_t \in \mathbf{R}^2$, $\mu \in \mathbf{R}$, have a smooth family of fixed points $x^*(\mu)$ at which the eigenvalues are complex conjugate. If there is a μ_0 such that

$$\operatorname{mod} \lambda(\mu_0) = 1 \quad \text{but} \quad \lambda^n(\mu_0) \neq \pm 1, \quad n = 1, 2, 3, 4$$

and

$$\frac{d \left(\operatorname{mod} \lambda(\mu) \right)}{d\mu} > 0$$

then there is an invariant closed curve bifurcating from $\mu = \mu_0$.

The analogy of this theorem with the Hopf bifurcation theorem for the continuous-time case is evident: while in the continuous-time case an equilibrium point looses its stability and bifurcates into closed orbits when the real parts of the characteristic equation vanish, the analogous criterion in the discrete-time case reads that an equilibrium looses its stability when the characteristic roots leave the unit circle[60] i.e., when mod λ exceeds 1. The Hopf bifurcation therefore occurs exactly at a μ_0 with mod $\lambda(\mu_0) = 1$. Furthermore, it is required that the roots do not become real when they are iterated on the unit cirle.

---

[59] *The following is a truncated version of Iooss (1979) and Guckenheimer/Holmes (1983).*

[60] *If the roots are real, the dominant root must be absolutely larger than 1 (cf. Section 2.1.1.1).*

The first four iterations λ^n must also be conjugate complex. Finally, again in analogy to the continuous-time case, the modulus must not be constant for varying μ at μ_0.[61]

As in the continuous-time case, this truncated theorem does not mention whether the bifurcation is subcritical or supercritical, *i.e.*, whether a closed orbit appears for $\mu < \mu_0$ or $\mu > \mu_0$.[62] Indeed, the stability of the closed orbit again depends on the coefficients of a third-order Taylor expansion.

It is relatively easy to examine whether the assumptions of the theorem are fulfilled. Write the characteristic equation as:

$$\lambda^2 + a\lambda + b = 0 \tag{4.3.97}$$

with the solution

$$\lambda_{1,2} = -a/2 \pm \sqrt{a^2/4 - b} \tag{4.3.98}$$

or, in the complex case, written as $\lambda_{1,2} = \beta_1 \pm \beta_2 i$ with $\beta_1 = -a/2$ and $\beta_2 = \sqrt{b - a^2/4}$. As the modulus is given by

$$\mathrm{mod}(\lambda) = \sqrt{\beta_1^2 + \beta_2^2}$$

it follows in this two-dimensional case that

$$\mathrm{mod}(\lambda) = \sqrt{a^2/4 + b - a^2/4} = \sqrt{b}. \tag{4.3.99}$$

Thus, it suffices to concentrate on the absolute part of the characteristic equation, which is the determinant of the Jacobian in the two-dimensional case.

As an example, consider once again the Kaldor model in a discrete version, which has simply been derived by replacing the differential operator by finite differences:

$$\begin{aligned}
\Delta Y_{t+1} &= Y_{t+1} - Y_t = \alpha\big(I(Y_t, K_t) - S(Y_t, K_t)\big) \\
\Delta K_{t+1} &= K_{t+1} - K_t = I(Y_t, K_t) - \delta K_t
\end{aligned} \tag{4.3.100}$$

or

$$\begin{aligned}
Y_{t+1} &= \alpha\big(I(Y_t, K_t) - S(Y_t, K_t)\big) + Y_t \\
K_{t+1} &= I(Y_t, K_t) + (1 - \delta)K_t.
\end{aligned} \tag{4.3.101}$$

The Jacobian is

$$J = \begin{pmatrix} \alpha(I_Y - S_Y) + 1 & \alpha(I_K - S_K) \\ I_Y & I_K + (1 - \delta) \end{pmatrix} \tag{4.3.102}$$

---

[61] *Recall that in the continuous-time case the real parts Re λ have to change for varying μ.*

[62] *See Guckenheimer/Holmes (1983), pp. 162-165 for details on the stability.*

with the determinant

$$\det J = \big(\alpha(I_Y - S_Y) + 1\big)\big(I_K + 1 - \delta\big) - \alpha I_Y(I_K - S_K). \qquad (4.3.103)$$

The eigenvalues are conjugated complex if

$$\det J > \frac{(\operatorname{tr} J)^2}{4}. \qquad (4.3.104)$$

Provided that the inequality holds, the bifurcation occurs at $\alpha = \alpha_0$ such that $\det J_{|\alpha=\alpha_0}$ $= 1$. Simple calculation yields

$$\big(\alpha(I_Y - S_Y) + 1\big)\big(I_K + 1 - \delta\big) - \alpha I_Y(I_K - S_K) = 1$$

$$\implies \quad \alpha_0 = \frac{\delta - I_K}{(I_Y - S_Y)(I_K + 1 - \delta) - I_Y(I_K - S_K)} \qquad (4.3.105)$$

which is positive if the denominator is positive.

The change of the modulus of the characteristic roots, $|\lambda(\alpha)|$, for an increase of the parameter α is given by

$$\frac{d\,|\,\lambda(\alpha)\,|}{d\alpha}\bigg|_{\alpha=\alpha_0} = \frac{d(\sqrt{\det J}\,)}{d\alpha}$$

$$= 1/2\Big(\big(\alpha(I_Y - S_Y) + 1\big)(I_K + 1 - \delta) - \alpha I_Y(I_K - S_K)\Big)^{-1/2}$$

$$\big((I_Y - S_Y)(I_K + 1 - \delta) - I_Y(I_K - S_K)\big)$$

$$= \frac{\delta - I_K}{2\alpha_0} > 0.$$

$$(4.3.106)$$

It follows that for $\alpha > \alpha_0$ the eigenvalues have a modulus larger than one, i.e., the fixed point is unstable. Therefore, a Hopf bifurcation occurs at $\alpha = \alpha_0$.[63] Without inspecting the coefficients of a specific third-order Taylor expansion of (4.3.101), again nothing can be said about the stability of the closed orbit. As was pointed out by Benhabib/Miyao (1981), there may however also arise some interest in the case of subcritical bifurcation, i.e., when the orbit is repelling: For initial points inside the circle, the corresponding fixed points $x^*(\alpha)$ are attractive. The circle thus can be interpreted as a boundary for all points which initiate a return of the system to its equilibrium path. Initial points

---

[63] It has been taken for granted that the iterations λ^n keep being conjugate complex roots.

outside the circle, however, will lead to an explosion of the system. This corresponds qualitatively to the notion of *corridor stability* introduced by Leijonhufvud (1973).

The Hopf bifurcation in discrete-time models has become popular in non-linear business cycle theory during the last years. For example, Cugno/Montrucchio (1984) studied a discrete version of Goodwin's predator-prey model, augmented by a mark-up pricing relation. An overlapping generations model with production can be found in Reichlin (1985). The overlapping generations model is considered a reasonable framework for deriving dynamic styructures of an economy from optimizing behavior in a general equilibrium context. While most dynamic general equilibrium models concentrate on the local or global stability properties of almost always unique equilibria, Reichlin's model demonstrates that the presence of non-linearities can imply periodic behavior of equilibrium solutions even in a standard neoclassical framework. A similar model is studied in Farmer (1986). Semmler (1987) detected the presence of closed orbits in a modification of Minsky's (1957) model of financial crises.

The well-known fact that discrete-time systems behave in a significantly different manner than continuous-time systems is apparant once again in the two economically equivalent versions of the Kaldor model with respect to the different bifurcation values. From a formal point of view, it is thus important to stress that in practical applications the numerically calculated bifurcation values refer genuinely to the model at hand. Approximations of a continuous-time system by a discrete one, or vice versa, may lead to an at least quantitatively different behavior. This will become more evident in the following sections dealing with chaotic motions because in that case a qualitatively different dynamic behavior may arise.

Chapter 5

Complex Motion in Business Cycle Models

The models described in the preceding chapters have been analyzed by means of mathematical techniques which belong to the nowadays standard and basic knowledge in the theory of dynamical systems. While the Poincaré-Bendixson theorem, the special features of the van der Pol equation or the Liénard equation etc. have been used for a fairly long time especially in engineering problems, it is the introduction of these concepts into economics which is relatively new. In this sense, it may be appropriate to label the techniques used in Chapter 4 as *classical* methods.

While during the first half of the century oscillation phenomena received mainly the attention of engineers alone, especially in electric circuit devices, a tremendous effort has been made by mathematicians and scientists since the mid-1960s to gain new insights into dynamical systems beyond the classically known features and to uncover new applications of dynamical systems theory in different branches of science. Forced by the intensive and steadily increasing usage of high-speed, large-scale computers, it was discovered that a large variety of dynamic phenomena exists in addition to those which could be dealt with using classic techniques. Furthermore, practical problems in different fields made it evident that the mathematical theory of dynamical systems was rather unsatisfactory. Problems such as phase transitions in laser devices in physics, the morphogenesis in biology and chemistry, thermodynamic phenomena far from equilibrium in chemistry, or turbulences in physics and meteorology could not be analyzed by means of standard methods. Inspired by E.N.Lorenz's pioneering work on turbulences in meteorology and R.Thom's work on morphogenesis, a revival of, for example, the mathematical field of differential topology was initiated, which by no means can be considered satisfactorily completed. Despite this open character of modern dynamical systems theory whose scientific route in the future is unclear, the outcomes of the theory such as the intensification of bifurcation theory, the catastrophe theory, synergetics, or chaos theory can also be viewed as having a potentially substantial influence on the analysis of economic dynamics and business cycle theory. Although in many cases it is not possible to apply the techniques introduced, for example, in physics directly to economics as well, these new methods at least show how restrictive the concentration on the usual methods in common business cycle theory has been in face of the large variety of possible complex behaviors.

As the mathematical apparatus of these new developments encloses a great number of definitions, theorems, and concepts, it would be far beyond the scope of this book and beyond the capabilities of the authors to provide a satisfactory mathematical overview. Rather, the basic ideas will be illustrated and those features stressed which are important for an economist concentrating on the technical usefulness of a mathematical theory in economic analysis.

5.1. Non-Linearities and Chaotic Movements

Starting with E.N. Lorenz' work on turbulences in fluids, one property of non-linear dynamical systems has received the attention of many scientists, which was coined *chaotic* or *irregular* movement.[1] For a long time the observable irregular and inharmonic time series of actual variables under consideration were roughly interpreted by the construction of models with basically regular and harmonic time paths on which exogenous stochastic influences were superimposed. In many cases it has not even been possible to construct such harmonic bases in the case of high complexities and unknown number of possibly important factors influencing the outcome. Often the best that can be done is to provide a stochastic description alone.

While this dilemma still exists in many practical studies which are confronted with highly complex actual time series, the discovery of chaotic properties of certain non-linear systems has shed another light on some irregularities. It has been discovered that dynamical systems, which are absolutely deterministic with respect to the numerical specification of the functions and hence the outcome at every point in time, may be able to generate time series which appear to be indistinguishable from pure random

---

[1] *Introductions to chaotic dynamics can be found in Ott (1981), Schuster (1984), and Thompson/Stewart (1986). Surveys with an emphasis on economic applications are contained in Chen (1988), Grandmont/Malgrange (1986), Kelsey (1988), and Lorenz (1989).*

numbers. Furthermore, these time series may be crucially dependent on the initial values of the variables and the numerical specification of the parameters. Arbitrarily small deviations of two initial values or small variations in the parameters can lead to completely different time paths.

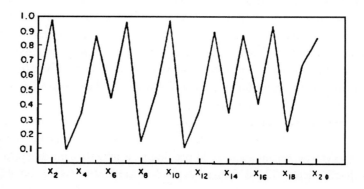

A Chaotic Time Series
Source: Li/Yorke (1975), p. 985
Figure 5.1

Figure 5.1 gives an example of a chaotic time series.[2] A trajectory will be called *chaotic in the Li/Yorke sense* if the following three properties hold:[3]

i) Every possible trajectory of a dynamical system moves arbitrarily close to every other one.

ii) No matter how close two distinct trajectories may come to each other, they must eventually move away.

iii) Even if a trajectory approximates a cycle of order k for a while, it must move away from that cycle.

If, in addition, two different but arbitrarily close initial points imply a divergence of the associated trajectories, i.e., if the dynamical system is *sensitive to initial conditions*, the dynamical system is said to be *chaotic*.

It is obvious that this irregular behavior of some dynamical systems also has some relevance to economics. If it cannot be excluded that a non-linear economic model under consideration has a chaotic regime for certain parameter values, then the relevance

---

[2] *The figure pictures a trajectory of the "logistic" equation, which will be presented below.*

[3] *See Day (1982), p. 408.*

of longer-term prognostications based on econometric estimation may be seriously restricted. From a practical point of view it is impossible to determine the exact initial values of all variables or the exact values of all estimated parameters; minor variations in these values can imply completely different time paths within the chaotic regime after some periods. Even the given accuracy of different computational devices may lead to drastic divergences after a few periods.

Most existing economic models dealing with the chaos property are discrete-time models that can be reduced to a one-dimensional dynamical system. The two-dimensional case is already much more difficult to handle, and only a few economic examples exist in this case. However, chaos does not only occur in discrete-time models, but may be a property of continuous-time models as well, in which the introduction of notions such as *strange attractors* plays an essential role.

5.1.1. Chaos in Discrete-Time Models

Consider the dynamical system

$$x_{t+1} = f(x_t, \mu); \quad x_t \in \mathbf{R}; \quad \mu \in \mathbf{R}, \tag{5.1.1}$$

with x_t as the value of the endogenous variable in period t and μ as an exogenously given parameter. The most popular contribution to chaotic dynamics stems from May (1976), who concentrated on the following special form of (5.1.1):

$$x_{t+1} = \mu x_t(1 - x_t), \quad x_t \in [0,1], \quad \mu \in [0,4]. \tag{5.1.2}$$

Equation (5.1.2) is the so-called *logistic equation*.

The logistic equation possesses a single extremum, and its graph is therefore called a *one-humped curve*. By increasing the parameter μ the graph of (5.1.2) is stretched upward. For all $\mu \in [0,4]$, the interval $[0,1]$ of the state variable x is mapped onto itself.[4] Figures 5.2.a and 5.2.b show two examples of the logistic equation for different values of μ.

The stationary equilibria (or fixed points) of (5.1.2), *i.e.*, the values of the state variable x for which $x_{t-1} = x_t = x_{t+1} \forall t$, are determined by the intersection of the graph of (5.1.2) and the 45^0-line. In addition to the origin as the trivial equilibrium point a second stationary equilibrium exists at

$$x^* = 1 - \frac{1}{\mu}. \tag{5.1.3}$$

---

[4] For $\mu > 4$ the extremum of (5.1.2) at $x_t = 0.5$ would be larger than $x_{t+1} = 1$.

For $\mu < 1$ the second equilibrium is negative and therefore does not belong to the admissible $x_t \in [0,1]$. For $\mu = 1$ the equilibrium coincides with the origin. These two cases will not be considered in the following. If $\mu > 1$, the second positive equilibrium point increases when μ is increased.

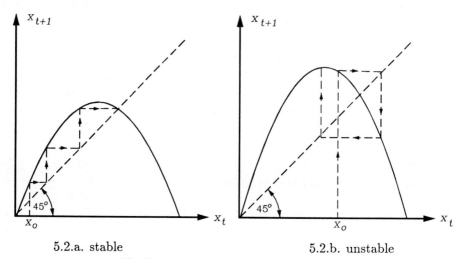

5.2.a. stable   5.2.b. unstable

The Logistic Equation for Different μ

Figure 5.2

As is well-known, the stability of a fixed point depends on the slope of $f(x_t)$ evaluated at x^*: the fixed point is stable as long as the slope of $f(x_t)$ is absolutely smaller than one. With

$$\frac{df(x_t)}{dx_t}\bigg|_{x=x^*} = \mu(1 - 2x^*) = 2 - \mu, \qquad (5.1.4)$$

it follows that the non-trivial fixed point is locally stable if $\mu \in (1,3)$.

The question arises of what happens when μ is increased beyond $\mu = 3$ and the equilibrium becomes unstable. Consider the so-called *second iterative* of equation (5.1.2), i.e., the map

$$f^2: \quad x_{t+2} = f(x_{t+1}) = f(f(x_t)) = f^2(x_t), \qquad (5.1.5)$$

which means that the mapping (5.1.2) has to be applied twice:

$$x_{t+2} = \mu(x_{t+1} - x_{t+1}^2) \quad \text{and} \quad x_{t+1} = \mu(x_t - x_t^2)$$

$$\Longrightarrow x_{t+2} = \mu(\mu(x_t - x_t^2) - \mu^2(x_t - x_t^2)^2). \qquad (5.1.6)$$

Figures 5.3.a and 5.3.b illustrate two graphs of the map f^2 for different μ. The graphs are characterized by three extrema; the inner extremum is stretched downward and the two outer extrema are stretched upward when μ is increased .

Depending on the value of the parameter μ one or three intersections with the 45^0-line are possible. First consider the case of a single point of intersection (cf. Figure 5.3.a). This fixed point of the second iterative is again stable as long as $|df^2(x_t)/dx_t| < 1$. In other words, if this fixed point is stable, it must be met every second period when transients have died out. However, as there is no other fixed point (point of intersection), and as this point corresponds with an intersection of the graph of the first iterative and the 45^0-line, it is also a fixed point of the first iterative. Figure 5.3.a is therefore just another presentation of the scenario of a stable fixed point depicted in Figure 5.2.a.

When μ is increased, three points of intersection of the graph of (5.1.6) and the 45^0-line will eventually emerge (cf. Figure 5.3.b). The former stable fixed point will loose its stability because the slope of f^2 will be greater than 1. At the two newly emerging fixed points the slope of f^2 will be absolutely smaller than unity. These fixed points of the map f^2 (or *fixed points of order 2*) will then be stable. This kind of stability still has to be interpreted. Consider a single point of intersection. This fixed point will be met every second period. But this is true for the second stable fixed point as well. It follows that the trajectory jumps between the two points of intersection from period to period. The stable equilibrium constellation consists therefore in a permanent switching between two values. In the following such a situation will be called a *period-2 cycle*.

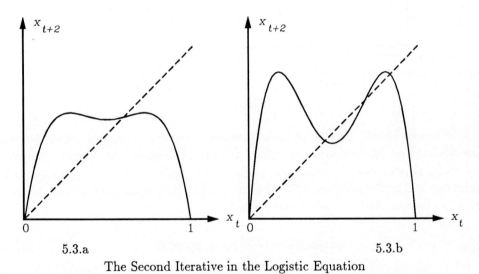

5.3.a   5.3.b

The Second Iterative in the Logistic Equation

Figure 5.3

If the parameter μ is increased even further, the slopes of f^2 will be absolutely larger than 1 evaluated at the two components of the period-2 cycle. The cycle will then become unstable. Each of the two period-2 fixed points bifurcates into two new stable fixed points and an unstable fixed point. Together with the unstable fixed point of the first iterative, seven fixed points therefore exist when the period-2 cycle looses its stability. The four stable fixed points form a period-4 cycle, *i.e.*, they are fixed points of the fourth iterative f^4.

The period of the cycle has doubled, and the afore mentioned bifurcation is therefore called a *period-doubling bifurcation*. Ongoing increases in the parameter μ will lead to successive period-doubling bifurcations. After n period-doubling bifurcations, a stable cycle with period 2^n exists. An illustration of this bifurcation behavior is depicted in Figure 5.4. Stable fixed points are located on the solid lines, while points on the dashed lines represent unstable fixed points.

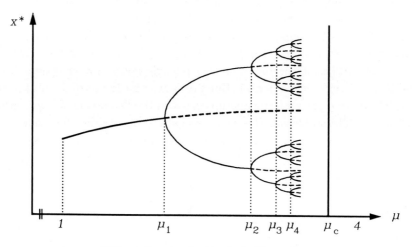

Bifurcation in the Logistic Equation
Figure 5.4

It can be shown that the distance between successive parameter values for which period-doubling bifurcations occur diminishes when μ is increased. In fact, there exists an accumulation point μ_c where the period of the cycle converges to infinity: it was demonstrated by Feigenbaum (1978) that the series of period-doubling bifurcation values of μ can be described by the following rule:[5]

$$\lim_{n \to \infty} \left(\frac{\mu_n - \mu_{n-1}}{\mu_{n+1} - \mu_n} \right) = \delta \approx 4.6692\ldots \tag{5.1.7}$$

where the number δ is called the *Feigenbaum number*. As δ is a constant, the sequence $\{\mu_n\}$ converges to a finite value. Thus, by increasing μ, the fixed points of period 2^n accumulate at a critical value μ_c. For the mapping (5.1.2) this critical value is approximately $\mu_c = 3.575$. For $\mu > \mu_c$, the situation changes drastically. Each of the

---

[5] *Cf. Collet/Eckmann (1980), p. 37.*

formerly stable fixed points has become unstable. Furthermore, for $\mu > \mu_c$ there are an infinite number of fixed points with different periods and an uncountable number of initial values x_o whose trajectories are aperiodic, *i.e.*, the trajectory never repeats itself. The interesting property of the fixed points is that odd periods can also occur now, which, however, appear only when μ is sufficiently larger than μ_c. A numerically exact plot of the bifurcations in the logistic equation is given in Figure 5.5.

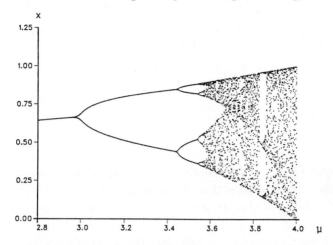

Numerical Plot of the Bifurcation in the Logistic Equation
Figure 5.5

Period-3 cycles play a dominant role in several mathematical theorems. The most popular result for one-dimensional discrete-time systems was provided by Li/Yorke (1975).[6]

Theorem 5.1   (Li/Yorke)

Let $J \subset \mathbf{R}$ be an interval and let $F : J \rightarrow J$ be continuous. Assume there is a point $a \in J$ for which the points $b = F(a)$, $c = F^2(a)$, and $d = F^3(a)$ satisfy

$$d \leq a < b < c \quad (\text{or} \quad d \geq a > b > c)$$

then

    i) for every $k = 1, 2, \ldots$ there is a periodic point in J having period k.

Furthermore,

---

[6] *Li/Yorke (1975), p. 987.*

ii) there is an uncountable set $S \subset J$ (containing no periodic points), which
satisfy the following conditions:

A) For every $p, q \in S$ with $p \neq q$

$$\limsup_{n \to \infty} |\ F^n(p) - F^n(q)\ | > 0$$

and

$$\liminf_{n \to \infty} |\ F^n(p) - F^n(q)\ | = 0.$$

B) For every $p \in S$ and periodic point $q \in J$,

$$\limsup_{n \to \infty} |\ F^n(p) - F^n(q)\ | > 0$$

The statement of the theorem corresponds with the verbal definition of chaos in the
sense of Li/Yorke (1975) mentioned above. By noting that the existence of a periodic
point with period three implies that the assumption $d \leq a < b < c$ will be fulfilled
somewhere, it is thus indeed possible to face chaos as soon as a period-3 point has been
detected.

The following theorem helps in understanding the complex behavior of discrete dynamical systems:[7]

Theorem 5.2   (Sarkovskii)

Consider the following ordering of all positive integers:

$$1 \prec 2 \prec 4 \prec 8 \prec 16 \ldots \prec 2^k \prec 2^{k+1} \prec \ldots$$

$$\ldots \ldots$$

$$\ldots \prec 2^{k+1}(2n+1) \prec 2^{k+1}(2n-1) \prec \ldots \prec 2^{k+1}5 \prec 2^{k+1}3 \prec \ldots$$

$$\ldots \prec 2^k(2n+1) \prec 2^k(2n-1) \prec \ldots \prec 2^k5 \prec 2^k3 \prec \ldots$$

$$\ldots \ldots$$

$$\ldots \prec 2(2n+1) \prec 2(2n-1) \prec \ldots \prec 2 \cdot 5 \prec 2 \cdot 3 \prec \ldots$$

$$\ldots \prec (2n+1) \prec (2n-1) \prec \ldots \prec 9 \prec 7 \prec 5 \prec 3.$$

If f is a continuous map of an interval into itself with a period p and $q \prec p$ in
this ordering, then f has a periodic point of period q.

---

[7] *Cf. Guckenheimer/Holmes (1983), p. 311.*

This special ordering of all integers deserves closer consideration. All odd integers starting with the number 3 have received the highest ranks, followed by all integers which can be expressed as an odd number times 2, 2^2, 2^3, etc. Finally, all integers which can be expressed as 2^n, $(n = 0, ..., \infty)$, have received the lowest ranks. Consider an arbitrary integer in this ordering. For example, if this number is 4, then the theorem implies that a mapping with a periodic point of period 4 also has a periodic point of period 2 and a periodic point of period 1.[8] If there is a periodic point of period m, where m can be expressed as the product of an odd number and 2^k, then there are periodic points of all lower orders. For example, a periodic point of period 20 implies the existence of all periodic points of even period. As soon as a period-three cycle has been detected, it follows that, according to the theorem, there are periodic points with every possible period.

It has to be stressed that the Li/Yorke theorem only provides a statement on the *existence* of aperiodic points and cycles of arbitrary order. However, for a certain $\mu > \mu_c$, μ_c given by the map in question, there is at most one stable period for many maps, which attracts nearly all initial points.[9] Then the dynamical system is not sensitively dependent on initial conditions. Thus, while for a special function and certain parameters the existence of aperiodic motions can be deduced theoretically, they may be numerically unobservable because only very few initial values lead to time paths which behave in that fashion through time. For practical economic problems, however, this may not be particularly important. Even if a stable periodic orbit exists, the convergence to that orbit may take so much time that it cannot be observed with the life span of an economist. In addition, existence of chaotic, aperiodic solutions are not the only non-linear phenomena which affect practical economics. According to Sarkovskii's theorem, the existence of a period-three cycle implies the existence of periodic solutions of all orders, which may be very large and essentially indistinguishable from aperiodic solutions.[10]

The preceding discussion of the dynamic behavior in the logistic equation is relevant because of a universal property of a family of one-dimensional maps: it was demonstrated by Feigenbaum (1978) that the special period-doubling behavior of (5.1.2) is generic in one-humped curves. The bifurcation values in different algebraic forms of (5.1.1) follow the same rule (5.1.7) as the logistic equation. The Feigenbaum number is

---

[8] *Alternatively, a period-4 point does not necessarily imply the existence of a period-8 point, which is ranked higher in this ordering.*

[9] *A proof that equation (5.1.2) has exactly one stable periodic orbit for every value of μ can be found in Guckenheimer et al. (1977), pp. 140-142. If there is a single stable periodic cycle, the (Lebesgue) measure of those points which do not converge to the stable periodic orbit is zero in that case (cf. Collet/Eckmann (1980), p.13).*

[10] *See also the discussion between Melese/Transue (1986) and Day (1986).*

therefore called a *universal constant*.[11]

5.1.2. Chaos and Business Cycles

The logistic equation with its distinguished dynamics described above belongs to the best-understood non-linear dynamical systems. Most economic examples of chaotic motion therefore concentrate on one-dimensional discrete-time systems. It was shown, for example, by Benhabib/Day (1981), Day (1982, 1983), Day/Shafer (1986), Gabisch (1984, 1985), Gaertner (1986), Grandmont (1985), Pohjola (1981), Stutzer (1980), and Woodford (1988) that chaotic motion can easily be generated in appropriately specified economic models. In the following, three examples of chaotic motion will be outlined which can now be called the prototype models of economic chaos.

Day (1982) reconsidered the standard neoclassical growth model, which in discrete time and assuming that the capital stock exists for exactly one period is expressed as[12]

$$Y_t = C_t + I_t$$
$$I_t = K_{t+1}$$
$$C_t = (1 - s)Y_t \qquad (5.1.8)$$
$$Y_t = F(K_t, L_t)$$
$$L_t = (1 + n)^t L_o$$

with the usual meaning of the symbols and n as the constant growth rate of the population. Provided that the production function is linear-homogeneous, the model reduces to

$$\frac{K_{t+1}}{L_t} = sF(K_t, L_t)/L_t$$
$$k_{t+1}(1 + n) = sf(k_t) \qquad (5.1.9)$$
$$k_{t+1} = sf(k_t)/(1 + n)$$

with $k_t = K_t/L_t$ as the capital-labor ratio.

As is well-known from the theoretical growth literature, the equilibrium growth path is asymptotically stable for a constant savings ratio and the usual properties of the production function. The question arises whether the difference equation (5.1.9) can be transformed into a one-humped logistic equation by modifying the genuine model (5.1.8), e.g., by a variable k-dependent savings rate or a modified production function. Of the several examples provided by Day (1982), the following one is chosen.

---

[11] *Compare also v. Trotha (1985).*

[12] *Though Day does not mention this deviation from standard neoclassical growth theory, the additional assumption is necessary to obtain the results presented below.*

Suppose that the production function can be described by

$$\frac{Y_t}{L_t} = Bk_t^\beta (m - k_t)^\gamma, \quad k_t \leq m = \text{constant}. \tag{5.1.10}$$

The component Bk_t^β is clearly a Cobb-Douglas-type element with $\beta \in (0, 1]$. The term $(m - k_t)^\gamma$ may be interpreted as the influence of pollution caused by an increasing k. With γ being small, $(m - k)^\gamma$ is close to unity for small values of k and falls to zero when k approaches m. Replacing $f(k_t)$ in (5.1.9) by (5.1.10) yields

$$k_{t+1} = \frac{sBk_t^\beta (m - k_t)^\gamma}{(1 + n)} = g(k_t), \tag{5.1.11}$$

and it is obvious that for $\beta = \gamma = m = 1$, (5.1.11) reduces to

$$k_{t+1} = \frac{sBk_t(1 - k_t)}{(1 + n)}, \tag{5.1.12}$$

which is formally identical to the logistic equation (5.1.2) with $\mu = sB/(1+n)$. Hence, it includes the possible occurrence of chaos for the appropriately chosen parameter values.

The more general form (5.1.11), however, can still be analyzed: Denote $\tilde{k}$ as that capital-labor ratio which maximizes (5.1.11), i.e.,

$$\frac{dk_{t+1}}{dk_t} = \frac{sB}{1 + n}\left(\beta k_t^{\beta-1}(m - k_t)^\gamma - k_t^\beta \gamma (m - k_t)^{\gamma-1}\right) = 0$$

$$\Longrightarrow \frac{\beta k_t^\beta (m - k_t)^\gamma}{k_t} = k_t^\beta \gamma \frac{(m - k_t)^\gamma}{m - k_t} \tag{5.1.13}$$

$$\Longrightarrow \tilde{k} = \frac{\beta m}{\gamma + \beta}.$$

Further, let k^c be the result of the backward iteration $k^c = g^{-1}(\tilde{k})$. By inspecting Figure 5.6 it can be seen that if $\tilde{k} < k^*$, where k^* denotes a steady-state fixed point, k^c will be smaller than $\tilde{k}$.

The parameters B, s, or n play essentially the same role as μ in the basic logistic equation (5.1.2). By increasing B, the graph of (5.1.11) is stretched upward. Consider the iteration of $\tilde{k}$: $g(\tilde{k}) = sB/(1 + n)\tilde{k}^\beta(m - \tilde{k})^\gamma$ and let k^m denote the maximal attainable capital-labor ratio, i.e., the intersection of the graph of (5.1.11) with the abscissa. A steady increase of B will eventually lead to $g(\tilde{k}) = k^m$. With $g(k^m) = 0$, it can easily be seen that the requirements of the Li/Yorke theorem are satisfied:

$$0 < k^c < \tilde{k} < k^m$$

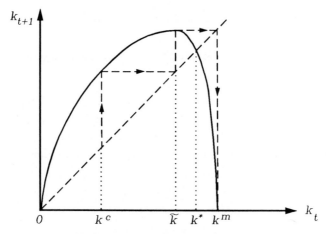

A Neoclassical Growth Model

Figure 5.6

$$\Rightarrow g(k^m) < k^c < g(k^c) < g(\tilde{k})$$

$$\Rightarrow g^3(k^c) < k^c < g(k^c) < g^2(k^c).$$

Thus, with appropriately chosen parameters for (5.1.11), there may be chaotic trajectories in this simple modified neoclassical growth model. Obviously, this result relies heavily on the postulated production function so that the model should be viewed as an exercise in finding the simplest examples of chaos in dynamic economic models. Other possible modifications of (5.1.8) leading to chaos include introducing a variable savings rate $s(k_t)$ or considering restricted growth.

Another example of chaotic motion can be found in Stutzer (1980), who demonstrates that transforming a continuous-time model into a discrete-time model can imply a change in a model's dynamic behavior. Instead of a constant, exogenously given population growth rate, it is assumed that this rate depends positively on per capita output:

$$\frac{N_{t+1} - N_t}{N_t} = a_1 - \frac{a_2 N_t}{Y_t}. \tag{5.1.14}$$

Together with a Cobb-Douglas-type production function

$$Y_t = a_3 N_t^\alpha, \quad \alpha \in [0,1], \tag{5.1.15}$$

(5.1.14) yields the non-linear one-dimensional difference equation:

$$N_{t+1} = a_1 N_t - \frac{a_2 N_t^2}{a_3 N_t^\alpha} + N_t$$

$$= N_t(1 + a_1 - \frac{a_2 N_t^{1-\alpha}}{a_3}). \tag{5.1.16}$$

A coordinate change $N_t = (a_3(1 + a_1)/a_2)^{1/(1-\alpha)} x_t$ leads to

$$x_{t+1} = (1 + a_1)x_t(1 - x_t^{1-\alpha}), \qquad (5.1.17)$$

which is equivalent to the logistic equation for $\alpha = 0$. The graph of (5.1.17) is again a one-humped curve for which a period-three cycle can be detected if the parameter a_1 is increased sufficiently. Hence, according to the Li/Yorke theorem or to Sarkovskii's theorem, there are aperiodic solutions for a_1 above a critical value.

The dynamical system (5.1.16), respectively (5.1.17), is a discrete-time version of Haavelmo's (1956) growth cycle model

$$\dot{N} = a_1 N - a_2 \frac{N^{2-\alpha}}{K}. \qquad (5.1.18)$$

Equation (5.1.18) is a version of a *Bernoulli differential equation* and exhibits monotonic convergence toward an equilibrium. Different time concepts can therefore involve drastically different kinds of dynamical behavior.

An example of an economic model with possibly chaotic dynamics, which does not rely heavily on arbitrary *ad-hoc* assumptions, was constructed by Grandmont (1985), who studied the dynamics of an overlapping generations model with perfect foresight.[13] The analysis is of particular importance because it demonstrates what kind of assumptions are necessary in constructing sound optimization processes in order to generate chaotic dynamics even in the analytically simplest case of perfect foresight. While not being a business cycle model in the macroeconomic sense of this book, the paper is relevant because it implictly reveals that it may be misleading to concentrate only on stability properties of stationary states: general equilibrium models may be characterized by complex motion.

Consider a standard overlapping-generations model[14] with two generations. Via savings decisions, the members of the young generation are making plans concerning the consumption in both the first and the second period of their life. As is well-known, the current consumption decisions of the young do not depend only on the current but also on the expected prices in the second period. Individuals are said to have perfect foresight if they anticipate future prices correctly, i.e., $p_{t+1} = p_{t+1,t}^e$, with p_{t+1} as the actual price in period $t + 1$ and $p_{t+1,t}^e$ as the price in that period expected in t. In order to make economic sense, perfect foresight expectations have to be the outcome of some kind of adaptation to a repeating pattern. The Rational Expectations literature usually refers to the unique, stationary, long-run equilibrium such that expectations are

---

[13] *Chaos in an overlapping-generations model was studied first by Benhabib/Day (1982), who introduced wealth in the utility function.*

[14] *See, e.g., Diamond (1965) and Samuelson (1958).*

stationary themselves. The effects of this structural assumption are demonstrated in Chapter 3. Suppose on the contrary that prices have displayed periodic behavior in the past with a sufficiently low periodicity. Perfect foresight expectations can then be justified when individuals have detected the periodicity of the time series of, for example, prices by learning. Suppose that these oscillating perfect foresight expectations exist. Then it can be shown that the overlapping-generations model is able to generate backward dynamics[15] which have led to correct and fulfilling expectations. The essential ingredients of the model that lead to cyclical behavior are the counteracting wealth and intertemporal substitution effects of a change in $p_t/p^e_{t+1,t}$. It can be shown that the offer curve of the individuals is represented by a backward-bending curve with suitable assumptions concerning the concavity of the utility functions.[16] It can further be shown that by introducing a parameter which expresses the old traders' risk aversion, the offer curves can be stretched such that period-three cycles emerge, which according to Sarkovskii's theorem imply the existence of cycles of all orders. The Rational Expectations approach to business cycles, of which the perfect foresight hypothesis is the extreme version, thus refers not only to stationary states with the usual exogenous shocks, but also encludes the case of endogenous cycles derived from optimizing behavior. However, some objections raised against the Rational Expectations approach still remain valid in this endogenous cycle model, namely that the model is basically an equilibrium model with no explicit price adjustment mechanism, that individuals must have a precise idea of the model of the economy, etc. Furthermore, the dynamics are essentially backward dynamics, implying that no statement on the relevant development of the system in the future can be provided.[17]

5.1.3. Chaos in Higher-Dimensional Systems

The fact that chaos in one-dimensional systems can easily be detected by the Li/Yorke theorem when the required non-linearities are given has led to an increasing number of examples, of which the models presented above are only a small sample. Though these

---

[15] *A backward dynamic time path of a variable is generated when the direction of time is reversed, i.e., the sequence of points $\{x_t\}_{t=0}^{t=-\infty}$ starting at $t = 0$ is considered. Backward dynamics therefore determine the values of the variables in the past which have led to the current values. The reason for this concentration on backward dynamics consists of the fact that the forward mapping, i.e., the usual mapping in dynamical economics, is a two-valued function in Grandmont's model, implying that the forward dynamics are not defined.*

[16] *The offer curve in this model is geometrically equivalent to a one-humped curve like that in Figure 5.5 which is reflected at the 45^0-line.*

[17] *A similar model can be found in Grandmont/Laroque (1985).*

models are usefulness pedagogical demonstrations of how easily chaos may be generated, several objections can be raised concerning the implications of chaos in these models for business cycle theory:

- The dimensional restriction requires either the study of partial economies, which are of little interest in business cycle theory, or the simplification, truncation, or aggregation of appropriate models, which is reminiscent of the bed of Procrustes.

- The typical bell-shaped functions of one-dimensional chaotic systems do not seem to be generic in standard economic models. In most existing models, the bell-shape of the first iterative has been produced by sometimes strong *ad-hoc* assumptions.

- One-dimensional, discrete-time dynamical systems typically display a sawtooth pattern. While this behavior, which is strongly reminiscent of noise, is highly informative because it reveals that seemingly stochastic processes can be generated in deterministic models, the requirements of business cycle models are usually not met. A business cycle model is characterized by time paths of the relevant variables displaying an upward or downward trend for a longer time interval, which in case of discrete-time models consists of several basic periods. One-dimensional models are unable to generate this desired kind of cyclical behavior.

- Finally, it may be argued that the irregular trajectories cannot unambiguously be interpreted as business cycles since the latter are usually considered to be much more regular.

As will be shown below, these objections only partly concern the chaotic dynamics in higher-dimensional systems. Trajectories of higher-dimensional systems can be smooth and can therefore appear to be much more regular than the time-series generated by one-dimensional discrete-time systems. Furthermore, examples of chaotic dynamical systems relying only on weak non-linearities can be provided.

The mathematical theory of chaos in higher-dimensional systems is still in progress and, basically, only little can be conjectured as to where the scientific route will end. Consequently, the economic literature on chaos in higher-dimensional systems is rather meager and it is not definitively clear whether these new developments are really relevant to business cycle theory. Nevertheless, in the following an attempt is made to present a very short overview of the mathematical theory and to outline the very few economic examples. It should not to be stressed that the presentation is far from being complete. Specifically, the concepts will usually only be mentioned and will not be discussed in detail. Rather, the main purpose of this section is to indicate the existence of possible new tools in dynamical economics and to provide incentives for future investigations of irregularly fluctuating economies.

Although it is possible to relate discrete- and continuous-time dynamical systems[18]

---

[18] *Compare, for example, Guckenheimer/ Holmes (1983), Section 1.5. A Poincaré*

via the so-called *Poincaré map*, both concepts will be sketched separately in the following sections.

Discrete-Time Higher-Dimensional Systems

As the Li/Yorke theorem is a very handy tool in establishing the existence of chaos (in the Li/Yorke sense) in one-dimensional systems, the question naturally arises of whether this theorem can be generalized to the *n*-dimensional case. An attempt to generalize the Li/Yorke theorem was provided by Phil Diamond as early as 1976.

Another concept for the detection of chaos in discrete-time systems, which has proven to be us as 1976.

Another concept for the detection of chaos in discrete-time systems, which has proven to be useful as soon as a model is numerically specified, was developed by Marotto (1978). Consider a discrete-time dynamical system

$$x_{t+1} = f(x_t), \quad x \in \mathbf{R^n}, \tag{5.1.19}$$

with a fixed point $x^* = f(x^*)$. A fixed point x^* is called an *expanding fixed point* if the eigenvalues of all points x in a neighborhood $B_r(x^*)$ of the equilibrium have a modulus larger than 1. An initial point located in this neighborhood, i.e., $x \in B_r(x^*)$, will therefore move away from the equilibrium.

Note that this notion of an expanding fixed point does not necessarily imply that a trajectory moves away from x^* everywhere. When $x \notin B_r(x^*)$ for an arbitrary r, the eigenvalues may be less than or equal to 1. Indeed, once a trajectory has reached a point outside $B_r(x^*)$, it is possible that the trajectory jumps back into $B_r(x^*)$ and even onto x^*. In such a case, the equilibrium is called a *snap-back repeller*.

Figure 5.7 illustrates this notion: A trajectory starting arbitrarily close to the fixed point x^*, i.e., at a point x_0 in Figure 5.7, is repelled from this fixed point, but after having left $B_r(x^*)$ suddenly jumps back to hit the fixed point exactly.

An interesting property of snap-back repellers was proved by Marotto:

Theorem 5.3   Marotto (1978)

If f possesses a snap-back repeller, then (5.1.19) is chaotic.

The definition of chaos used by Marotto is essentially the same as Li/Yorke's definition in **R**. The emphasis is placed on the existence of aperiodic motion and not on the sensitive dependence on initial conditions.

---

   map is constructed as the series of unidirectional intersection points of a flow and a cross-section.

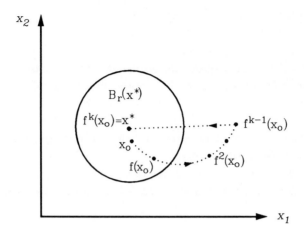

A Snap-Back Repeller
Figure 5.7

The advantage of Marotto's concept consists of the fact that it can be relatively easily handled once the model under investigation is numerically specified: by regarding the backward iteratives starting at equilibrium, chaos has been established as soon as that trajectory enters the ball $B_r(x^*)$ again with r numerically calculated before such that x^* is an expanding fixed point.

Herrmann (1986) was able to detect such a snap-back repeller in a version of the Kaldor model, which has been extensively discussed in the preceding sections:

$$\Delta Y_{t+1} = \alpha\big(I(Y_t, K_t) + C(Y_t) - Y_t\big)$$
$$\Delta K_{t+1} = I(Y_t, K_t) - \delta K_t. \tag{5.1.20}$$

The equilibrium is assumed to be unstable, *i.e.*, the modulus of the eigenvalues is larger than one. For nonequilibrium values of (Y_t, K_t) the eigenvalues decrease when the system moves away from the stationary state. It can be shown that the modulus will eventually become smaller than one when (Y_t, K_t) lie outside a circle with radius r around the equilibrium.[19] It has to be noted, however, that the result of any numerical example cannot be generalized to hold for the entire range of parameter values in a certain model. The concept of snap-back repellers requires a separate numerical study for each numerical specification of a model.

---

[19] *The numerical procedure makes use of a backward iteration technique: the equilibrium point is iterated backwards. When the backward iteration leaves the circle and returns to a small neighborhood of the equilibrium, a snap-back repeller exists.*

Continuous-Time Higher-Dimensional Systems

While chaos in discrete-time systems may already occur in one-dimensional systems, a minimal dimension of $n = 3$ is required in continuous-time systems in order to encounter irregular behavior.[20] Naturally, the study of three-dimensional continuous-time models has received most attention in dynamical systems theory.

The following passages attempt only to outline some concepts of chaos in these continuous-time systems[21] and concentrate on those results which may have some potential relevance to business cycle theory.

The essential notion in an investigation of chaos in continuous-time models is that of a *strange attractor*. Out of several different definitions, the following seems to be the most comprehensive one:

Definition 5.1   (Ruelle (1979))

Consider the n-dimensional dynamical system

$$\dot{x} = f(x, \mu), \quad x \in \mathbf{R^n}, \quad \mu \in \mathbf{R}. \tag{5.1.21}$$

A bounded set $A \subset \mathbf{R^n}$ is a *strange attractor* for (5.1.21) if there is a set U with the following properties:

i) U is an n-dimensional neighborhood of A.

ii) For every initial point $x(0) \in U$, the points $x(t)$ remain in U for all $t > 0$; the trajectory starting at $x(0)$ becomes and stays as close to A as one wants for t large enough. This means that A is *attracting*.

iii) There is a sensitive dependence on initial conditions when $x(0)$ is in U, i.e., small variations of the initial value $x(0)$ lead to essentially different trajectories after a short time. This makes A a *strange* attractor.

iv) The attractor is indecomposable, i.e., it cannot be split into two different attractors.

The existence of a strange attractor in a continuous-time dynamical system implies chaos, i.e., highly irregular behavior. Figure 5.8 shows the *Lorenz attractor*, investigated

---

[20] *This follows directly from the Poincaré-Bendixson theorem, which implies that the most complex behavior of a planar system consists of limit cycles. Compare Guckenheimer/Holmes (1983), p. 50f. and Lichtenberg/Liebermann (1982), p. 383, fn.1. Recall also the fact that in planar systems trajectories cannot intersect, which implies a regular behavior.*

[21] *See Rössler (1977) for an overview and a categorization of chaos in three- and four-dimensional systems.*

by the meteorologist E.N.Lorenz(1963), which nowadays serves as a prototype model for a continuous-time chaotic system. The time-paths of the dynamical system are irregular because every time the trajectory enters the region where the two wings come together, the system is highly sensitive to the very exact position: an observer cannot *a priori* decide to which of the two wings of the attractor the trajectory will move.

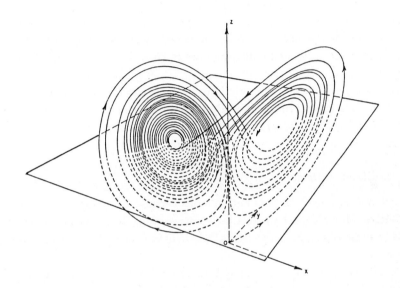

The Lorenz Attractor
Source: Guckenheimer/Holmes (1983), p.95
Figure 5.8

The discovery of strange attractors in different dynamical systems has been a major focus of research in dynamical systems theory during the last decade. Business cycle theory as one of the most important economic fields for applying dynamical systems theory should therefore be potentially interested in results on these complex dynamics. As long as the algebraic structure is not precisely specified, however, it is usually difficult to provide sufficient conditions for the occurrence of strange attractors. Only a few particular families of dynamical systems exist which are known to possess the capability of generating chaotic dynamics under certain conditions. Two families of dynamical systems seem to be particularly relevant for business cycle theory.

i) *Coupled Oscillator Systems:*

Consider an n-dimensional continuous-time system

$$\dot{x} = f(x); \qquad x \in \mathbf{R}^n. \tag{5.1.22}$$

If (5.1.22) allows for oscillatory behavior the diffential equation is said to be an *oscillator*. It was demonstrated in Chapter 4 that non-linear two-dimensional systems can only have stable or unstable equilibria or limit cycles.

A dynamical system is called a *coupled oscillator system* if it can be written as

$$\begin{aligned} \dot{x} &= f(x, y) \\ \dot{y} &= g(x, y) \end{aligned} \; ; \quad x, y \in \mathbf{R}^n, \tag{5.1.23}$$

i.e., the motion in the two subsystems is influenced by the motion in the other subsystems. If at least three subsystems like the ones in (5.1.22) are coupled, chaotic motion can result.

Economic examples of coupled oscillator systems can be found in Goodwin (1947) in a study of interdependent markets, in Puu (1987) with an example from international trade, and in Larsen/Mosekilde/Rasmussen/Sterman (1988) in an investigation of long-run business cycles. A survey is contained in Lorenz (1989).

ii) *Forced Oscillator Systems:*

A dynamical system like (5.1.21) is autonomous because time does not enter the equations explicitly. Though most models in business cycle theory are constructed in the framework of these autonomous systems, the behavior of certain models depends explicitly on time.

Let (5.1.21) be a two-dimensional system and write it as a second-order differential equation, *i.e.*,

$$\ddot{x} + g(x)\dot{x} + h(x) = 0. \tag{5.1.24}$$

An oscillator is called a *forced oscillator* when (5.1.24) is turned into

$$\ddot{x} + g(x)\dot{x} + h(x) = k(t), \tag{5.1.25}$$

with $k(t)$ as a periodic function, *i.e.*, the endogenous (and permanent) oscillation is periodically disturbed by an exogenous force. If the amplitude of the forcing term is strong and its frequency differs sufficiently from the autonomous system's own frequency, chaotic motion can emerge in the solution of (5.1.25).

Economic examples of forced oscillator systems can be found in Puu (1987) and Lorenz (1989).

5.1.4. Numerical Techniques and the Empirical Evidence of Chaos

The concepts mentioned above allow the existence of chaotic motion to be analytically deduced. In several cases, for example when the difference equation has the form of a one-humped curve, it is possible to apply the Li/Yorke theorem or Sarkovskii's theorem and to establish the existence of chaos. However, in many cases it may be difficult or analytically impossible to detect a period-three cycle, and the question arises whether it is possible to apply numerical methods in investigating irregular behavior. Suppose that for a certain dynamical system a time series has been generated which looks like that in Figure 5.1. Though it is tempting to immediately interpret that series as being chaotic, this conclusion is not justified because the series can be regular with a high period. For example, if this period is m, then the series repeats in exactly the same pattern after m periods of time. Numerical examples show that even for cycles of relatively low period it may be impossible to distinguish regular time series from completely irregular series by simple visual inspection. It is therefore necessary to introduce more sophisticated methods of time series analysis in the investigation of irregular motion.

Power Spectral Analysis

Spectral analysis has proven to be very useful in the analysis of periodic patterns of time series. It is beyond the scope of this book to provide a satisfactory introduction to this subject.[22] We will therefore concentrate only on the interpretations of the results of the appropriate algorithms.[23] For example, consider a sinusoidal motion with a frequency $\tilde{f}$ measured in terms of 2π. A frequency of $\tilde{f} = 1$ means that the length of the cycle is exactly 2π, i.e., there is one complete sinusoidal wave movement in the interval $[0, 2\pi]$. Frequencies with $\tilde{f} \neq 1$ indicate that the cycle has not been completed in $[0, 2\pi]$, i.e., $\tilde{f} < 1$, or that another cycle has already started in $[0, 2\pi]$, i.e., $\tilde{f} > 1$. In spectral analysis a given time series is divided into different harmonic series with different frequencies. For example, if a time series consists of two overlapping harmonic series, spectral analysis attempts to isolate these two harmonic series and to calculate the frequencies involved. Furthermore, spectral analysis provides information on the contribution of each harmonic series to the overall motion, i.e., on whether there are dominating frequencies. Graphically, the results of these spectral-analytical considerations can be illustrated in so-called *power spectrum* diagrams, in which power spectra are plotted against frequencies. A power spectrum can loosely be defined as each frequency's contribution to the overall motion of the time series. For example, if there is no periodic component in a given series, the power spectrum will be a smooth monotonic

---

[22] *See, e.g., Granger/Hatanaka (1964) or König/Wolters (1972) for good surveys.*

[23] *This may especially be justified because several numerical program packages include routines for spectral analysis so that the mathematical details can be neglected at this place.*

curve.[24] If there are frequencies for which the associated values of the power spectrum are significantly higher than for others, spectral analysis indicates the existence of periodic behavior. A single peak in the power spectrum therefore implies the existence of a cycle with the associated frequency in the actual time series under investigation.

The relevance of these considerations for the investigation of irregular behavior is obvious: when a regular series which appears to be irregular is analyzed by this spectral method, the power spectrum displays a peak at a certain frequency. When a time series is considered in which several frequencies (and therefore cycles of different periods) are involved, the power spectrum has several distinguishable peaks at different frequencies. As an irregular or chaotic time series does not possess a dominating frequency, the power spectrum displays peaks at each frequency.

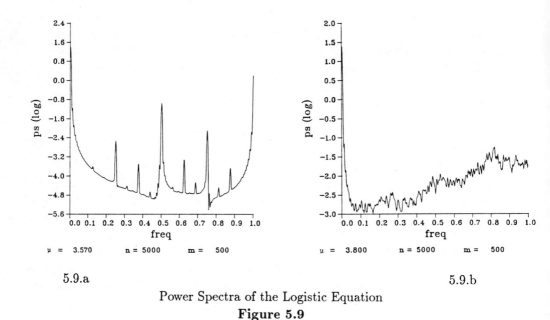

5.9.a   5.9.b

Power Spectra of the Logistic Equation
Figure 5.9

Figures 5.9.a and 5.9.b represent power spectra of the logistic equation for different values of the bifurcation parameter μ.[25] Figure 5.9.a illustrates the power spectrum for a value $\mu < \mu_c$ of the bifurcation parameter. It is evident from Figure 5.4 that the logistic equation is characterized by period doubling when μ is sufficiently close to μ_c. Consequently, the power spectrum exhibits distinguishable peaks at frequencies with

---

[24] *Depending on the particular algorithm this curve will have different shapes. Typically, the power spectrum for non-oscillating time-series is negatively sloped.*

[25] *Frequencies are measured in units of π in both figures.*

equal distance. Figure 5.9.b illustrates the power spectra for μ in the chaotic region. It is obviously impossible to isolate a single frequency which dominates the other ones.

Power spectra are especially useful in investigations of higher-dimensional dynamical systems which usually cannot be examined by analytical methods anymore. However, it may be difficult to distinguish chaotic behavior from complicated but period behavior in these systems, because subharmonics are typically involved which also appear as peaks in the power spectrum.

Lyapunov Exponents and Correlation Dimensions

The calculation of Lyapunov exponents and correlation dimensions represents the standard procedure for detecting chaotic motion in a time series. It is beyond the scope of this book to provide a satisfactory survey of these techniques. Therefore, these concepts will only briefly be described below.[26]

Time series generated by deterministic chaotic dynamical systems possess a particular structure in contrast to time series generated by stochastic processes. The emerging structure is due to two phenomena which are distinguished only for expository purposes:

- Given an arbitrary set of initial points, the geometric region containing these initial points will be stretched in one direction and contracted into another one under the action of the dynamical system, *e.g.*, for a single iteration of a mapping.

- The stretching cannot take place in a single direction for all iterations because the set would quickly contain infinite coordinates. In addition to stretching and contraction, chaotic dynamical systems are thus characterized by a folding of a set of initial conditions.

The stretching, contraction, and folding take place in each period. The first iteration generates a set which is already much more geometrically complicated. After several iterations, the set looks like a wildly twisted object.

Lyapunov exponents are numbers which reflect the stretching and contraction on an attractor in different directions (dimensions). An n-dimensional dynamical system possesses n different Lyapunov exponents. For example, consider a dynamical system with an asymptotically stable equilibrium. The iteration of initial points located in a given set implies that the size of this set shrinks from iteration to iteration. In the limit, the former set of initial points has been mapped to the single equilibrium point by successive iterations. In other words, this former set contracted in every direction.

---

[26] *More information on these concepts and on other numerical techniques can be found in Lorenz (1989), Chapter 5.*

The Lyapunov exponents λ_i of the system are all negative in this case. In fact, when a dynamical system possesses an attractor, for example in the form of a stable single equilibrium point or a stable limit cycle, the sum of the Lyapunov exponents is always negative.

The particular type of an n-dimensional dynamical systems' behavior is determined by the individual Lyapunov exponents λ_i, $i = 1, \ldots, n$. If all exponents are negative, the attractor is a single equilibrium point. If one of the exponents equals zero, a cyclical component is involved in the motion. If one of the exponents is positive and the sum of all exponents is still negative, the dynamical system exhibits chaotic motion. As a positive Lyapunov exponent implies an exponential stretching of a given set of initial points, two nearby initial points will exponentially diverge under the action of the dynamical system. The presence of positive Lyapunov exponents is therefore identical with the sensitive dependence on initial conditions mentioned in Section 5.1.1.

When a dynamical system is given, Lyapunov exponents can be calculated directly. However, in most cases time-series analysis deals with a single observed variable, the generating dynamical system of which is unknown. It is thus desirable to obtain information about the original dynamical system (if it exists) from the observed univariate time series. A technique which recently has found much attention *embeds* a time series in an artifial m-dimensional object. Take the first m observations and put them together in an m-dimensional vector. Then consider the second observation and its $m - 1$ successors and put them together in a second vector. Take the third observation and its successors, etc. The procedure finally yields a number of m-dimensional vectors that represent points in an m-dimensional phase space. The number m is called the *embedding dimension*. The interesting property of this procedure is that, under certain conditions, the emerging geometric object in the m-dimensional space is equivalent with the object formed by the trajectory of the original dynamical system. These reconstructed attractors constitute a prerequisite for the numerical calculation of Lyapunov exponents of an actual time series.

The second tool for numerically investigating chaotic time series also relies on the construction of embeddings and is concerned more with the phenomenon of folding a set of points on an attractor. Imagine a trajectory starting at a given initial point in, for example, three-dimensional phase space. The trajectory will move in a particular fashion in a subset of $\mathbf{R}^3$ and it will be bounded. Eventually, the trajectory may come close to the initial point. This may also be the case for the trajectory starting at another initial point, but the time both trajectories need to re-enter a neighborhood of the two nearby initial points can be considerably different. Inspite of this dynamic uncorrelation of initial points and points in their neighborhood, it is worthwhile to investigate the geometric correlation of nearby points, *i.e.*, how close two points on the same or different trajectories may come in phase space. The *correlation dimension* is an index for measuring this geometric correlation. The calculation of this dimension is essentially a counting procedure in which the number of points located in a neighborhood of a certain point is successively determined for all points and varying neighborhoods.[27]

The important property of correlation dimensions is that deterministic dynamical systems and purely stochastic systems behave essentially different in this procedure: the correlation dimension of a stochastic system increases permanently when the embedding dimension m is increased. On the contrary, it converges to a finite limit if the time series under consideration is generated by a deterministic system. Moreover, if the deterministic system generates a regular period motion, its correlation dimension will be an integer and will be identical with the usual (Euclidian) dimension of the trajectory on the attractor. For example, when a two-dimensional system possesses a limit cycle, *i.e.*, a one-dimensional geometric object, the calculated correlation dimension will be equal to 1. In the case of chaotic motion, the correlation dimension, D^C, will be a noninteger.[28]

The relevance of these two numerical tools for the analysis of actual time series can be summarized as follows:

- The correlation dimension provides information on the minimum (Euclidian) dimension of a dynamical system which possibly generated the time series. If the correlation dimension has a value between two successive integers, *i.e.*, $\ell - 1 \leq D^C \leq \ell$, it follows that the dimension of the dynamical system is at least equal to ℓ. A low correlation dimension indicates the presence of nonlinearities in a deterministic dynamical system. If the correlation dimension is very large and still increases for increasing values of m, the system is probably stochastic.

- If the largest Lyapunov exponent is positive, the time series exhibits chaotic motion. Occasionally, the chaos property may also be derived from a possibly noninteger value of the correlation dimension.

In addition to these two tools, several more sophisticated techniques for distinguishing

---

[27] *The precise expression is*

$$D^C(m) = \lim_{\varepsilon \to 0} \frac{\ln C(\varepsilon, m)}{\ln \varepsilon},$$

with ε as the size of the neighborhood, m as the embedding dimension, $C(\varepsilon, m)$ as the number of points located in the neighborhood of size ε of all points, and D^C as the correlation dimension.

[28] *The object is then said to have a fractal dimension. In fact, the procedure for calculating correlation dimensions is a numerical approximation of determining more general concepts of fractal dimensions. Specific difficulties in calculating correlation dimensions suggest that the fractal character should not be overestimated in practical work.*

random and deterministic non-linear motion have been developed which are particularly relevant to economic time series analysis.[29]

Empirical Evidence of Chaotic Motion in Actual Economic Time Series

The application of the two standard procedures presented in the last section requires relatively large data sets on the order of several tens of thousands of observations. Of course, economic time series are typically much shorter, say on the order of 50-500 observations. From the beginning, the empirical results presented below should be evaluated with caution.

In the following, only a very short summary of some recent results will be presented. These non-linear time-series analyses can roughly be divided into investigations of macroeconomic and microeconomic/mesoeconomic data.

Business cycle theory (in the sense of this book) is concerned with fluctuation of major macroeconomic variables like the national product or the stock of money. The erratic nature of GNP's fluctuations is obvious, and in Chcal environments. It is therefore of particular interest to answer the question whether the observable erratic fluctuations are really due to exogenous random influences, or whether they are endogenously generated by a nonlinear structure of the economy.

Pioneeering work on this topic was undertaken by Brock (1986). In an investigation of US GNP data, Brock calculated low correlation dimensions and positive Lyapunov exponents but the data did not pass additional tests. Frank/Stengos (1988) performed a similar study for Canadian GNP data and arrived at qualitatively identical conclusions. Similar results were obtained by Frank/Gencay/Stengos (1988) who analyzed time series from Japan, Italy, the United Kingdom, and Germany. The Japanese data seemed to offer some evidence of non-linear structure, but the data for the other countries rejected the hypothesis of chaotic motion. While it seems hasty to deny the presence of chaos in all possible international GNP data sets, it can at least be said that the available studies do not support the possibility of deterministic chaos.

It may be argued that the very small sample and the quality of the data explain the findings. The entries in macroeconomic time series are always calculated according to a specific aggregation scheme. For example, different procedures in *i)* evaluating different goods, *ii)* in distinguishing stocks and flows or durable and nondurable goods, or in *iii)* disregarding double entries, etc., will lead to different aggregated data. It has been argued that standard, simple-sum techniques generate a high degree of noise particularly in aggregated monetary data. Barnett/Chen (1986) calculated correlation

---

[29] *Cf. Brock (1986) for a concise introduction to several different concepts including residual diagnostics and re-shuffling diagnostics.*

dimensions and Lyapunov exponents for Divisa monetary indices which are compatible with neoclassical aggregation theory. For data sets with more than seven hundred entries the reported correlation dimensions are astonishingly low and the Lyapunov exponents are slightly positive. The presence of chaos can therefore not be excluded from these time series. Larger data sets were investigated by Scheinkman/LeBaron (1986) in a study of daily stock return rates. The correlation dimensions are typically larger but still relatively low (< 7). It seems as if the availability of large data sets constitutes the main prerequisite in empirical investigations of chaotic motion. Financial and monetary data on the microeconomic level are therefore the best candidates for chaotic motion because the sample sizes are typically larger than on the macroeconomic level.

Summarizing, the existing literature has uncovered two phenomena:

- Some investigated time series have low correlation dimensions, indicating that non-linearities in the economy or parts of it cannot be ignored. Exogenous stochastic shocks might not be as relevant as claimed by linear business cycle models.

- Chaotic motion cannot be falsified in all economic time series, but it seems as if its presence is exceptional.

These empirical findings do not imply that the theoretical investigation of chaotic motion in economics is completely worthless. It can be argued that a model should be evaluated according to its capability to generate the same outcome as reality. Even if assumptions are made which do not survive empirical tests, an abstract model may be able to provide a satisfactory picture of real life. The Rational Expectations literature is a good example of this procedure: although Rational Expectations or Perfect Foresight are artifacts without much empirical justification, the models outlined in Chapter 3 can obviously be quite helpful in explaining several aspects of the cycle. Analogously, deterministic models which allow for chaotic motion can be viewed as a theoretical attempt to generate erratic fluctuations without claiming that actual time series are indeed chaotic. The qualitative difference between purely stochastic and chaotic time series can then be ignored in many practical cases: inspite of the fact that chaotic time series potentially allow for some degree of predictability when compared with random series, the presence of noise in the measurements will probably almost always change the empirical findings on the value of, for example, correlation dimensions in practical field studies.

5.2. Catastrophe Theory and Business Cycle Theory

Of the more recent developments in dynamical systems theory the branch called *catastrophe theory* has found particular interest - especially in popular presentations - and has led to much confusions probably because of the irritating label of the theory. Furthermore, catastrophe theory was controversial among mathematicians for some time because it was not clear whether the label 'theory' was an adequate description of this field. It seems, however, that this initial debate about the relevance of catastrophe theory has settled down and that there is an agreement that it is at least a very useful method in studying dynamical systems heuristically. Moreover, catastrophe theory is able to elucidate what the structural requirements for a model are if certain dynamical phenomena are to be explained.

Catastrophe theory is characterized by a property that probably contributed to the initial confusion, namely that the underlying mathematics are rather sophisticated while on the other hand in practical applications of the theory nearly no mathematics are involved at all. In order to get an idea of the immanent mechanisms, a very short introduction to catastrophe theory will be provided, which may nevertheless appear to be rather extensive in space.[30]

5.2.1. Basic Ideas of Catastrophe Theory

The aim of catastrophe theory is the analysis and classification of sudden jumps - or *catastrophes* - in the behavior of dynamical systems. Consider a one-dimensional function, parametrized by an m-dimensional vector α:[31]

$$V = V(x, \alpha), \quad x \in \mathbf{R} \quad \alpha \in \mathbf{R}^m \tag{5.2.1}$$

Without loss of generality, the function V can be represented by a polynomal because any sufficiently smooth one-dimensional function can be expressed by a Taylor-expansion.[32] Let

$$V(x, \alpha) = x^n + \alpha_1 x^{n-1} + \ldots + \alpha_n x^0, \quad n \leq m, \tag{5.2.2}$$

---

[30] *Introductions to the theory are, e.g., Saunders (1980), Arnold (1984), and Zeeman (1977), ch. 1-2.*

[31] *Actually, a family of functions is therefore considered.*

[32] *Compare for the following Saunders (1980), pp. 17 ff. and Poston/Stewart (1978), pp. 92 ff.*

be such a polynomal with some α_i being possibly equal to zero. It can easily be imagined that, for a given n, the graph of the polynomal (5.2.2) has different geometric shapes when some parameters vanish. For example, the graph of x^4, i.e., $\alpha_i = 0$, $i = 1, 2, 3, 4$ and $n = 4$, is quite different from that of $x^4 + \alpha_1 x^3$. Depending on the number of vanishing α's, one or several extrema of the function may occur.

The question arises whether for a given n a parameter constellation exists for which the function (5.2.2) is structurally stable. A function like (5.2.2) with some α_i being possibly equal to zero is said to be *structurally stable* if the number and the character of the extrema of the function do not change when some of these α_i become positive.[33] For example, the expression x^4 is not structurally stable because $x^4 + \alpha_1 x^3$ has additional extrema. It can be shown that for $n = 4$ the polynomial $x^4 + \alpha_2 x^2 + \alpha_3 x$ *is* structurally stable. This structurally stable form of the polynomal (5.2.2) for a given n is called the *universal unfolding* of x^n. The number of parameters which is necessary to stabilize x^n for a given n is called the *codimension* of the unfolding, e.g., x^4 has codimension two.

Catastrophe theory proves that for a codimension ≤ 4, exactly seven different universal unfoldings exist, including four unfoldings in the one-dimensional case (5.2.2) and three unfoldings in the two-dimensional case. In other words, once the number of parameters α_i is specified, only a small number of structurally stable functions exist. This is the essential result of Thom's famous theorem, in which the universal unfoldings are labelled *elementary catastrophes*.

Denote the derivative of an unfolding with respect to x, V_x, as the *equilibrium surface* of V if $V_x = 0$. Until now, no relationship to dynamical systems has been established. Consider a dynamical system

$$\dot{z} = g(z), \quad z \in \mathbf{R}^n. \tag{5.2.3}$$

Assume that the variables can be divided into *fast* and *slow* variables. Let, e.g., z_1 adjust infinitely fast to its equilibrium value.[34] In that case the other slow variables $z_2, \cdots, z_n$ can be interpreted as "parameters" which change very slowly. In the short-run, we will consider only the fast variable z_1 and the equilibrium constellation

$$\dot{z}_1 = 0 = g_1(z_1, \cdots, z_n). \tag{5.2.4}$$

---

[33] *Note that this definition of structural stability refers to a function and not to dynamical systems. Recall that a dynamical system is structurally stable if the solution curves are topologically equivalent when a parameter is varied.*

[34] *This procedure is similar to the so-called adiabatic approximation which has found interest especially in physics. (Haken (1983b)). An economic application of the adiabatic approximation can be found in Medio (1984), where a non-linear dynamic input-output model is investigated.*

Note that we concentrate only on the value of z_1 that prevails after the (infinitely fast) adjustment to the equilibrium value of z_1, i.e., for each parameter constellation the fast variable has already adjusted.[35]

With $z_2, \cdots, z_n$ treated as parameters, re-write (5.2.4) as

$$\dot{z}_1 = 0 = g_1(z_1, \alpha), \quad z_1 \in \mathbf{R}, \quad \alpha \in \mathbf{R}^{n-1}$$

or, by letting $z_1 = x$ and $m = n - 1$:

$$\dot{x} = 0 = f(x, \alpha), \quad x \in \mathbf{R}, \quad \alpha \in \mathbf{R}^m.$$

Suppose that a function $F(x, \alpha)$ exists such that $F_x = f(x, \alpha) = \dot{x}$. A dynamical system which can be derived from such a function $F(x, \alpha)$ is called a *gradient system*.[36] The function $F(x, \alpha)$ is formally identical to the function $V(x, \alpha)$ mentioned above. In the following presentation we will concentrate only on dynamical systems $\dot{x} = f(x, \alpha)$ for which the associated $F(x, \alpha)$ are universal unfoldings $V(x, \alpha)$, i.e., structurally stable functions. The function $f(x, \alpha) = 0 = F_x(x, \alpha) \cong V_x(x, \alpha)$ describes the equilibrium surface of the system. Catastrophe theory therefore deals exclusively with dynamical systems whose equilibrium surface $f(x, \alpha) = 0$ has the form of the equilibrium surface of a universal unfolding.

In order to uncover the properties of these equilibrium surfaces, it is necessary to consider the *singularity set S*, which in the one-dimensional case is described by

$$V_{xx} = 0, \tag{5.2.5}$$

i.e., the second derivative must be equal to zero.[37] Geometrically, the singularity set consists of all parameter combinations for which the equilibrium surface is tangent to

---

[35] *In the long-run, however, it cannot be assumed anymore that the parameters, i.e., the slow variables, are constant. The long-run dynamics are characterized by $\dot{z}_i \neq 0, i = 2, \cdots, n$ and a z_1 which always takes on its appropriate equilibrium values.*

[36] *While in other sciences these functions $F(x, \alpha)$, which are so-called potentials, can often be defined, economic theory formally start with a differential equation system in most applications. If these dynamical systems are gradient systems, then a potential, from which the system is derived, naturally exists. If, however, such a potential cannot be defined, the application of catastrophe theory may not be valid. A weaker condition than that of the existence of a potential is the existence of a stable Lyapunov-function, whose existence must be established in every individual case.*

[37] *In the multi-dimensional case, the determinant of the Hessian matrix, i.e., the matrix of second-order derivatives, must be equal to zero.*

the direction of the variable x. The projection of the singularity set on the parameter space is called the *bifurcation set B*.

The reason why the universal unfoldings are called elementary catastrophes will become immediately clear by a geometric description of the simplest catastrophes. Consider the analytically simplest catastrophe, namely the *fold catastrophe*. Its universal unfolding is given by $V(x) = x^3 + \alpha_1 x$, which is illustrated in Figure 5.10.[38]

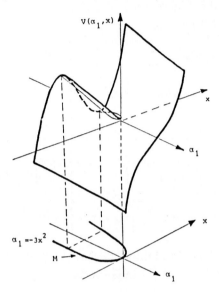

The Fold Catastrophe
Source: Ursprung (1982), p. 129.
Figure 5.10

The equilibrium surface is defined as:

$$M : \quad 3x^2 + \alpha_1 = 0. \tag{5.2.6}$$

The equilibrium surface is therefore a parabola whose singularity set, which is a subset of M, is described by:

$$S : \quad 6x = 0. \tag{5.2.7}$$

It follows that the singularity set consists of the single point $(x = 0, \alpha_1 = 0)$. In addition, the bifurcation set is the single point $\alpha_1 = 0$.

It must suffice at this place to proclaim that $V(x, \alpha)$, respectively $F(x, \alpha)$, tends to take on its minimal value. It follows that - for a given α_1 - the state variable 'falls'

---

[38] *Compare Ursprung (1982), p. 129.*

into the fold once it has passed the upper ridge respectively the front branch of the equilibrium surface. The lower ridge is obviously the locally stable locus of the system, while for state variable values lower than those on the front branch of M the system 'breaks down'. [39] Only the upper branch of M in Figure 5.10 is therefore locally stable. By increasing the parameter α_1 exogenously from α_1' over α_1'' to the bifurcation point, it can be seen that the possibly smooth change of α_1 leads to a sudden jump - or a catastrophe - at $\alpha_1 = 0$ (cf. Figure 5.11).

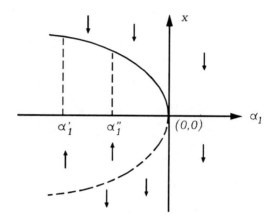

The Equilibrium Surface of the Fold
Figure 5.11

The second catastrophe, the *cusp catastrophe*, is the one which has found most interest because it describes a richer dynamical behavior and can still be handled quite sufficiently in geometric terms. The unfolding of the cusp catastrophe,

$$V(x) = x^4 + \alpha_1 x^2 + \alpha_2 x, \tag{5.2.8}$$

has an equilibrium surface

$$M: \quad 4x^3 + 2\alpha_1 x + \alpha_2 = 0, \tag{5.2.9}$$

and a singularity set

$$S: \quad 12x^2 + 2\alpha_1 = 0. \tag{5.2.10}$$

The bifurcation set can be obtained by eliminating x from M and S, yielding

---

[39] *The term should be used for illustration purposes only. Correctly speaking, the dynamics are no longer defined by elementary catastrophe theory because that theory refers to local stabilities only.*

$$B: \quad 8\alpha_1^3 + 27\alpha_2^2 = 0. \tag{5.2.11}$$

Note that this is exactly the discriminant[40] of the equilibrium surface equation. It follows that the bifurcation set equation implies that (5.2.9) has three real roots, which either all coincide if $\alpha_1 = \alpha_2 = 0$, or two of them coincide if α_1 and α_2 are distinct. As the unfolding is an object in four-dimensional space, a geometric presentation of the cusp catastrophe has to start with the equilibrium surface (cf. Figure 5.12).

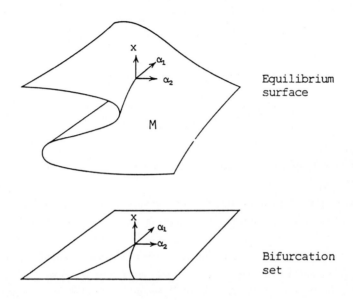

Equilibrium
surface

Bifurcation
set

The Cusp Catastrophe
Source: Saunders (1980), p. 43.
Figure 5.12

The term 'cusp catastrophe' is immediately obvious from the shape of the bifurcation set. Noting that the state variable is always situated on 'top' of the equilibrium surface, it becomes apparent that as soon as the parameters are changed such that the state variable reaches the singularity set at II (cf. Figure 5.13) after having moved on the upper part of the surface, the variable x will jump down to the lower part of M in Figure 5.12.

If the long-run movement of α_2 is such that a motion on the lower part from III to IV occurs, then there will be another jump back to the upper part at IV, which again belongs to the singularity set. Considering these motions in the parameter space only,

---

[40] *Cf. equation (4.3.84).*

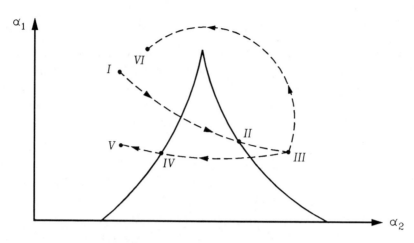

Motions in the Cusp Catastrophe
Figure 5.13

it follows that catastrophes occur exactly every time the bifurcation set is crossed from the outside (cf. Figure 5.13).

The dynamic paths of the parameters as the slow variables have been drawn under the assumption that the parameter α_1 is changing very slowly and that it is dominated by the movement of α_2. However, once the system is located at III, it is as well imaginable that α_1 moves more rapidly such that a return to the upper sheet occurs via a route around the cusp point. In this case, no catastrophes occur because the bifurcation set is crossed from the outside. Which route will actually be followed depends, of course, on the adjustment speeds of the slow variables.

The other different elementary catastrophes are naturally more difficult to illustrate and require the constancy of one or more parameters in order to be presented graphically. As this is beyond the scope of this book and as most applications of catastrophe theory deal with the fold or the cusp, the interested reader is referred to Poston/Stewart (1978) for a detailed description of other elementary catastrophes.

It has to be stressed that the elementary catastrophes have a local character and that the theory deals essentially with bifurcations of stable fixed points into stable and unstable ones. Systems which undergo other kinds of bifurcations are generally not suited to be treated by catastrophe theory. For example, systems that give rise to limit cycles (for example after a Hopf bifurcation) can be shown to lack a stable Lyapunov-function in some cases. The incorporation of dynamical phenomena such as limit cycles would be the subject of a 'general' catastrophe theory, which would include all kinds of structural instabilities. As such a generalization is not in sight, phenomena like limit cycles can be treated only under special assumptions about the systems. For example, in the van der Pol oscillator presented in Section 4.3.4., which can be viewed as an algebraically specified Kaldor model, a relatively strong damping is required, *i.e.*, a high value of the coefficient of $\dot{Y}$ in the presentation as a second-order differential equation.[41]

The foregoing introduction to catastrophe theory has hopefully revealed some characteristics of the theory, which - in turn - have even led to the critique that it is not a theory, at all. Once a potential can be defined, the motion on the equilibrium surface depends on the dynamics of the slow variables. Without a more or less explicit knowledge of these slow dynamics, nothing can be said about the actual dynamics of the state variables. Furthermore, if a complete dynamical system has been defined, catastrophe theory can give no description of the dynamic behavior of the system which is more enlightening or more definite than the insights provided bu other mathematical tools. Consequently, most applications of catastrophe theory can be found in problems for which little is known about the formal dynamics of the system. What catastrophe theory can indeed reveal, however, is the highest possible dynamic complexity which can arise in a certain model. If, for example, a closed orbit can be observed in an empirical study, then it is clear from catastrophe theory that a model which attempts to explain this actual phenomenon cannot be of the fold catastrophe type because the equilibrium surface of the fold admits only once-and-for-all catastrophes. Closed orbits thus require at least a cusp catastrophe model, while this model, on the other hand, would not make it sure that orbits arise exclusively. In this sense, catastrophe theory can be viewed as a method of excluding certain kinds of dynamic behavior if a model is known whose structure does not allow for a simple solution. Catastrophe theory may thus be considered as a "negative" theory.

5.2.2. The Kaldor Model in the Light of Catastrophe Theory

An early application of catastrophe theory in business cycle theory stems from Varian (1977), who presented an augmented version of the familiar Kaldor model[42]

$$\dot{Y} = \alpha\big(I(Y, K) - S(Y, K)\big)$$
$$\dot{K} = I(Y, K) - D \qquad\qquad (5.2.12)$$
$$\dot{W} = \gamma(W^* - W)$$

---

[41] *For a description of the van der Pol oscillator as a cusp catastrophe see Saunders (1980), pp. 68-72.*

[42] *Actually, Varian starts with the usual two-dimensional version of the Kaldor model and introduces wealth in a second version. As will become clear from the following discussion, the two-dimensional system is, of course, a special form of (5.2.12) and can be better understood in catastrophe-theoretic terms if it is embedded in a 3-dimensional presentation.*

with W as 'wealth', W^* as the long-run equilibrium value of wealth, γ as the wealth adjustment coefficient, and D as autonomous and constant depreciation. The investment function is of the well-known Kaldor type. Suppose that savings is negatively related to wealth in such a way that not only the income-independent part of savings but also the marginal propensity to save falls if wealth is increased (cf. Figure 5.14).

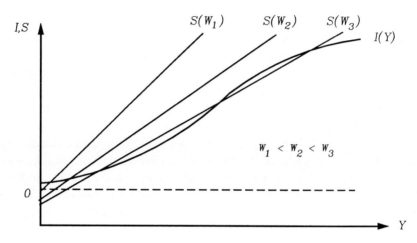

The Dependence of Savings on Wealth
Figure 5.14

Thus, depending on the value of W, there may exist one or three intersections with the investment curve in Figure 5.14, implying different stability properties. If wealth is very low, there can only be one intersection of the functions, independent of the magnitude of K. By increasing wealth, however, a point will be reached where for certain K multiple equilibria in the goods market exist. Graphically, the scenario looks like the cusp catastrophe (cf. Figure 5.15).

Obviously, by looking at the manifold from the front, the $\dot{Y} = 0$ - surface in this model is identical to that of the original Kaldor model if a fixed value of W is assumed. If the variable K and W are interpreted as very slow variables, the manifold $\dot{Y} = 0$ indeed describes the state of the system at every point in time.

Remembering that there may be problems with catastrophe theory if it should be applied to dynamical systems undergoing a Hopf bifurcation, it is useful to construct a stationary equilibrium, i.e., a fixed point of the complete system, which is locally stable (cf. point E in Figure 5.15).

By inspecting the goods market adjustment equation, it can easily be seen that the system always operates on top of the manifold. Let W be fixed on a high level for a while. The usual phase-space of the Kaldor model under the assumption of a locally stable fixed point is illustrated in Figure 5.16.a., whereas Figure 5.16.b. shows

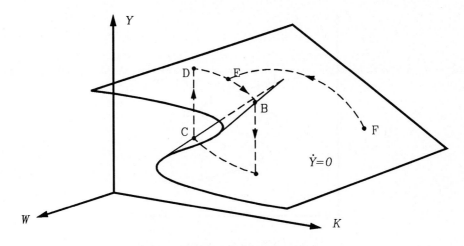

A Three-Dimensional Kaldor-Model
Figure 5.15

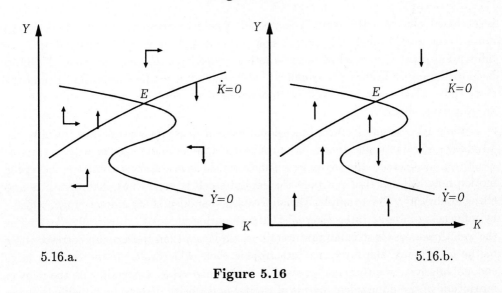

5.16.a.   5.16.b.

Figure 5.16

the dynamics if the adjustment speed in the goods market tends to infinity relative to the implicit adjustment speed of capital. It can be seen that the positively sloped branch of $\dot{Y} = 0$ is repelling, implying that in Figure 5.15 the state variable Y is always located on top of the manifold. With Y on that manifold, the dynamics of the system are completely determined by the dynamics of the slow variables. With W still being fixed, a complete cycle can be generated. Suppose that there is a small exogenous disturbance of the equilibrium E (cf. Figure 5.17). If the disturbance is very small, the system returns to E fairly rapidly according to the dynamics of K. However, once K

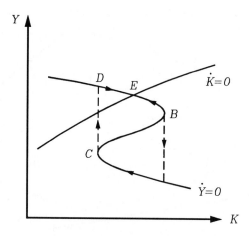

Single Orbit in the Varian Model
Figure 5.17

is increased such that the point B is crossed, a catastrophe occurs and income jumps down to the lower branch of $\dot{Y} = 0$. A slow movement along $\dot{Y} = 0$ is initiated until the bifurcation point C is reached where another catastrophe occurs and where Y jumps back to the upper branch. Gradually, Y will tend back to the equilibrium E and the story ends. Thus, there is a 'cycle' with only one single rotation which was initiated by an exogenous shock.

While this essentially two-dimensional version does not provide new results, the advantage of catastrophe theory is uncovered if the complete system with a variable wealth is considered: the exogenous shock which is necessary to initiate the cyclic motion may be such that not only the capital stock is varied but that wealth is also changed abruptly. For example, Varian assumes a sudden stock market crash, which - by influencing interest rates - can affect the valuation of wealth drastically. As long as the wealth decrease is so small that wealth is still larger than the amount corresponding to the cusp point, the foregoing catastrophic cycle will result. If the crash is large enough, however, wealth may decrease below the cusp value. Depending on the relative magnitude of the adjustment speeds of capital and wealth, it may be possible that the return to the long-run equilibrium may occur via a route around the cusp point (cf. Figure 5.18).

As a catastrophe can occur only when the bifurcation set is crossed from the inside, it is obvious in this case that no catastrophe occurs. Usually, the route around the cusp point on the non-singularity part of the manifold M takes more time than the catastrophic route over the singularity set. Economically, the two routes can be interpreted as a depression with a following slow recovery, or a recession with a fast return to the equilibrium values, respectively. Figure 5.19 illustrates these two possible forms of a

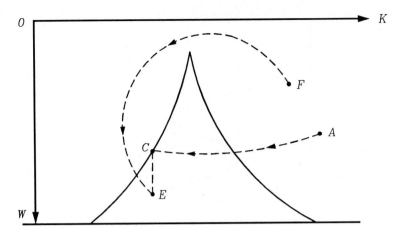

Fast and Slow Returns to Equilibrium
Figure 5.18

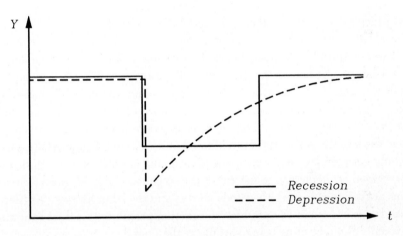

Recession and Depression
Figure 5.19

recovery in a Y-vs.-time diagram.

If the dynamic system is modelled such that the long-run stationary equilibrium is locally unstable, i.e., if it is located on the upward-sloping sheet of the manifold, it is possible to encounter endogenous cycles (cf. Figure 5.20). As was pointed out in the introduction, catastrophe theory can be applied if the damping in the oscillator is strong enough. In the Kaldor model this is the case if the expression $(I_Y - S_Y)$ is small.[43]

Of course, this kind of 'cyclic' behavior should not be confused with the harmonic

---

[43] *See Section 4.3.4.2.. for a discussion of the Liénard-van der Pol oscillator.*

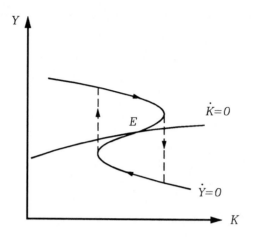

Catastrophes and Unstable Equilibria
Figure 5.20

oscillation which arises if the system generates limit cycles.[44]

The application of catastrophe theory in the original two-dimensional Kaldor model basically does not provide new insights into this standard business cycle model, but it is well suited as an illustration of the basic ideas of catastrophe theory. Among the other examples of the usuage of catastrophe theory in economics, a disequilibrium model by Blad (1981) dealing with the dynamics of the Malinvaud model (Malinvaud (1977)) is of interest in the present context. The paper is an example of the advisory character of catastrophe theory: the static Malinvaud model of a rationed economy with production distinguishing between four different types of rationing regimes of prices and wages in a highly aggregated economy has to get rid of the so-called region of *under-consumption*, where firms are rationed in both the goods market and the labor market. As there are no inventories, the existence of the production function prohibits this dual rationing. The region is usually thought of as being shrunk to the boundary between the neighboring regimes of repressed inflation and Keynesian unemployment. While the Malinvaud model is very helpful in macroeconomic discussions, its conceptual shortcoming leads to a discontinuity of the vector field of price and wage changes if these are modelled according to the usual excess demand hypothesis. By asking the question of how the simplest dynamics have to be modelled such that the solution paths of prices and wages are smooth in the neighborhood of the boundary, Blad introduced fold catastrophe dynamics which indeed provide the desired results under certain assumptions. While reminding of a fight against the vanes of a windmill, the paper is important from a

---

[44] *Compare also George (1981) for a Kaldor-type three-dimensional system, which is very similar to Varian's model and in which an unstable long-run equilibrium is assumed.*

methodological point of view because it uncovers the heuristical character of catastrophe theory, which becomes apparent in Blad's paper in the formulation of potentials which lack any kind of economic meaning, at all.[45]

An empirical investigation of the stagflation phenomenon in the light of catastrophe theory can be found in Fischer/Jammernegg (1986).

5.3. Structural Instability and Business Cycle Theory – Conclusions

The methods and instruments introduced in the preceding sections should have made it evident that a large variety of dynamical phenomena exists beyond those which can be grasped in, e.g., standard multiplier-accelerator business cycle models. While all deterministic linear business cycle models and all analyses making use of standard methods in non-linear models can at best uncover harmonic oscillations with constant frequencies, the phenomena like bifurcations, chaotic dynamics, or catastrophes show that it may be worthwhile to consider the appropriate methods and concepts in dynamical economic systems and hence in business cycle theory. Even in very simple – while often highly arbitrary – business cycle models, these phenomena can be shown to exist. While the linear business cycle models have often been critizised because of their obvious failure to describe actual time series with their typical irregularities – which suggest that the harmonics should be superimposed by exogenous, stochastic influences – chaotic non-linear business cycle models are able to generate time series endogenously, which are similar to actual empirical time series. This seems to suggest a supplementary attitude toward dynamical economic systems. Once the territory of non-linearities has been entered – and there is no economically motivated, qualitative reason to refer to the restrictive linear case only – it must be taken into account that absolutely deterministic models (in the sense of the specification of the model's structure and the definiteness of the behavioral functions) can generate a large variety of dynamical patterns if certain parameters are appropriately chosen. Moreover, once certain parameters in some dynamical systems have been fixed, it is not possible to trace the dynamic paths into the future with definite preciseness because the technical restrictions of computation facilities imply that it is conceptually impossible to avoid the sensitivity to initial conditions of these systems. As the numerical values of economic variables are never known with absolute accuracy, long-term predictions may therefore be prevented in these systems.

At a first glance, the impact of these "strange" dynamics on the development of economics seems to be rather negative: if the task of economics is not only to describe and to explain economic phenomena in a historical fashion, but also to provide arguments in forecasting future events in a real economy, then the presence of endogenously

---

[45] *See for the problem of smooth dynamics in the Malinvaud model also Blad/Zeeman (1982).*

generated exotic phenomena as explained above can lead to a failure of economics. Especially in econometrics, the most sophisticated model structure and parameter estimation may be viewed as superfluous if exact forecastings are made impossible by the dynamic properties of the model.

The positive aspect of chaotic dynamical systems consists in the fact that they can generate seemingly stochastic time series without referring to arbitrarily postulated exogenous influences. While it is certainly inappropriate to deny the influence of exogenous forces completely, explanations of the business cycle should not rely mainly on exogenous forces. Irregular components of the cycle should be explained - at least partly - by the immanent dynamics. The application of chaotic dynamical systems may therefore be fruitful in analyzing past business cycles.

It has often been argued that dynamical systems must be structurally stable in order to make any sense. In analogy to experimental sciences, it is claimed that a descriptive model must lead to the same qualitative result if the experiment is repeated in a minimally changed environment. The immanent attitude toward reality which is apparent from this claim is characterized by the conviction that reality is indeed stable in this structural sense. If reality is stable, then structurally unstable systems may nevertheless be well-suited to describe actual phenomena as long as the system does not operate in the neighborhood of bifurcation values.[46]

Real economies do not have to be structurally stable, however. The conviction that small variations in the environment of a real system do not lead to drastically and qualitatively different kinds of behavior is a heritage of the mechanistically oriented 19th century. Guided basically by a weltanschauung favouring the idea of deterministic harmonics, complex phenomena which could not be explained by the usual models led either to the postulate of actually involved but analytically neglected influences, or essentially harmonic dynamics were thought of as being superimposed by purely stochastic influences. Modern science, however, is rich in experimental examples of structurally unstable systems, which suggest a revision of fundamental attitudes toward reality. The theoretical and interdisciplinary field of synergetics[47], the thermodynamic theory of dissipative structures[48], etc., constitute basic approaches to the modelling of observed structural instabilities in comprehensive terms. While it is accordingly adequate to work with structurally unstable models even in the 'hard' sciences in many cases,[49]

---

[46] *Actually, it has to be made precise which definition of structural stability is underlaid. The definition of structural stability used in this book is only one of several concepts. See Vercelli (1984), app., for a discussion of different concepts of structural stability and their implications for economic theory.*

[47] *Cf. Haken (1983b).*

[48] *Cf. Glansdorff/Prigogine (1977).*

[49] *Note in this context that the Hamiltonian dynamics in mechanics, which are used*

the notion of structural instability may also be tempting in descriptions of dynamical economic phenomena. Indeed, it has been emphasized by Vercelli (1984) that the works of Marx, Schumpeter, and also Keynes can be reinterpreted by using the general notion of structural instability. While it is not always easy to distinguish between dynamic and structural instability, it seems evident that, e.g., the Schumpeterian analysis of an evolutionary economy is guided by an implicitly present idea of structural instability. If the economy is understood as a dissipative dynamical system, i.e., a system which permanently experiences the insertion and loss of energy, then the Schumpeterian innovation shocks may be viewed as energy implementations leading to a qualitatively different dynamic behavior. While an economy without innovative forces is compelled to remain at the (disadvantageous) stable equilibrium, the innovation shocks can lead to cyclical behavior away from equilibrium. Economies with this kind of behavior are similar to phenomena in physics and biology, and it is tempting to apply the appropriate concept of self-organization[50] to dynamical economics as well.[51] While a final statement on the usefulness of such an approach seems hasty, the study of structurally unstable systems in economics may possibly be a fruitful subject of future research and may constructively supplement the basically equilibristic and mechanistic world view that is dominating dynamical economics.

---

in economics mainly in optimal growth models, are typically structurally unstable. See Abraham/Marsden (1980).

[50] See the detailed presentation in Haken (1983a) or Glansdorff/Prigogine (1977).

[51] Cf. Fehl (1983) and Silverberg (1984).

References

Abraham, R.M./Marsden, J.E. (1978): Foundations of Mechanics. Reading, Mass.: Benjamin/Cummings.

Allen, R.G.D. (1963): Mathematical Economics. London: MacMillan.

Allen, R.G.D. (1967): Macroeconomic Theory. London: MacMillan.

Alexander, J.C./Yorke, J.A. (1978): Global Bifurcation of Periodic Orbits. American Journal of Mathematics, 100, pp. 263-292.

Alexander, S.S. (1958): Rate of Change Approaches to Forecasting-Diffusion Indexes and First Differences. Economic Journal, 68; reprinted in: **Readings** (1966), pp. 626-640.

Andronov, A.A./Chaikin, C.E. (1949): Theory of Oscillations. Princeton: Princeton University Press.

Arnold, V.I. (1984): Catastrophe Theory. Berlin-Heidelberg-New York: Springer.

Arrow, K.J./Hahn, F.H. (1971): General Competitive Analysis. San Francisco: Holden-Day.

Assenmacher, W. (1984): Lehrbuch der Konjunkturtheorie. München-Wien: Oldenbourg.

Azariadis, C./Guesnerie, R. (1986): Sunspots and Cycles. Journal of Economic Theory, 40, pp. 725-737.

Barnett, W./Chen, P. (1988): The Aggregation-Theoretic Monetary Aggregates are Chaotic and have Strange Attractors: An Econometric Application of Mathematical Chaos. In: **Barnett, W.A. et al.** (eds.): Dynamic Econometric Modelling. Cambridge: Cambridge University Press.

Baumol, W.J. (1958): Topology of Second Order Linear Difference Equations With Constant Coefficients. Econometrica, 26, pp. 258-285.

Baumol, W.J. (1970): Economic Dynamics. 3rd ed., New York: MacMillan.

Begg, D.K.H. (1982): The Rational Expectations Revolution in Macroeconomics. Baltimore: John Hopkins Press.

Begg, D.K.H. (1983): Rational Expectations and Bond Pricing: Modelling the Term Structure with and without Certainty Equivalence. Economic Journal, 94, suppl., pp. 45-58.

Benassy, J.P. (1982): The Economics of Market Disequilibrium. New York: Academic Press.

Benassy, J.P. (1984): A Non-Walrasian Model of the Business Cycle. Journal of Economic Behavior and Organization, 5, pp. 77-89.

Benhabib, J./Day, R.H. (1980): Erratic Accumulation. Economic Letters, 6, pp. 113-117.

Benhabib, J./Day, R.H. (1981): Rational Choice and Erratic Behaviour. Review of Economic Studies, 48, pp. 459-471.

Benhabib, J./Day, R.H. (1982): A Characterization of Erratic Dynamics in the Overlapping Generations Model. Journal of Economic Dynamics and Control, 4, pp. 37-55.

Benhabib, J./Miyao, T. (1981): Some New Results on the Dynamics of the Generalized Tobin Model. International Economic Review, 22, pp. 589- 596.

Benhabib, J./Nishimura, K. (1979): The Hopf-bifurcation and the Existence of Closed Orbits in Multisector Models of Optimal Economic Growth. Journal of Economic Theory, 21, pp. 421-444.

Bergstrom, A.R. (1972): A Model of Technical Progress, the Production Function and Cyclical Growth. Economica, 29, pp. 357-370.

Black, S.W./Russel, R.R. (1969): An Alternative Estimate of Potential GNP. Review of Economic Studies, 51, pp. 70-76.

Blad, M.C. (1981): Exchange of Stability in a Disequilibrium Model. Journal of Mathematical Economics, 8, pp. 121-145.

Blad, M.C./Zeeman, E.C. (1982): Oscillations between Repressed Inflation and Keynesian Equilibria Due to Inertia in Decision Making. Journal of Economic Theory, 28, pp. 165-182.

Blatt, J.M. (1978): On the Econometric Approach to Business Cycle Analysis. Oxford Economic Papers, 30, pp. 292-300.

Blatt, J.M. (1980): On the Frisch Model of Business Cycles. Oxford Economic Papers, 32, pp. 467-479.

Blatt, J.M. (1983): Dynamic Economic Systems - A Post-Keynesian Approach. Armonk: M.E.Sharpe.

Blinder, A.S./Fischer, S. (1981): Inventories, Rational Expectations, and the Business Cycle. Journal of Monetary Economics, 8, pp. 277-304.

Boldrin, M. (1984): Applying Bifurcation Theory: Some Simple Results on Keynesian Business Cycles. DP 8403, University of Venice.

Boyce, W.E./DiPrima, R.L. (1977): Elementary Differential Equations and Boundary Value Problems. 3rd ed., New York: Wiley.

Boyd, I./Blatt, J.M. (1988): Investment Confidence and Business Cycles. Berlin-Heidelberg-New York: Springer.

Branson, W.H. (1979): Macroeconomic Theory and Policy. 2nd ed., New York: Harper and Row.

Breuss, F. (1982): Potential Output und gesamtwirtschaftliche Kapazitätsauslastung. Monatsberichte des Österreichischen Instituts für Wirtschaftsforschung, 2, 1982, pp. 104-118.

Brock, W.A. (1986): Distinguishing Random and Deterministic Systems: Abridged Version. Journal of Economic Theory, 40, pp. 168-195.

Broida, A.L. (1955): Diffusion Indexes. The American Statistician, 9, pp. 7-16.

Brunner, K./Cukierman, A./Meltzer, A.H. (1980): Stagflation, Persistent Unemployment and the Permanence of Economic Shocks. Journal of Monetary Economics, 6, pp. 467-492.

Brunner, K./Cukierman, A./Meltzer, A.H. (1983): Money and Economic Activity, Inventories and Business Cycles, Journal of Monetary Economics, 11, pp. 281-319.

Burns, A.F. (1954): The Frontiers of Economic Knowledge. Princeton University Press.

Burns, A.F./Haavelmo, T. (1968): Business Cycles. In: International Encyclopedia of the Social Sciences. Vol. 2, pp. 226-249.

Burns, A.F./Mitchell, W.C. (1946): Measuring Business Cycles. Studies in Business Cycles No.2, National Bureau of Economic Research, New York.

Cagan, P. (1956): The Monetary Dynamics of Hyperinflation. In: **Friedman, M.** (ed.): Studies in the Quantity Theory of Money. Chicago: The University of Chicago Press.

Carter, M./Maddock, R. (1984): Rational Expectations. Macroeconomics of the 1980s? London: MacMillan.

Cass, D./Shell, K. (1983): Do Sunspots Matter? Journal of Political Economy, 91, pp. 193-227.

Chang, W.W./Smyth, D.J. (1971): The Existence and Persistence of Cycles in a Non-Linear Model: Kaldor's 1940 Model Re-examined. Review of Economic Studies, 38, pp. 37-44.

Chen, P. (1988): Empirical and Theoretical Evidence of Economic Chaos. System Dynamics Review, 4, pp. 81-108.

Christiano, L.J. (1981): A Survey of Measures of Capacity Utilization. IMF Staff Papers, 28, pp. 144-198.

Clark, C. (1984): Is there a long cycle? Banca Nationale Del Lavoro Quarterly Review, 150, pp. 307-320.

Clark, C.W. (1976): Mathematical Bioeconomics. New York: John Wiley.

Clark, J.M. (1917): Business Acceleration and the Law of Demand: A Technical Factor in Economic Cycles. Journal of Political Economy, 25, pp. 217-235.

Clower, R.W. (1965): The Keynesian Counterrevolution: A Theoretical Appraisal. In: **Hahn, F.H./Brechling, F.P.R.** (eds.): The Theory of Interest Rates. London: Macmillan.

Coddington, E.A./Levinson, N. (1955): Theory of Ordinary Differential Equations. New York: MacGraw-Hill.

Collet, P./Eckmann, J.-P. (1980): Iterated Maps on the Interval as Dynamical Systems. Basel-Boston: Birkhaeuser.

Cugno, F./Montrucchio, L. (1982a): Stability and Instability in a Two Dimensional Dynamical System: a Mathematical Approach to Kaldor's Theory of the Trade Cycle. In: **Szegoe, G.P.** (ed.): New Quantitative Techniques for Economic Analysis. New York: Academic Press, pp. 265-278.

Cugno, F./Montrucchio, L. (1982b): Cyclical Growth and Inflation: a Qualitative Approach to Goodwin's Model with Money Prices. Economic Notes, 11, pp. 93-107.

Cugno, F./Montrucchio, L. (1984): Some New Techniques for Modelling Non-Linear Economic Fluctuations: A Brief Survey. In: **Goodwin, R.M. et al.** (1984), pp. 146 - 165.

Dana, R.A./Malgrange, P. (1984): The Dynamics of a Discrete Version of a Growth Cycle Model. In: **Ancot, J.P.** (ed.): Analysing the Structure of Economic Models. The Hague: Martinus Nijhoff, pp. 205-222.

Davidson, P. (1984): Reviving Keynes' Revolution. Journal of Post Keynesian Economics, 6, 1984, pp. 561-575.

Day, R.H. (1978): Cobweb Models with Explicit Suboptimization. In: **Day, R.H./ Cigno, A.** (eds.): Modelling Economic Change: The Recursive Programming Approach. Amsterdam: North Holland.

Day, R.H. (1982): Irregular Growth Cycles. American Economic Review, 72, pp. 406-414.

Day, R.H. (1983): The Emergence of Chaos from Classical Economic Growth. Quarterly Journal of Economics, 98, pp. 201-213.

Day, R.H. (1984): Disequilibrium Economic Dynamics. Journal of Economic Behaviour and Organisation, 5, pp. 57-76.

Day, R.H. (1986): Unscrambling the Concept of Chaos Through Thick and Thin: Reply. Quarterly Journal of Economics, 101, pp. 425-426.

Day, R.H./Shafer, W. (1986): Keynesian Chaos. Journal of Macroeconomics, 7, pp. 277-95.

De Baggis, H.F. (1952): Dynamical Systems with Stable Structures. In: **Lefschetz, S.** (ed.): Contribution to the Theory of Non-Linear Oscillations. Vol. II., pp. 37-59, Princeton University Press.

Debreu, G. (1959): Theory of Value. New Haven-London: Yale University Press.

De Foville, A. (1888): Essai de Météorologie Economique et Sociale (1), Journal de la Société de Statistique de Paris, 29, pp. 243-249.

DeLong, J.B./Summers, L.H. (1986): Are Business Cycles Symmetrical? In: **Gordon, R.J.** (ed.): The American Business Cycle - Continuity and Change, pp. 166-178. Chicago: The University of Chicago Press.

Dernburg, T.F./Dernburg, J.D. (1969): Macroeconomic Analysis. Reading, Mass.: Addison-Wesley.

Desai, M. (1973): Growth Cycles and Inflation in a Model of the Class Struggle. Journal of Economic Theory, 6, pp. 527-545.

Deutsche Bundesbank (1973): Das Produktionspotential in der Bundesrepublik Deutschland. Monatsberichte, 25, No. 10, pp. 28-34. English Translation in Deutsche Bundesbank (1973), Monthly Reports.

Deutsche Bundesbank (1981): Neuberechnung des Produktionspotentials für die Bundesrepublik Deutschland. Monatsberichte, 33, pp. 32-38.

Diamond, P.A. (1965): National Debt in a Neoclassical Growth Model. American Economic Review, 55, pp. 1126-1150.

Diamond, P. (1976): Chaotic Behaviour of Systems of Difference Equations. International Journal of Systems Science, 7, pp. 953-956.

Dornbusch, R./Fischer, S. (1978): Macroeconomics. New York: McGraw-Hill.

Downs, A. (1959): An Economic Theory of Democracy. New York: Harper.

Dumenil, G./Levy, D. (1985): The Dynamics of Competition: A Restoration of the Classical Analysis. Mimeo: CEPREMAP.

Dumenil, G./Levy. D. (1986): The Macroeconomics of Disequilibrium: A Classical View. Mimeo: CEPREMAP.

Economic Report of the President together with the Annual Report of the Council of Economic Advisors. Washington, D.C., 1962.

Economic Report of the President together with the Annual Report of the Council of Economic Advisors. Washington, D.C., 1977.

Evans, M.K. (1969): Macroeconomic Activity. New York: Harper and Row.

Farmer, R.E.A. (1986): Deficits and Cycles. Journal of Economic Theory, 40, pp. 77-88.

Fehl, U. (1983): Die Theorie dissipativer Strukturen als Ansatzpunkt für die Analyse von Innovationsproblemen in alternativen Wirtschaftsordnungen. In: **Schüller, A. et al.** (eds.): Innovationsprobleme in Ost und West. Stuttgart: Fischer.

Feigenbaum, M. (1978): Quantitative Universality for a Class of Non-Linear Transformations. Journal of Statistical Physics, 19, pp. 25-52, and 21, pp. 669-706.

Fischer, E.O./Jammernegg, W. (1986): Empirical Investigation of a Catastrophe Extension of the Phillips Curve. The Review of Economics and Statistics, pp. 9 -17

Fischer, S. (ed.) (1980a): Rational Expectations and Economic Policy. Chicago: The University of Chicago Press.

Fischer, S. (1980b): On Activist Monetary Policy with Rational Expectations. In: **Fischer, S.** (1980a), pp. 211-247.

Flaschel, P. (1984): Some Stability Properties of Goodwin's Growth Cycle. A Critical Elaboration. Zeitschrift für Nationalökonomie, 44, pp. 63-69.

Flaschel, P. (1985): Macroeconomic Dynamics and Effective Demand. Some Corrections. Metroeconomica, 37, pp. 135-56.

Flaschel, P./Krüger, M. (1984): Endogenous Aspirations in a Model of Cyclical Growth. Richerche Economiche, 38, pp. 598-612.

Flaschel, P./Semmler, W. (1985): Classical and Neoclassical Competitive Adjustment Processes. Mimeo: University of Bielefeld.

Frank, M./Gencay, R./Stengos, T. (1988): International Chaos? European Economic Journal, 32, pp. 1569-1584.

Frank, M./Stengos, T. (1988): The Stability of Canadian Macroeconomic Data as Measured by the Largest Lyapunov Exponent. Economics Letters, 27, pp. 11-14.

Freeman, C./Clark, J./Soete, L. (1982): Unemployment and technical innovation - A study of long waves and economic development. London : Frances Pinter.

Frey, B.S. (1978): Politico-Economic Models and Cycles. Journal of Public Economics, 9, pp. 203-220.

Frey, B.S./Garbers, H. (1972): Der Einfluß wirtschaftlicher Variablen auf die Produktivität der Regierung. Jahrbücher für Nationalökonomie und Statistik, 186, pp. 281-295.

Frey, B.S./Kirchgaessner, G. (1977): A Basic Dilemma in Democracy. DP 95, Department of Economics, University of Konstanz.

Frey, B.S./Lau, L.Y. (1968): Towards a Mathematical Model of Government Behaviour. Zeitschrift für Nationalökonomie, 28, pp. 355-380.

Frey, B.S./Ramser, H.-J. (1976): The Political Business Cycle: A Comment. Review of Economic Studies, 43, pp. 553-555.

Frey, B.S./Schneider, F. (1978a): An Empirical Study of Politico-Economic Interaction in the United States. Review of Economics and Statistics, 60, pp. 174-183.

Frey, B.S./Schneider, F. (1978b): A Politico-Economic Model of the United Kingdom, Economic Journal, 88, pp. 243-253.

Friedman, B.M. (1979): Optimal Expectations and the Extreme Information Assumption of "Rational Expectations" Macromodels. Journal of Monetary Economics, 5, pp. 23-41.

Friedman, M. (1968): The Role of Monetary Policy. American Economic Review, 58, pp. 1-17.

Frisch, R. (1933): Propagation Problems and Impulse Problems in Dynamic Economics. In: Economic Essays in Honor of Gustav Cassel. London: Allen & Unwin.

Gabisch, G. (1980): Konjunktur und Wachstum. In: Kompendium der Wirtschaftstheorie und Wirtschaftspolitik, Band 1, pp. 275-332. 3rd ed. (1988). München: Vahlen.

Gabisch, G. (1984): Nonlinear Models of Business Cycle Theory. In: **Hammer, G./Pallaschke, D.** (eds.), (1984): Selected Topics in Operations Research and Mathematical Economics. Berlin-Heidelberg-New York: Springer, pp. 205-222.

Gabisch, G. (1985): Nichtlineare Differenzengleichungen in der Konjunkturtheorie. In: **Gabisch, G./v.Trotha, H.** (1985), pp. 5-25.

Gabisch, G. (1987): Nonlinearities in Dynamic Economic Systems. Atlantic Economic Journal, 15, pp. 22-31.

Gabisch, G./v.Throtha, H. (1985) (eds.): Dynamische Eigenschaften nicht-linearer Differenzengleichungen und ihre Anwendungen in der Oekonomie. GMD - Studien, 97, Sankt Augustin.

Gaertner, W. (1986): Zyklische Konsummuster. Jahrbücher für Nationalökonomie und Statistik, 201, pp. 54-65.

Gandolfo, G. (1983): Economic Dynamics: Methods and Models. 2nd ed., Amsterdam: North-Holland.

Gater, R. (1931): Die Konjunkturprognose des Harvard-Institutes. Zürich: Ginberger.

George, D. (1981): Equilibrium and Catastrophes in Economics. Scottish Journal of Political Economy, 28, pp. 43-61.

Georgescu-Roegen, N. (1971): The Entropy Law and Economic Progress. Cambridge, Mass.: Harvard University Press.

Gerard-Varet, L.A./Jordan, R./Kirman, A. (1984): Rational Expectations Equilibria with Stochastic Quantity Rationing. Paper presented at the **ESEM**, Madrid 1984.

Glansdorff, P./Prigogine, I. (1977): Thermodynamic Theory of Structure, Stability and Fluctuations. London-New York: Wiley.

Goldberg, S. (1958): Introduction to Difference Equations. New York: Wiley.

Goodwin, R.M. (1947): Dynamical Coupling with Especial Reference to Markets Having Production Lags. Econometrica, 15, pp. 181-204.

Goodwin, R.M. (1951): The Non-linear Accelerator and the Persistence of Business Cycles. Econometrica, 19, pp. 1-17.

Goodwin, R.M. (1967): A Growth Cycle. In: **Feinstein, C.H.** (ed.): Socialism, Capitalism and Economic Growth. Cambridge: Cambridge University Press 1969. Revised version in: **Hunt, E.K./Schwarz, J.G.** (eds.) (1969): A Critique of Economic Theory, pp. 442-449, Harmondsworth: Penguin.

Goodwin, R.M. (1987): The Economy as an Evolutionary Pulsator. In: **Vasko, T.** (ed.): The Long Wave Debate, pp. 27-34. Berlin-Heidelberg-New York: Springer.

Goodwin, R.M./Krüger, M./Vercelli, A. (eds.) (1984): Non-linear Models of Fluctuating Growth. Berlin-Heidelberg-New York: Springer.

Gordon, R.A. (1952): Business Fluctuations. New York: Harper & Brothers.

Gordon, R.J. (1973): The Welfare Cost of Higher Unemployment. Brookings Papers on Economic Activity, 1973.1, pp. 133-195.

Grandmont, J.-M. (1985): On Endogenous Competitive Business Cycles. Econometrica, 53, pp. 995-1045.

Grandmont, J.-M./Laroque, G. (1985): Stability of Cycles and Expectations. CEPREMAP 8519.

Grandmont, J.-M./Malgrange, P. (1986): Nonlinear Economic Dynamics: Introduction. Journal of Economic Theory, 40, pp. 3-12.

Granger, C.W.J./Hatanaka, M. (1964): Spectral Analysis of Economic Time Series. Princeton: Princeton University Press.

Guckenheimer, J. (1973): Bifurcation and Catastrophe. In: **Peixoto, M.M.** (ed.): Dynamical Systems. New York-London: Academic Press, pp. 95-109.

Guckenheimer, J./Holmes, P. (1983): Nonlinear Oscillations, Dynamical Systems, and Bifurcations of Vector Fields. New York-Berlin-Heidelberg: Springer.

Guckenheimer, J./Oster, G./Ipaktchi, A. (1977): The Dynamics of Density Dependent Population Models. Journal of Mathematical Biology, 4, pp.101-147.

Guesnerie, R. (1986): Stationary Sunspot Equilibria in an N Commodity World. Journal of Economic Theory, 40, pp. 103-127.

Haken, H. (1983a): Synergetics. An Introduction. 3rd ed., Berlin-Heidelberg-New York: Springer.

Haken, H. (1983b): Advanced Synergetics. Berlin-Heidelberg-New York : Springer.

Herrmann, R. (1986): Vergleich der dynamischen Eigenschaften stetiger und diskreter zweidimensionaler Konjunkturmodelle. Dissertation Göttingen.

Hicks, J.R. (1950): A Contribution to the Theory of the Trade Cycle. Oxford: Oxford University Press. 2nd ed. (1965), Oxford: Claredon Press.

Hirsch, M. W./Smale, S. (1974): Differential Equations, Dynamical Systems, and Linear Algebra. New York: Academic Press.

Ichimura, S. (1955): Towards a General Non-Linear Macrodynamic Theory of Economic Fluctuations. In: **Kurihara, K.K.** (ed.): Post-Keynesian Economics. New Brunswick: Rutgers University Press, pp. 192-226.

Intriligator, M. (1971): Mathematical Optimization and Economic Theory. Englewood Cliffs: Prentice Hall.

Iooss, G. (1979): Bifurcations of Maps and Applications. Amsterdam: North Holland.

Iooss, G./Joseph, D.D. (1980): Elementary Stability and Bifurcation Theory. New York-Heidelberg-Berlin: Springer.

Jäger, K. (1984): Persistenz und zyklische Schwankungen der Unterbeschäftigung in Gleichgewichtsmodellen mit rationalen Erwartungen. Zeitschrift für Wirtschafts- und Sozialwissenschaften, 104, pp. 645-673.

Kaldor, N. (1940): A Model of the Trade Cycle. Economic Journal, 50, pp. 78-92.

Kaldor, N. (1971): A Comment. Review of Economic Studies, 38, pp. 45-46.

Kalecki, M. (1935): A Macroeconomic Theory of the Business Cycle. Econometrica, 3, pp. 327-344.

Kalecki, M. (1937): A Theory of the Business Cycle. Review of Economic Studies, 4, pp. 77-97.

Kalecki, M. (1939): A Theory of the Business Cycle. In: **Kalecki, M.** (1972): Essays in the Theory of Economic Fluctuation, pp. 116-149. London: Allen & Unwin.

Kalecki, M. (1943): Studies in Economic Dynamics. London: Allen & Unwin.

Kalecki, M. (1954): Theory of Economic Dynamics. London: Unwin University Books.

Kelsey, D. (1988): The Economics of Chaos or the Chaos of Economics. Oxford Economic Papers, 40, pp. 1 -31.

King, R.G./Plosser, C.I. (1984): Money, Credit, and Prices in a Real Business Cycle. American Economic Review, 74, pp. 363-380.

Kirchgaessner, G. (1984): Optimale Wirtschaftspolitik und die Erzeugung politisch-ökonomischer Konjunkturzyklen. Meisenheim: Hain.

Klein, L.R. (1964): A Post-war Quarterly Model: Description and Application. Models of Income Determination, Conference on Research in Income and Wealth. Princeton University Press.

Klein, L.R./Preston, R.S. (1967): Some New Results in the Measurement of Capacity Utilization. American Economic Review, 57, pp. 34-58.

Kondratieff, N.D. (1935): The Long Waves in Economic Life. Review of Economic Statistics, 17, pp. 105-115.

König, H./Wolters, J. (1972): Einführung in die Spektralanalyse ökonomischer Zeitreihen. Meisenheim: Anton Hain.

Koopmans, T.C. (1947): Measurement without Theory. The Review of Economic Statistics, 29; reprinted in: **Readings** (1966), pp. 186-203.

Koopmans, T.C. (1949): A Reply. The Review of Economics and Statistics, 31; reprinted in: **Readings** (1966), pp. 218-225.

Krelle, W. (1959): Grundlagen einer stochastischen Konjunkturtheorie. Zeitschrift für die gesamte Staatswissenschaft, 115, pp. 472-494.

Krelle, W. (1981): Erich Preisers Wachstums- und Konjunkturtheorie als einheitliche dynamische Theorie. In: **Mückl, W.J./Ott, A.E.** (eds.): Gedenkschrift für Erich Preiser. Passau: Passavia Universitätsverlag.

Krengel, R. (1970): Die Berechnung des industriellen Produktionspotentials in der Bundesrepublik Deutschland mit Hilfe von Zeitreihen des Brutto-Anlagevermögens. Beiträge zur Strukturforschung des DIW, 10, pp. 40-44.

Kromphardt, J./Dörfner, J. (1974): The Capacity of the Smithies Model to Explain the Growth Trend by Endogenous Forces. Econometrica, 42, pp. 667-677.

Kromphardt, J. (1984): Ansätze der Konjunkturtheorie. In: **Bombach, G. et al.** (eds.): Perspektiven der Konjunkturforschung. Tübingen: J.C.B. Mohr.

Kuh, E. (1966): Measurement of Potential Output. American Economic Review, 56, pp. 758-776.

Kydland, F./Prescott, E.C. (1980): A Competitive Theory of Fluctuations and the Feasibility and Desirability of Stabilization Policy. In: **Fischer, S.** (1980a), pp. 169-187.

Kydland, F./Prescott, E.C. (1982): Time to Build and Aggregate Fluctuations. Econometrica, 50, pp. 1345-1370.

Laidler, D.E.W. (1976): An Elementary Monetarist Model of Simultaneous Fluctuations in Prices and Output. In: **Frisch, H.** (ed.): Inflation in Small Countries. Berlin-Heidelberg-New York: Springer, pp. 75-89.

Larsen, E.R./Mosekilde, E./Rasmussen, S./Sterman, J. (1988): Entrainment between the Economic Long Wave and other Macroeconomic Cycles. Mimeo. Physics Laboratory III, The Technical University of Denmark.

Lefschetz, S. (1948): Lectures on Differential Equations. Princeton: Princeton University Press.

Leijonhufvud, A. (1973): Effective Demand Failures. Swedish Journal of Economics, 75, pp. 27-48.

Levinson, N./Smith, O.K. (1942): A General Equation for Relaxation Oscillations. Duke Mathematical Journal, 9, pp. 382-403.

Li, T.Y./Yorke, J.A. (1975): Period Three Implies Chaos. American Mathematical Monthly, 82, pp. 985-992.

Lichtenberg, A.J./Liebermann, M.A. (1982): Regular and Stochastic Motion. New York-Heidelberg-Berlin: Springer.

Liénard, A. (1928): Etude des oscillations entretenues. Revue Generale de l' Electricite, 23, pp. 901-46.

Lindbeck, A. (1976): Stabilization Policy in Open Economics with Endogenous Politicians. American Economic Review, Papers and Proceedings, 66, pp. 1-19.

Long, J.B./Plosser, C.I. (1983): Real Business Cycles. Journal of Political Economy, 91, pp. 39-69.

Lorenz, E. N. (1963): Deterministic Non-Period Flows. Journal of Atmospheric Sciences, 20, pp. 130-141.

Lorenz, H.-W. (1987a): Strange Attractors in a Multisector Business Cycle Model. Journal of Economic Behavior and Organization, 8, pp. 397-411.

Lorenz, H.-W. (1987b): International Trade and the Possible Occurrence of Chaos. Economics Letters, 23, pp. 135-138.

Lorenz, H.-W. (1989): Nonlinear Dynamical Economics and Chaotic Motion. Berlin-Heidelberg-New York: Springer. Forthcoming.

Lotka, A.Y. (1925): Elements of Physical Biology. Baltimore: Wiliams and Wilkens.

Lucas, R.E. (1973): Some International Evidence on Output-Inflation Tradeoffs. In: **Lucas, R.E.** (1981), pp. 131-145.

Lucas, R.E. (1975): An Equilibrium Model of the Business Cycle. In: **Lucas, R.E.** (1981), pp. 179-214.

Lucas, R.E. (1981): Studies in Business-Cycle Theory. Cambridge, Mass.: The MIT Press.

Lucas, R.E./Prescott, E.C. (1974): Equilibrium Search and Unemployment. In: **Lucas, R.E.** (1981), pp. 156-178.

Lucas, R.E./Sargent, T.J. (1979): After Keynesian Macroeconomics. In: **Lucas, R.E./Sargent, T.J.** (1981), pp. 295-319.

Lucas, R.E./Sargent, T.J. (eds.) (1981): Rational Expectations and Econometric Practice. Minneapolis: The University of Minnesota Press.

MacRae, D.C. (1977): A Political Model of the Business Cycle. Journal of Political Economy, 85, pp.239-263.

Malinvaud, E. (1977): The Theory of Unemployment Reconsidered. Oxford: Basil-Blackwell.

Marotto, F.R. (1979): Snap-Back Repellers Imply Chaos in R^n. Journal of Mathematical Analysis and Applications, 72, pp. 199-223.

Marsden, J.E./McCracken, M. (1976): The Hopf-bifurcation and its Applications. New York-Heidelberg-Berlin: Springer.

May, R.M. (1976): Simple Mathematical Models With Very Complicated Dynamics. Nature, 261, pp. 459-467.

McCallum, B. (1980): Rational Expectations and Macroeconomic Stabilization Policy. Journal of Money, Credit and Banking, 12, pp. 716-746.

McCallum, B. (1986): On 'Real' and 'Sticky-Price' Theories of the Business Cycle. Journal of Money, Credit, and Banking, 18, pp. 397-414.

McCallum, B. (1988): Postwar Developments in Business Cycle Theory: A Moderately Classical Perspective. Journal of Money, Credit, and Banking, 20, pp. 459-471.

Medio, A. (1980): A Classical Model of Business Cycles. In: **Nell, E.J.** (ed.): Growth, Profits, and Property. Cambridge: Cambridge University Press.

Medio, A. (1984): Synergetics and Dynamic Economic Models. In: **Goodwin, R.M. et al.** (1984), pp. 166-191.

Medio, A. (1987): Oscillations in Optimal Growth Models. Journal of Economic Behavior and Organization, 8, pp. 413-427.

Melese, F./Transue, W. (1986): Unscrambling Chaos Through Thick and Thin. Quarterly Journal of Economics, 101, pp. 419-423.

Mertens, D. (1961): Die kurzfristige Kapazitätsauslastungsrechnung des DIW. Vierteljahresschrift zur Wirtschaftsforschung, 1, pp. 72-90.

Metzler, L.A. (1941): The Nature and Stability of Inventory Cycles. Review of Economic Studies, 23, pp. 113-129.

Minford, P./Peel, D. (1983): Rational Expectations and the New Macroeconomics. Oxford: M. Robertson.

Minsky, H.P. (1957): Monetary Systems and Accelerator Models. American Economic Review, 47, pp. 859-882.

Mitchell, W.C./Burns, A.F. (1938): Statistical Indicators of Cyclic Revivals. Bulletin 69, National Bureau of Economic Research, New York; reprinted in: **Moore, G.H.** (1961), Ch. 6.

Moore, G.H. (1950): Statistical Indicators of Cyclic Revivals and Recessions. Occasional Paper 31, National Bureau of Economic Research, New York; reprinted in: **Moore, G.H.** (1961), Ch. 7.

Moore, G.H. (1954): Analysing Business Cycles. The American Statistician, 8, pp. 13-19.

Moore, G.H. (1955): The Diffusion of Business Cycles. In: **Solo, R.A.** (ed.): Economics and Public Interest. New Brunswick: Rutgers University Press; reprinted in: **Moore, G.H.** (1961), Ch. 8.

Moore, G.H. (1961): Business Cycle Indicators. Vol. 1, Princeton: Princeton University Press.

Moore, G.H. (1979): The Forty-second Anniversary of the Leading Indicators. In: **Fellner, W.** (ed.): Contemporary Economic Problems. Washington, D.C.: American Enterprise Institute; reprinted in: **Moore, G.H.** (1980), Ch. 20.

Moore, G.H. (1980): Business Cycles, Inflation and Forecasting. National Bureau of Economic Research: Studies in Business Cycles No.24, Cambridge, Mass.: Ballinger.

Muth, J.F. (1961): Rational Expectations and the Theory of Price Movements. Reprinted in: **Lucas, R.E./Sargent, T.J.** (1981), pp. 3-22.

Nerlove, M. (1958): Adaptive Expectations and Cobweb Phenomena. Quarterly Journal of Economics, 72, pp. 227-240.

Nordhaus, W.D. (1975): The Political Business Cycle. Review of Economic Studies, 42, pp. 169-190.

Okun, A.M. (1962): Potential GNP: Its Measurement and Significance. American Statistical Association. Proceedings of the Business and Economic Statistics Section. 98-104. Reprinted in: **Okun, A.M.** (1970).

Okun, A.M. (1970): Political Economy of Prosperity. Washington, D.C.: The Brookings Institution.

Ott, A.E. (1972) (ed.): Wachstumszyklen. Berlin: Duncker & Humblot.

Ott, E. (1981): Strange Attractors and Chaotic Motions of Dynamical Systems. Review of Modern Physics, 53, pp. 655-671.

Pasinetti, L.L. (1960): Cyclical Fluctuations and Growth. Oxford Economic Papers, 12, pp. 215-241.

Patinkin, D. (1965): Money, Interest and Prices. 2nd ed., New York: Harper & Row.

Persons, W.M. (1919a): Indices of Business Conditions. Review of Economic Statistics, 1, pp. 5-107.

Persons, W.M. (1919b): An Index of General Business Conditions. Review of Economic Statistics, 1, pp. 111-205.

Persons, W.M. (1919c): General Business Conditions. Review of Economic Statistics, 1, Supplement, August 1919, pp. 2-8.

Phelps, E.S. et al. (1969): Microeconomic Foundations of Employment and Inflation. New York: Norton.

Phillips, A.W. (1954): Stabilisation Policy in a Closed Economy. Economic Journal, 64, pp. 290-323.

Phillips, A.W. (1963): An Appraisal of Measures of Capacity. American Economic Review, 53, pp. 275-292.

Ploeg, F. van der (1983): Predator-Prey and Neoclassical Models of Cyclical Growth. Zeitschrift für Nationalökonomie, 43, pp. 235-256.

Ploeg, F. van der (1985 a): Optimal Government Policy in a Small Open Economy with Rational Expectations and Uncertain Election Outcomes. Paper presented at the World Congress of the Econometric Society, Boston/Mass., August 1985.

Ploeg, F. van der (1985 b): Classical Growth Cycles, Metroeconomica, 37, pp. 221-230.

Ploeg, F. van der (1986): Rational Expectations, Risk and Chaos in Financial Markets. Economic Journal, 96, Supplement, pp. 151-162.

Pohjola, M.J. (1981): Stable and Chaotic Growth: the Dynamics of a Discrete Version of Goodwin's Growth Cycle Model. Zeitschrift für Nationalökonomie, 41, pp. 27-38.

Popper, K. (1934): Die Logik der Forschung. Wien: Springer. 8th ed., (1984), Tübingen: J.C.B.Mohr. Engl. Transl.: The Logic of Scientific Research. 10th ed., London: Hutchinson.

Poston, T./Stewart, I. (1978): Catastrophe Theory and its Applications. Boston: Pitman.

Preiser, E. (1933): Grundzüge der Konjunkturtheorie. Tübingen: J.C.B.Mohr (Paul Siebeck).

Prigogine, I. (1980): From being to becoming. San Francisco: W.H.Freeman.

Puu, T. (1987): Complex Dynamics in Continuous Models of the Business Cycle. In: **Batten,D./Casti, J./Johansson, B.** (eds.): Economic Evolution and Structural Change. Berlin-Heidelberg-New York: Springer.

Ramser, H.J. (1983): Preis-Lohn-Dynamik im Modell der neuen Keynesianischen Makroökonomik. In: **Bombach, G. et al.** (eds.): Makroökonomik heute: Gemeinsamkeiten und Gegensätze. Tübingen: J.C.B. Mohr.

Ramser, H.J. (1987): Beschäftigung und Konjunktur. Berlin-Heidelberg-New York: Springer.

Rasche, R.H./Tatom, J.A. (1977): Energy Resources and Potential GNP. Review of the Federal Reserve Bank of St.Louis, 59, pp. 10-21.

Readings in Business Cycle Theory (1966), American Economic Association Series. London: Allen and Unwin.

Reichlin, P. (1985): Equilibrium Cycles and Stabilization Policies in an Overlapping Generations Model with Production. Mimeo. Columbia University, New York.

Rose, H. (1967): On the Non-Linear Theory of the Employment Cycle. Review of Economic Studies, 34, pp. 153-173.

Rössler, O.E. (1977): Continuous Chaos. In: **Haken, H.** (ed.): Synergetics. A Workshop. Berlin-Heidelberg-New York: Springer.

Ruelle, D. (1979): Strange Attractors. Mathematical Intelligencer, 1979, 2, pp. 126-137.

Ruelle, D./Takens, F. (1971): On the Nature of Turbulence. Communications in Mathematical Physics, 20, pp. 167-192.

Sachverständigenrat (1970): Jahresgutachten zur Begutachtung der gesamtwirtschaftlichen Entwicklung. Mainz: Kohlhammer.

Sachverständigenrat (1988): Jahresgutachten zur Begutachtung der gesamtwirtschaftlichen Entwicklung. Mainz: Kohlhammer.

Samuelson, P.A. (1939): Interactions Between the Multiplier Analysis and the Principle of Acceleration. Review of Economic Statistics, 21, pp. 75-78.

Samuelson, P.A. (1947): Foundations of Economic Analysis. Cambridge, Mass.: Harvard University Press.

Samuelson, P.A. (1958): An Exact Consumption-Loan Model of Interest with or without the Social Contrivance of Money. Journal of Political Economy, 66, pp. 467-482.

Samuelson, P.A. (1971): Generalized Predator-Prey Oscillations in Ecological and Economic Equilibrium. In: **Merton, R.C.** (ed.) (1972): The Collected Scientific Papers of P.A. Samuelson, Vol. III, pp. 487-90, Cambridge, Mass.: MIT-Press

Samuelson, P.A. (1972): A Universal Cycle? In: **Merton, R.C.** (ed.) (1972): The Collected Scientific Papers of P.A. Samuelson, Vol. III, pp. 473-86, Cambridge, Mass.: MIT-Press.

Sargent, T.J. (1979): Macroeconomic Theory. New York: Academic Press.

Sato, Y. (1985): Marx-Goodwin Growth Cycles in a Two-Sector Economy. Zeitschrift für Nationalökonomie, 45, pp. 21-34.

Saunders, P.T. (1980): An Introduction to Catastrophe Theory. Cambridge: Cambridge University Press.

Scheinkman, J.A./LeBaron, B. (1986): Nonlinear Dynamics and Stock Returns. Mimeo. Department of Economics. University of Chicago.

Schinasi, G.J. (1981): A Non-Linear Dynamic Model of Short-Run Fluctuations. Review of Economic Studies, 48, pp. 649-656.

Schinasi, G.J. (1982): Fluctuations in a Dynamic, Intermediate-Run IS-LM Model: Applications of the Poincaré-Bendixon Theorem. Journal of Economic Theory, 28, pp. 369-375.

Schönfeld, P. (1967): Probleme und Verfahren der Messung der Kapazität und des Auslastungsgrades, Zeitschrift für die gesamte Staatswissenschaft, 123, pp. 25-59.

Schumpeter, J.A. (1939): Business Cycles. Volume I. New York-London: McGraw-Hill.

Schuster, H.G. (1984): Deterministic Chaos – An Introduction. Weinheim: Physik-Verlag.

Semmler, W. (1987): A Macroeconomic Limit Cycle Model with Financial Perturbations. Journal of Economic Behavior and Organization, 8, pp. 469-496.

Shiller, R.J. (1978): Rational Expectations and the Dynamic Structure of Macroeconomic Models. Journal of Monetary Economics, 4, pp. 1-44.

Silverberg, G. (1984): Embodied Technical Progress in a Dynamic Economic Model: The Self-Organization Paradigm. In: **Goodwin, R.M. et al.** (1984), pp. 192-208.

Simonivits, A. (1982): Buffer Stocks and Naive Expectations in a Non-Walrasian Dynamic Macromodel: Stability, Cyclicity and Chaos. The Scandinavian Journal of Economics, 84, pp. 571-581.

Skott, P. (1985): Vicious Circles and Cumulative Causation. Thames Papers in Political Economy. London: Thames Polytechnic.

Slutzky, E. (1937): The Summation of Random Causes as the Source of Cyclic Processes. Econometrica, 5, pp. 105-146.

Smithies, A. (1957): Economic Fluctuations and Growth. Econometrica, 25, pp. 1-52.

Solow, R.M./Stiglitz, J.E. (1968): Output, Employment, and Wages in the Short Run. Quarterly Journal of Economics, 82, pp. 537-60.

Stähle, H. (1928): Das Beobachtungsverfahren der wirtschaftlichen Wechsellagen des Harvard-University Committee on Economic Research. Schmollers Jahrbuch, 52, pp. 261-310.

Sterman, J.D. (1985): A Behavioral Model of the Economic Long Wave. Journal of Economic Behavior and Organization, 6, pp. 17-53.

Strigel, W.H. (1977) (ed.): In Search for Economic Indicators. Berlin-Heidelberg-New York: Springer.

Stutzer, M. (1980): Chaotic Dynamics and Bifurcation in a Macro-Model. Journal of Economic Dynamics and Control, 2, pp. 253-276.

Takayama, A. (1974): Mathematical Economics. Hinsdale, Ill.: The Dryden Press.

Thom, R. (1977): What is Catastrophe Theory about? In: **Haken, H.** (ed.): Synergetics. A Workshop. Heidelberg-New York: Springer.

Thurow, L./Taylor, L. (1966): The Interaction between the Actual and Potential Rates of Growth of the Economy. Review of Economic Studies, 48, pp. 351-360.

Tichy, G. (1982): Neuere Entwicklungen in der Konjunkturtheorie. IFO-Studien, 28, pp. 213-238.

Thompson, J.M.T./Stewart, H.B. (1986): Nonlinear Dynamics and Chaos. Chichester-New York: John Wiley.

Torre, V. (1977): Existence of Limit Cycles and Control in Complete Keynesian Systems by Theory of Bifurcations. Econometrica, 45, pp. 1457-1466.

v.Trotha, H. (1985): Familien chaotischer Abbildungen des Einheitsintervalls . In: **Gabisch, G./v.Trotha, H.** (1985), pp. 157-161.

Ursprung, H.W. (1982): Die elementare Katastrophentheorie: Eine Darstellung aus der Sicht der Oekonomie. Berlin-Heidelberg-New York: Springer.

Varian, H.R. (1979): Catastrophe Theory and the Business Cycle. Economic Inquiry, 17, pp. 14-28.

Varian, H.R. (1981): Dynamical Systems with Application to Economics. In: **Arrow, K.J./Intriligator, M.D.** (eds.): Handbook of Mathematical Economics, Vol. I, Amsterdam: North Holland, pp. 93-110.

Vasko, T. (ed.): The Long Wave Debate. Berlin-Heidelberg-New York: Springer.

Velupillai, K. (1978): Some Stability Properties of Goodwin's Growth Cycle Model, Zeitschrift für Nationalökonomie, 39, pp. 245-257.

Vercelli, A. (1984): Fluctuations and Growth: Keynes, Schumpeter, Marx, and the Structural Instability of Capitalism. In: **Goodwin, R.M. et al.** (1984), pp. 209-231.

Vining, R. (1949a): Koopmans on the Choice of Variables to be Studied and of Methods of Measurement. Review of Economic Studies, 31. Reprinted in **Readings** (1966), pp. 204-217.

Vining, R. (1949b): A Rejoinder. Review of Economic Studies, 31. Reprinted in **Readings** (1966), pp. 226-230.

Vogt, W. (1969): Fluktuationen in einer wachsenden Wirtschaft unter klassischen Bedingungen. In: **Bombach, G.** (ed.): Wachstum, Einkommensverteilung und wirtschaftliches Gleichgewicht. Berlin: Duncker und Humblot, pp. 61-72.

Volterra, V. (1931): Lecons sur la Theorie Mathematique de la Lutte pour la Vie. Paris: Gauthier-Villars.

Vosgerau, H.-J. (1984): Einige Problemkomplexe der Konjunkturforschung. In: **Bombach, G. et al.** (eds.): Perspektiven der Konjunkturforschung. Tübingen: J.C.B. Mohr.

Wagemann, E. (1928): Konjunkturlehre. Berlin: Hobbing.

Wallich, H.C. (1968): The American Council of Economic Advisers and the German Sachverstaendigenrat: A Study in the Economics of Advice. Quarterly Journal of Economics, 82, pp. 349-379.

Wenig, A. (1975): Beschäftigungsschwankungen, Einkommensverteilung und Inflation. Zeitschrift für die gesamte Staatswissenschaft, 131, pp. 1-42.

Wenig, A. (1979): Konjunkturtheorie. In: **Beckmann, M. et al.** (eds). Handwörterbuch der Mathematischen Wirtschaftstheorie, pp. 141-154. Wiesbaden: Beck.

Wold, H. (1954): A Study in the Analysis of Stationary Time Series. Stockholm.

Woodford, M. (1986): Stationary Sunspot Equilibria in a Finance Constrained Economy. Journal of Economic Theory, 40, pp. 128-137.

Woodford, M. (1988): Imperfect Financial Intermediation and Complex Dynamics. In: **Barnett, W.A./Geweke, J./Shell, K.** (eds.): Economic Complexity: Chaos, Sunspots, Bubbles, and Nonlinearity. Cambridge: Cambridge University Press.

Zarnowitz, V. (1985): Recent Work on Business Cycles in Historical Perspective. Journal of Economic Literature, 23, pp. 523-580.

Zarnowitz, V./Moore, G.H.: Major Changes in Cyclical Behavior. In: **Gordon, R.J.** (ed.): The American Business Cycle - Continuity and Change, pp. 519-582. Chicago: The University of Chicago Press.

Zeeman, E.C. (1977): Catastrophe Theory. Selected Papers 1972-77. Reading, Mass.: Addison-Wesley.

Name Index

Subject Index

W

World economic forecast up to year 2000

W. Krelle (Ed.)

The Future of the World Economy

Economy Growth and Structural Change

1989. 124 figures. 704 pages.
ISBN 3-540-50467-2

Economy growth and structural change – the future of the world economy – is analysed in this book. Conditional forecasts are given for the economic development of the most important world market countries till the year 2000. The driving forces of economic growth are identified and forecasted, in connection with collaborating scholars in most of these countries and with international organizations. This information is used in solving a coherent world model. The model consists of linked growth models for each country (or groups of countries). The solutions show that the inequality in international income distribution will further increase and that the CMEA and OECD countries will approximately keep their relative positions, with some changes within these groups.
Structural change is also analysed.
The book closes with chapters on special features of the future economic development: on the international dept problem, on long waves, on structural change in the world trade, on the emergence of service economics and on the comparison of GDP and NMP national accounting.

Springer-Verlag Berlin
Heidelberg New York London
Paris Tokyo Hong Kong

H.-J. Vosgerau (Ed.)

New Institutional Arrangements for the World Economy

1989. 26 figures. 492 pages. (Studies in International Economics and Intitutions).
ISBN 3-540-50480-X

As technical progress in transportation of goods and people, communication and transmission of information proceeds, the economic interdependencies between nations grow stronger and stronger – at least potentially. Whether this intensification of economic transactions can really materialize, depends upon the political, social, legal and economic institutions within which they take place. Existing institutional arrangements have to a large extent to be adapted to changing needs. These problems are analysed in four areas: exchange stabilization, international financial markets, protectionism and the Uruguay GATT round, and organization of international production.

G. Fels, G. M. von Furstenberg (Eds.)

A Supply-Side Agenda for Germany

**Sparks from –the United States
–Great Britain
–European Integration**

1989. 7 figures. VI, 439 pages.
ISBN 3-540-50544-X

This book deals with supply-side economics and the needed reorientation it would bring to West German policy. The change would add up to an overall strategy for freeing markets, for removing government-imposed distortions, and for using free-market approaches to correct distortions imposed by pressure groups. It would equip the country to follow the lead of the United States and Great Britain in starting to escape from the tangle in which taxes, regulations, and unemployment have grown in step. The impending completion of the European internal market in 1992 adds urgency to this task.

Springer

Studies in Contemporary Economics

Editors: **D. Bös, G. Bombach, B. Gahlen, K. W. Rothschild**

Springer-Verlag Berlin
Heidelberg New York London
Paris Tokyo Hong Kong

D. Laussel, W. Marois, A. Soubeyran (Eds.)

Monetary Theory and Policy

Proceedings of the Fourth International Conference on
Monetary Economics and Banking
Held in Aix-en-Provence, France, June 1987

1988. 22 figures, 34 tables. XVIII, 383 pages.
ISBN 3-540-50322-6

In Part I the reader will find new results on some specific topics of monetary theory, which are of growing importance in contemporary literature: the role of expectations in models, the trade-off between inflation and unemployment, credit contracts under imperfect information, and money supply. The papers in Part II are concerned with the game theoretic approach to monetary policy making: the time inconsistency problem is revisited in different frameworks using for instance repeated game theory, and coordination between fiscal and monetary policy is studied as a game between the Treasury and the Central Bank.

B. C. J. van Velthoven

The Endogenization of Government Behaviour in Macroeconomic Models

1989. 12 figures. XII, 367 pages. ISBN 3-540-50925-9

The purpose of this book is to discuss the issues involved in and to make a contribution to the endogenization of public sector behaviour in macroenonomic models.

G. Rübel

Factors Determining External Debt
An Intertemporal Study

1988. VI, 264 pages. ISBN 3-540-50504-0

Against the background of the international debt problem which originated with the oil shocks of the seventies, this book undertakes a theoretical analysis of the factors determining aggregate external debt, using the example of a raw material importing country.